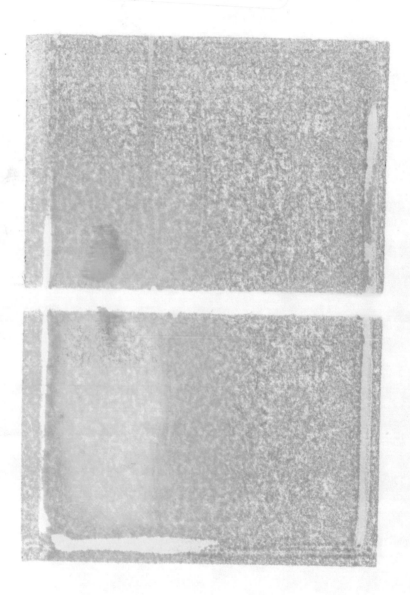

DICTIONARY
of
BUSINESS
FINANCE
and
INVESTMENT

1 4.95

DICTIONARY

of

BUSINESS

FINANCE

and

INVESTMENT

By NORMAN D. MOORE

DRAKE PUBLISHERS INC.

NEW YORK • LONDON

Published in 1976 by
Drake Publishers Inc.
801 Second Ave.
New York, N.Y.   10017

ISBN; 0-8473-1197-X
LC: 74-29447

Printed in The United States of America

Encyclopedic dictionary of

WORDS
and
PHRASES

Common to the world of business,
the financial community,
and the stock market

PREFACE

With the passing of time nations rise and fall, governments change, and social systems develop to fit the times. As society expands and progresses through new technological developments, the tendency arises to divide into areas of concentrated interests. The more that people specialize in their occupations and social activities, the more their language tends to specialize also. Each group develops its own jargon, or words and phrases that are peculiar to that group's activity.

Understanding only a few terms of a specialized activity has little benefit other than the satisfaction of understanding. However, a determined effort to study that terminology can actually yield a useful skill in that field. Investment is mostly a matter of gathering facts. Experience amounts to making personal gains and losses to verify the facts already learned.

This *DICTIONARY of BUSINESS, FINANCE, and INVESTMENT* attempts to rise above the role of a dictionary. That is, instead of offering only an alphabetized listing of terminology, each term is presented as a building block of the entire subject. This is done by explaining each basic term first, then listing related terms, finally, any other subject that might cast light upon the subject is given as a reference.

Throughout the preparation of the dictionary the author followed the concept that the reader's position, and not the author's, is the primary consideration. Thus, the text is not prepared as a compilation of facts and ideas of interest only to the author. Rather, information that is sought by many professionals, investors, and other individuals is organized as conveniently as possible, in a breezy style to hold the reader's interest.

The writer felt that information is of no value if it is obscured from the reader in lofty, linguistic starchiness. Accordingly, a great deal of effort has been expended to make the book interesting. The author will consider this effort successful if the users *read* the book out of interest rather than *refer* to it out of need. If the readers then are able to gain sufficient skill to improve their performance in the areas of business and investment, the entire purpose of the book will have been accomplished.

Norman D. Moore

Author

Note to investors

There are numerous charts used to illustrate various terms in this volume. The proportional charts in many of the illustrations use a special kind of logarithmic graph paper designed by the author. These charts are not available from any retail outlets at the time of this printing. Investors wishing to obtain these materials may write to this publisher for information about availability.

GUIDE TO DICTIONARY USAGE

The fields of business, finance, and investment have considerable overlap, and they reach into the lives of a vast number of people. Nevertheless, there is a special jargon in use among those who are actively involved. Jargon is the use of expressions not normal to the language to describe activities peculiar to a specific group of people. Since these specialized words and phrases are coined by the users, there are times that different terms develop to apply to the same subject. Then, too, some terms can have several different meanings. This dictionary reports variations as they have been found.

To aid the reader in getting the most usefulness from the book we have formulated policies and guide lines as follows:

1. If several terms apply to the same subject, that subject will be defined under each term unless they appear on the same page.

2. Definitions are as complete as is practical to reduce unnecessary cross referencing.

3. Each definition lists any similar terms, defines the other terms that differ only slightly emphasizing the differences, lists opposing terms, and gives references to any other terms that might expand on the subject.

4. If a major topic has other sub-topics, all will be listed under the major heading and then listed separately in their own alphabetical locations in the book.

5. Terms that consist of initials only are listed in alphabetical sequence at the beginning of each alphabetical chapter. Next, complete words are listed.

For example, under "A" the initials *ADR* and *ASE* appear first. Next, the complete words begin with *Accelerated depreciation, Account executive*, etc.

6. Alphabetizing of terms considers word groupings ahead of absolute alphabetical sequence. For example, all terms which begin with the word *market* are listed in a group by alphabetical order of the second word of the term: *Market, Market average, Market breadth, Market equity, Market order*, etc., ending with *Market volume*. Then the next grouping begins with *Marketability*. In absolute alphabetizing *Marketability* would come between *Market* and *Market average*. For convenience in researching multiple references and also in respect to simple cross referencing of similar terms, grouping is more practical.

7. If additional information would expand the subject, a reference will be given to another term. The term will be printed in capital letters with the statement "see . . ." or "notice . . .".

8. If sub-headings are necessary, they will either be enumerated and printed in standard type, or they will be printed in italics, depending upon the circumstances. Words appearing within a definition in italics are for emphasis.

A

ADR

American depository receipt. A negotiable security which gives evidence of ownership of blocks of a foreign security that are being held on deposit in a foreign branch of an American bank. They are used to simplify trading in foreign securities. An American who buys an ADR pays for it in American dollars, and dividends are paid in American dollars. The disadvantages are that the investor must pay a slightly higher price to cover bank charges, and the voting rights go to the bank instead of the ADR holder.

AMEX

Another name for the American Stock Exchange. Also called ASE, the curb market, or curb exchange, and, sometimes, even the other market. See American Stock Exchange for more information about trading

1

privileges and membership seats. Also see STOCK EXCHANGE for a list of other exchanges.

A S E

American stock exchange, often referred to as AMEX. A stock exchange or trading center for securities, much like the New York Stock Exchange. It is a smaller exchange, and generally lists smaller and newer corporations than does the New York Exchange. Some securities may be traded on *both* exchanges. Brokers are admitted to the exchange for trading by membership only. Membership is gained by purchasing a seat and meeting certain exchange requirements which include licensing and certain financial requirements. Compliance with federal regulations is also a condition of membership. There are 650 seats available.

Sometimes referred to as the other exchange, the American Exchange is one of the two national exchanges, along with the New York Exchange. There are a number of regional exchanges located in some of the major cities of the United States. See STOCK EXCHANGE for a list of other exchanges.

Accelerated depreciation

A method for amortizing the cost of an asset at a variable rate. Heavier deductions are made in early years so that the value carried on the books will be similar to actual market value for the asset. There are several methods of calculating these deductions, they are as follows:

1. Double deductions for the first year.

2. Extra 20 % deduction for the first year.

2

3. Declining balance . . . charging off a given percent of the remaining value each year. For example, deducting 30 % each year of the value remaining from the preceding year.

4. Sum-of-the-digits . . . charging off diminishing fractions of the value each year. The fraction is arrived at by assigning successive numbers to each year of the expected life, then totaling the numbers. Thus, for a 7 year life the years are numbered 1, 2, 3, 4, 5, 6, and 7 for a total of 28. On the first year 7/28 of the purchase price is written off. On the second year 6/28 is claimed, the third year 5/28 is claimed, and so on.

These methods are also called accelerated amortization. See DEPRECIATION for comparison to straight line depreciation, allowed depreciation, and allowable depreciation.

Account executive
1. A registered representative of any broker or dealer trained and licensed by the NASD and state agencies to sell securities. Also called a customer's man or customer's broker. Although technically incorrect, most people refer to him as "my broker".
2. In advertising and sales related activities in other business areas an account executive is a person responsible for all business relations between his company and one or more client companies.

Account representative
The person who handles security trading orders for the investor. A registered representative of any broker or dealer. He is specially trained and is licensed by the

National Association of Security Dealers (NASD) and by state agencies to sell securities. Also called a registered representative, account executive, or customer's broker. To most people he is just "my broker", although the term is technically incorrect.

Accounts payable

An accounting term that refers to all of the current liabilities or debts of a company that must be paid within the near future. For normal bookkeeping purposes it will include suppliers, utilities, rental payments, legal fees, royalties, and any other amount due to creditors outside the company. There may be times, however, that other amounts may be included. For annual reports or especially for an audit, everything must find a place as an asset or liability. Unpaid wages and salaries, interest and dividends due to be paid, and, at times, *potential* liabilities are included, even though invoices have not yet been received.

Accounts receivable

An accounting term that refers to the amount of money due to a company for all goods or services sold on credit. It is counted on the books as a current asset or one which can be converted into cash in the near future. The near future, in this case, is interpreted as one year.

Accrued interest

Bond interest that has been accumulating since the last payment was made. The buyer of such a bond pays the market price plus the accrued interest. Exceptions include bonds that are in default and income bonds. The bond prices may be quoted as "with interest" or "and interest".

Accumulation plan
A plan for purchasing shares of an investment company on an installment basis. See *special features* under the listing of INVESTMENT COMPANY for comparisons of several types of installment purchases of mutual funds or investment company shares.

Acid test
A shortcut method for calculating the liquidity or financial resistance of a company to sudden economic disturbances. The acid test is the comparison of the "quick ratio" to industry standards. The quick ratio is determined by subtracting the value of inventory from current assets, then dividing by current liabilities. In normal times a ratio between 1 and 1.5 is acceptable. Less than 1 is considered alarming. During 1974 the average of all manufacturers had dropped to less than .90. In 1955 the average of all manufacturers was 1.36.

Acquisition
The process of buying or acquiring some asset. The term is sometimes applied to the purchase of a block of stock, but more often it is used to mean the buying of the entire company or all of its outstanding stock. Acquisitions used to be methods for a growing company to expand its line of products or improve its strength in certain areas. In recent years it has become an end in itself, that is, growing for the sake of growing and showing higher profits every year. This trend led to the age of the conglomerate, or a company which will buy any kind of a smaller company with no regard to product compatibility, as long as it can be expected to boost earnings. With this purpose in mind there have been cases where a smaller company using

5

leverage could buy a larger one. See PYRAMID and WORKING CONTROL.

Acquisition cost

A sales charge or commission charged for investment in mutual funds. It is called a load or front end load. A few mutual funds have no sales charge and are referred to as no load funds. In addition, there is usually a small maintenance fee charged monthly or quarterly by *both* front end load funds and no load funds.

Across the board

A term suggesting a widespread and complete action. For example, a company giving across the board pay raises gives the raise to all employees, or, if the company makes an across the board price increase, all of its products would receive a higher price. It does not mean that the price hike would be uniform, but there would be some changes on each.

Activity

The volume of security trading whether speaking of a single issue or the market as a whole. It is considered an important indicator for use in measuring public emotion. Most often people use the term market volume, but the term activity appears in certain indexes and in written discussions of market theory.

Actual market

The price at which a security can be bought today. It is also called market price or current market for a security.

Add-on-loan

A loan in which the interest is calculated at the stated

rate for the full period of contract for the full amount of principal, then added to the principal at the beginning before payments are calculated. Interest paid on this type loan is higher than if the interest were calculated on the monthly unpaid balance. In the final months of such a contract you are still paying interest on the full amount of principal, even though much of the principal has been paid off. This is a very common type loan policy for consumer loans. Also see INTEREST for other forms of loan repayment with examples of interest calculation.

Adjustment

A change in statistics made in order to account for a new development. For example, earnings figures may be revised to account for a stock split or a loss carry forward. The resulting figures are more representative in comparison to previous quarters or years. In the financial statements an adjusted figure will be shown preceded by a letter "a".

Advance-decline index

A leading indicator showing the cumulative net difference between stock price advances and declines. It is used as a measure of the breadth of market movements and the disparity between current price averages and the normal condition.

Advances and declines

An index that is widely followed as an indicator of investor interest and that is interpreted by some to forecast market trends. It records the cumulative difference between the number of stocks on the New York Stock Exchange which rise and those which decline daily compared to the prices of the previous day.

Advancing market

Generally rising stock prices or an up market. Also see STRONG MARKET, UPTREND, BULL MARKET, RALLY and RECOVERY.

Advisory service

An organization which sells information and makes recommendations to investors. Many such services employ experts who study certain segments of the securities market and publish their findings in newsletters, charts, and reference books.

Affiliated company

A company in which there is 5% or more ownership of the outstanding voting shares held by another corporation either directly or indirectly. The designation arises from certain regulations concerning financial reports that publicly held corporations are required to publish. Also see SUBSIDIARY for distinctions.

After market

1. The market formed by supply and demand which develops for a security after the issue is originally offered to the public. Also called a secondary market.
2. In other areas of business an after market is the demand for accessory products to be used with some major product line. The major product is aimed at the primary market. For example,

automobiles are reaching a primary market while mirrors, tape players, tires and other replacement parts make up the secondary or after market for autos.

Agency security

Securities sold by federal agencies such as the Federal Home Loan Bank and Federal National Mortgage Association. See FANNIE MAE.

Agent

A person or company which acts on the behalf of others. For example, a securities broker who buys or sells securities for his customer, buys from, or sells to a third party. He charges a fee or commission for his services. He is occasionally called an intermediary. Manufacturer's representatives are also agents, since they sell goods for the manufacturer to dealers. Note the difference from a DEALER or PRINCIPAL who buys and sells for his own account. When the dealer resells a product, he charges a mark up for profit instead of a commission, as is charged by a broker or agent.

Aggressive investing

A term applied to securities buying that is aimed at rapid growth rather than safety of principal or production of income. The term would be more correct to say agressive *trading* rather than investing since the aggressive person may sell frequently to realize profits on every price swing. The term aggressive means to accept greater risks in the hope of getting greater profits. The inherent risks require a very active effort in research and monitoring of an account to take the best advantage of fast moving opportunities for profits or to avoid fast moving setbacks. This is also called speculating. Note the difference from DEFENSIVE INVESTING. Also compare terms INVESTING and TRADING and the terms LONG TERM and SHORT TERM.

All or none offering

When new issues are being prepared for sale to the public, there are times when investment bankers are not willing to underwrite the issue. This may be because the market climate looks unfavorable. Underwriting is buying the entire issue outright for resale to the public. If a complete sellout is critical to the issuer, the investment bankers may act as agents only and offer the stock to the public with the provision that if the complete offering is not sold by a specified date, the orders will be cancelled and all money returned to the subscribers. This is the all or none provision. At times another method will be used where the agents offer the new issue on a best efforts basis. In this case there is no obligation to sell any definite portion of the issue. The offering still has a termination date, but proceeds of the sale are kept, and unsold shares remain unissued.

All or none order

A securities trading order issued by an investor to his broker that can be either a market order or a limited order, but it is to be executed in its entirety or not at all. Unlike the fill or kill order which is canceled if not promptly executed, the all or none can remain open until filled. Bids or offers are not accepted for these all or none orders in stocks, but if such an order is received for bonds, and there are more than 50 bonds involved, bids or offers can be taken. See BUY and

SELL ORDERS for a list of other kinds of orders used in securities trading.

Allowable depreciation

The amount of depreciation that *could have been* claimed on a capital asset if none was actually claimed for any reporting period. The amount is *added to* the value of an asset. It is reasoned that the deductions save taxes; therefore, the absence of deductions should increase tax liability. Note the difference from ALLOWED DEPRECIATION which is the actual amount of depreciation written off under accepted accounting practices. See DEPRECIATION for explanations of different methods for calculating depreciation.

Allowed depreciation

The amount of depreciation allowed by the IRS to be written off or subtracted from income for normal replacement of capital equipment. This is the actual amount claimed as a deduction if it is within accepted accounting procedures allowed by the IRS. Notice the difference from ALLOWABLE DEPRECIATION which, in the absence of any write off, *increases* the value of the asset and the tax liability. See DEPRECIATION for comparisons and examples.

Alternative order

An order to a broker to do either of two alternatives, such as either buy a particular stock at a limited price or buy on a stop order. If the conditions lead to executing one of the alternatives, then the other is cancelled. It can also apply to sell orders as well as to buy orders. Also called either/or orders. See BUY

ORDERS or SELL ORDERS for a list of other kinds of orders used in securities trading.

Amalgamation

The combining of two or more separate businesses into one entirely new one while the original companies cease to exist. Also called a consolidation. Notice the difference from MERGER. See CONGLOMERATE and HOLDING COMPANY for other forms for joining corporate forces.

American depository receipt

Also called an ADR. A negotiable security which gives evidence of ownership of blocks of foreign securities that are being held in deposit in a foreign branch of an American bank. They are used to simplify trading in foreign securities. An American who buys an ADR pays for it in American dollars, and dividends are paid on it in American dollars. The advantages are speed and simplicity for the investor. The disadvantages are that the investor must pay a slightly higher price to cover bank charges; also, the voting rights go to the bank instead of the ADR holder.

American Stock Exchange

Also called AMEX or ASE. An exchange or securities trading center much like the New York Stock Exchange. It is a smaller exchange and generally lists smaller and newer corporations than the New York Exchange. Some securities may be traded on *both* exchanges. Brokers and dealers are admitted to the exchange for trading by membership only. Membership is gained by purchasing a seat and meeting certain financial requirements. Compliance with federal regulations is also a condition of membership.

There are 650 seats available.

Sometimes referred to as the curb exchange in reference to its origin, which was actually on the sidewalk in New York, it is sometimes called the other exchange, also. The American Exchange is one of the two national exchanges along with the New York Exchange. There are a number of regional exchanges located in some of the major cities of the United States. See STOCK EXCHANGE for a list of other exchanges.

American Stock Exchange price-change index

A composite index composed of the total of all stock and warrant prices for issues traded on a given day on the American Stock Exchange divided by the total number of shares listed on the exchange. It is updated periodically throughout each day. The index is interpreted as an indicator of market strength. Also, see INDEXES, AVERAGES and COMPOSITES for more information on technical indicators.

Amortization

The process of gradually reducing a liability or charging off a capital expenditure over a period of time. See DEPRECIATION, STRAIGHT LINE DEPRECIATION, and ACCELERATED DEPRECIATION for different methods of amortizing or writing off expenses.

Amortize

To write off the cost of something on a gradual basis, such as:

1. Annual deductions from income for depreciation of equipment.
2. Costs of tooling spread over a given number of units

---

of finished products.

3. Spreading development costs over several years of production and sales.

4. Spreading the cost of a bond premium over the years to maturity.

Analyst

A professional person whose business is studying and reporting the financial conditions and future prospects for public corporations. He studies financial reports and financial publications, talks to company officers, and may even loiter around company headquarters to get grapevine information of value in forecasting the company's prospects for future profit. See FUNDA-MENTAL ANALYSIS, TECHNICAL ANALYSIS and OPTIMAL ANALYSIS for different approaches to analysis of securities or the markets for them.

... And interest

An expression that means that a bond price so quoted will have an added cost to the buyer equal to the interest accrued since the last payment. Bonds in default or income bonds do not trade with accrued interest and are said to be traded flat. "And interest" is sometimes stated as "with interest". Bonds quoted as "and interest" appear to cost the investor more, but the extra cost is recovered as soon as the first interest payment is received. In like manner, the seller of the bond seems to get an extra price for the bond, but it is really his portion of the interest payment for the period that he held the bond.

Annual meeting

A yearly meeting of stockholders of a corporation for

the purpose of electing the Board of Directors and voting on matters of major importance such as entering new fields of business activity, setting major company policy, or matters that require revisions of the articles of incorporation.

Annual report

A yearly report distributed by a corporation to its shareholders which includes financial statements (balance sheet, income statement, and statement of capital), reports from various officers reviewing major events of the past year, and a forecast of progress for the next several years.

Annualize

Translating a quarterly report or statistics from some other short period to indicate what a full year of operation would produce with the same rate of change.

Annuity bond

A bond which bears no maturity date. It will continue drawing interest indefinitely. Also called a continued bond, irredeemable bond, and perpetual bond. See BONDS for other types of bonds and comparisons between them.

Antitrust

An action or policy which is designed to prevent monopolistic business activities. Competing companies acting together to exert united power are considered to be in violation of antitrust laws. Also, a company which buys out its major competition to dominate a market, or a company which by its own success becomes the largest single supplier of its product, may also be considered in violation of anti-trust laws. The laws were designed to prevent one company from controlling an entire market, but sometimes bigness alone is considered an evil.

Appraisal

A professional evaluation of the market value of some asset by an independent expert. Often appraisals are sought by persons seeking to buy some property if the buyer himself does not have a good knowledge of that property. Sellers may also seek appraisals in order to set a fair selling price.

Appreciation

Another term for growth or increase in value. With securities, appreciation is called paper profits since the gain is on paper only. At the time of sale the profit becomes real or is realized. It is then a taxable gain.

Approved list

Also called eligible list. A list of securities that are acceptable for investment by mutual funds or other financial institutions. In some states the list is prepared by the state government itself for use by mutual funds, banks, insurance companies, pension funds and other financial institutions operating within the state. The list, if prepared by the state, is then called the legal list. The list is composed of high quality securities meeting certain specifications. In the absence of such a list in a state or sometimes in addition to it, there is a broadly defined prudent man rule imposed upon these institutions and other fiduciaries.

Arbitrage

A trading technique used to take advantage of differences in the price of a security in different markets by making a purchase in one market and selling in the other market.

Arithmetical chart

A chart used for all manner of graphs including stock prices. It is laid out in a grid pattern with all lines equally spaced, each successive line representing the same numerical value in a progression. Also called a linear chart. See page 18 for arithmetical chart. See STOCK CHARTS for other charts used for securities charting.

Arm-in-arm

A term referring to personal interests involved in a business transaction. Persons involved in a business transaction or relationship where personal or other interests may be served in such a way that questions are raised about motives, are said to be involved in an arm-in-arm or too friendly a deal.

Arm's length

The opposite condition to the arm-in-arm situation listed above. A business transaction where participants take precautions to avoid criticism about being too friendly or having personal motives, or avoiding personal benefits or even the appearance of personal benefits from the transaction.

Arrears

An amount that is due but unpaid. A bond which has interest payments in arrears is said to be in default.

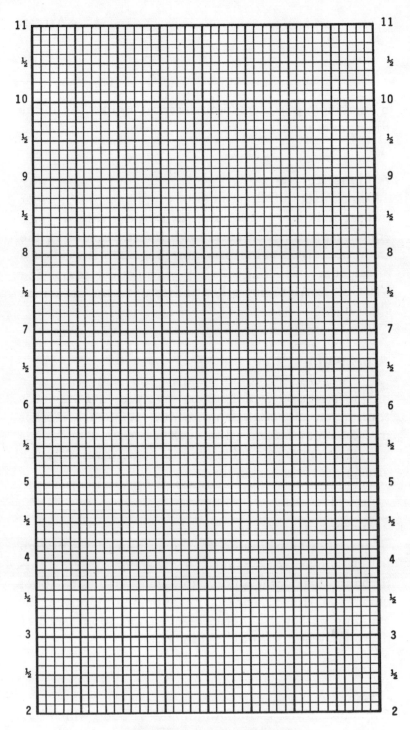

ARITHMETICAL CHART

18

Asked price

A price requested by the *selling* party for any particular stock. If bid and asked prices are quoted by a broker, the asked price represents the lowest price that anyone has offered to accept for that stock at that particular time, while the bid is the highest that anyone has offered to pay for it. The buyer need not make the purchase if he considers the price too high. If a broker is asked for a quote on a given stock, he may say . . . "The asking price is . . . ", which means the seller is willing to negotiate. However, if he reports . . . "Bid and asked is . . . ", it is a firm quote to buy from you at the bid price or sell to you at the asked price.

Assessment bonds

Those bonds issued by a municipality which will be repaid by property assessment taxes. See BONDS for other types of bonds and comparisons between them.

Asset value

Total value of assets after deducting all liabilities. Usually stated as per share value. It is calculated by dividing total assets by the number of shares outstanding and reported as the net asset value or NAV. Usually the market value of the security is much higher than the NAV, but, in times of economic uncertainty and other market pressures, the market prices of even good stocks can be pushed well below the NAV.

Assets

Everything owned and due to a person or a corporation. It includes several categories as they are listed on financial statements, such as:

1. Fixed assets: real estate and equipment.

2. Current assets: cash, securities, notes, inventories, and accounts receivable.

3. Intangible assets: patents, license agreements, trade marks, and good will.

4. Other assets: life insurance cash value, investments in subsidiaries, and, sometimes, the items listed in No. 3.

If the intangible assets are listed separately, the investments may also be moved into the current asset list. When listing the value of assets, the total value is shown. Any indebtedness is listed separately under LIABILITIES.

Associated press index

A composite of 60 industrial stocks, 15 railroad stocks and 15 utility stocks. An indicator of general market conditions. It is published in some periodicals instead of the popular Dow Jones Industrial Averages. It has a slightly broader coverage of the market than the DJI, and it has the dubious value of having a proprietary or original index for the public to follow. It is commonly featured in many local newspapers.

Assumed bond

Another name for a guaranteed bond, or a bond that is guaranteed by someone other than the issuer. For example, a parent corporation may guarantee the repayment of an issue by a subsidiary. See BONDS for other types and comparisons between them.

At market

An order issued by an investor to a broker to purchase or sell a security at whatever price is current when the transaction is made. Usually called a market order. See

BUY or SELL ORDERS for a list of other kinds of orders used in securities trading.

At the close order

A market order which is to be executed at or as near the close of the market as practicable. If the order is not filled, or if any portion of it is not filled, then the order is cancelled. Also called a fill or kill order, or an immediate or cancel order. See BUY or SELL ORDERS for a list of other kinds of orders used in securities trading.

At the opening only order

A market or limited price order issued by an investor to his broker which is to be executed at the opening of the market or not at all, and any such order or portion of such order which is not executed is cancelled. Also called a fill or kill order, or an immediate or cancel order. Also see BUY or SELL ORDERS for a list of other kinds of orders used in securities trading.

Auction

A term sometimes used to describe the stock exchanges. It is properly applied because the trading floor prices are agreed upon by bid and asked prices between buyers and sellers. If sellers cannot find buyers at the prices they want, they lower the price until a buyer accepts. Also, if demand grows strong, the sellers will ask higher prices.

Audit

An examination of a company's books financial records by outside accountants in order to assure the company or some regulatory agency that the company's financial statements are a true account of the company's condition.

Authorized common stock

The maximum amount of common stock that can be issued by a corporation according to its charter. The number is originally decided upon by the incorporators and recorded in the articles of incorporation. If the Board of Directors later decides to change the number of shares authorized, they may do so by a proper action of the board and file amended articles with state regulatory agencies. There may be a considerable difference between the amount of stock authorized and the amount issued or outstanding. The company need not issue all that is authorized, and it may repurchase some of the outstanding shares if it chooses. Repurchased shares are held as treasury shares for reissue at any time, or they can be used for acquisitions or employee stock option plans. There are times when a company may repurchase some of its outstanding stock and retire it altogether.

Automatic dividend reinvestment

An optional feature in many mutual funds which provides for reinvestment of all income distributions (usually capital gains distributions are automatically reinvested unless the investor requests payment) for greater growth.

Average down

To buy additional shares in a stock that you already own when the market price is declining. The purpose is to lower the *average* price paid which reduces the amount of recovery necessary in order to break even. It is a defensive practice which does work and can be recommended for the unsophisticated investor. A skilled trader, however, may find a better prospect for investing the same amount of money to get a stronger growth. Research and skill are required to find those opportunities if they exist.

Average investor

The little man, small investor, odd lot trader or unsophisticated investor. 80% of all investors fit in this category, in spite of the fact that 80% of the stock is held and traded by the institutions. The average investor has a poor record, but some of the big ones can turn in equally bad performances.

Averages, indexes, indicators, and composites

Different types of numerical indicators used for measuring the stock market or economic conditions. These indicators are charted and followed carefully in the hope that they can indicate future moves. Variations and combinations are so numerous that the terms are almost interchangeable. There are basic meanings, however, with the distinctions as follows:

1. Averages: A numerical quantity that results from adding a series of stock prices or other numbers, then dividing the total by the number of entries. In some averages a divisor is not used, but each entry is multiplied by a weighting factor. This type average is more properly called an index, composite, or weighted average. Some of the more commonly used are listed on the next five pages.

2. Indexes: Numerical quantities that bear some relationship to stock market prices and economic conditions. For example, the comparison of yields

on high grade bond sales to the yields on low grade bond sales is supposed to give an index to measure investor confidence in the stock market. The flow into lower grade bonds is taken as an indication that investors are much more confident and can accept greater risks.

3. Indicators: Data compiled and charted which reports certain business or economic conditions and is interpreted as a possible stock market influence. As an example, durable goods orders give an indication of what business management expects and is planning for.

4. Composites: Any set of numbers which combines data from different sources to provide a reference for conditions of the market or the economy. Some composites combine stock and bond prices. Others combine prices from different industries and use weighted multipliers to adjust answers. Others will combine two or more other indexes.

Some of the most commonly used averages, indexes, indicators, and composites are as follows:

Advance-decline index: A leading index showing the cumulative net differences between stock price advances and declines. It is used as a measure of market breadth.

American Stock Exchange Price Change Index: An average of all American Stock Exchange common stock and warrant prices. An indicator for general market trends.

Associated Press Index: A composititie of 60 industrial stocks, 15 railroad stocks, and 15 utility stocks. An indicator of general market conditions.

Barron's Confidence Index: An index comparing yield on high grade bonds to yield on low grade bonds. An indicator which often anticipates market moves.

Dow Jones Bond Averages: An average of six bond groups. It indicates bond market strength.

Dow Jones Composite: A total of all 65 stocks which are included in the Dow Jones Industrial Average, Dow Jones Transportation Average and Dow Jones Utilities Average. It is a more representative index of market conditions than the Dow Jones Industrial alone, which is the most commonly quoted indicator of market trend.

Dow Jones Industrial Average: A composite of 30 large industrial stocks. This is the most widely followed of all market indicators for general market conditions. Companies composing the average are listed under the separate heading DOW JONES INDUSTRIAL AVERAGE.

Dow Jones Transportation Average: A composite of 20 railroad, trucking, and shipping line stocks. An indicator of the conservative side of the market. While this average usually moves together with the industrial average, a strong divergent move is interpreted as an indication of the beginning of a major trend reversal.

Dow Jones Utilities: A composite of 15 major utility stocks. An indicator of strength in the defensive portion of the stock market.

High-low Index: A dual line index showing new yearly highs and lows on a 10 week moving average basis. A market breadth indicator which often confirms major trend changes where the two lines cross.

New York Stock Exchange Composite Index: A weighted average of all NYSE common stocks. A good indicator of general market conditions.

New York Stock Exchange Volume Index: A total number of all shares traded daily. An indicator of market breadth which can also be plotted against other indicators to measure investor attitude.

New York Times Stock Average: An average of 25 industrial and railroad stocks. A general market indicator.

Odd-lot Index: A composite of odd-lot sales. An indicator of small investor attitudes. Odd-lot trades usually hold steady through major trends but increase just before the market tops out.

Odd-lot Short Sales: A composite of odd-lot short selling which indicates small investor attitudes. Unusually heavy short selling by odd-lotters usually will pinpoint a market bottom.

Price-earnings Ratio Line: A calculated index which shows where market prices for a given stock would be if traded at an arbitrarily selected acceptable P-E ratio. Acceptable ratios are calculated by plotting moving averages of earnings over several years. It is intended as an index of desireability of investment in given securities.

Short Interest Ratio: An index comparing uncovered short positions to average volume over a 30 day period. A ratio above 1.5 is considered bullish, and below 1.0 is considered bearish in investor attitudes.

Standard and Poor's Composite Index: A composite of 500 common stocks (425 industrial stocks, 20 railroad stocks, 55 utility stocks). A general market indicator which is considered more indicative than the more popular Dow Jones Indistrial Average because it represents approximately 90% of the market value of all common stocks listed on the New York Stock Exchange.

Standard and Poor's 100 Industry Groups: Individual indexes for each of 100 separate industries. Indexes computed weekly of stock prices in each industry to show areas of strength and weakness in the general market.

Trend Lines Market Barometer: A composite index composed of a number of other key indexes in weighted values. It indicates bullish and bearish conditions in general market attitude.

Other Indicators: Many other indicators are used in the analysis and forecasting of market and economic conditions. Some of the most common in use are the computed and charted quantities listed below:

Average Work Week
Bank Reserves
Business Inventories
Business Failures
Corporation Profits after Taxes
Disposable Income
Gross National Product
Housing Starts
Installment Debt
Lay Off Rate
Margin Rate
New Orders, Durable Goods
Prime Interest Rate
Potential Purchasing Power
Retail Sales Trading Volume
Unemployment Rate

There are literally hundreds of indexes and indicators

in use by the securities industry and economic experts. The Government Printing Office publishes the *Business Conditions Digest*, which contains hundreds of indexes. In addition, there are many commercial publications which employ others.

Averaging

Also called dollar cost averaging. A formula for investing in which the investor buys at regular intervals at a fixed dollar amount each time. The number of shares purchased each time may vary because of market price fluctuations. The object is to reduce the *average* cost per share by buying fewer shares when the price is high and more shares when the price is low. It is strictly a long term device for the unsophisticated investor. Dollar cost averaging as an investment formula or technique is a method of overcoming a lack of knowledge that has something of the same theory involved as averaging down but averaging down is a more professional approach to normal investing. In this approach the investor is not committing any regular amounts but is following normal investment procedures and practices. The averaging comes when the price declines on a stock he owns. As near the bottom of a decline as possible, the investor buys additional shares to reduce his average cost. If the price declines further, he may again buy more to continue lowering his average cost. Also see FORMULA INVESTING.

B

B-unit

A unit of trading for international transactions of very large proportions. Its value varies from day to day but to a lesser degree than individual currencies. It is composed of five different currencies: the American dollar, German mark, French and Swiss francs, and the British pound, in equal proportions. The B-unit was devised as an alternative to the EURCO when the dollar began to regain strength on international markets, and people wanted something involving the dollar but were not willing to trust the dollar completely. Involving the dollar with other currencies in a trade deal has the effect of averaging out the value of those major currencies. The B-unit is one of the so called CURRENCY BASKETS or CURRENCY COCKTAILS. Also see EURCO for differences.

Baby bond

A type of bond introduced a few years ago with a face

value of less than the customary $1,000. Some were priced as low as $100. The object of the lower price was to permit more people to purchase them and thus complete an offering of bonds during a period of investor resistance. The bookkeeping chores and nuisance for the brokers led to their discontinuance. See BONDS for other types of bonds and comparisons between them.

Back office, Back room

The bookkeeping department of a brokerage firm. That portion of a broker's business involved in recording transactions, securing transfers of securities, and other accounting operations. The non-selling activities of a brokerage.

Backlog

1. In business operations: the value of orders received but not yet ready for delivery.
2. In investments: the liquid assets held . . . cash, government bonds, life insurance surrender value and other high grade investments that are readily marketable.

Bail out

Selling out of a stock at the earliest possible moment with no regard for losses. A panic sale or distress sale. Also called dumping or unloading.

Balance sheet

A financial report on a specific date including liabilities, assets, net worth or deficit, and other related information. Arranged so that the value of assets are listed in one column and liabilities are listed in another. Subtracting liabilities from assets gives the capital or net worth of a company.

Balanced funds

Mutual funds which keep a balance between stocks and bonds in their portfolios. It is thought that stocks in such a fund can provide the growth of capital while bonds offer the safety. See INVESTMENT COMPANIES for other types of funds and descriptions of each. Also see INVESTMENT COMPANY ACT OF 1940 for definitions, purposes, and limitations.

Bank debits

In national economics, the total number of check transactions made during any given period of time through all the nation's banks. The figure is used as an index of business activity.

Bankruptcy

A procedure entered into by an individual or a business whereby the federal courts administer the dissolution or reorganization and settlement of debt and the protection of a debtor. The Bankruptcy Act passed in 1898 and modified in 1938 consists of fourteen chapters. The first seven chapters establish the structure of the system, define the rights and duties of bankrupt parties and their creditors, and the procedures that must be followed. Chapters 8 through 14 authorize special procedures for specific cases. If recovery seems hopeless, a straight bankruptcy is filed under which all the assets are sold and distributed by the court to creditors. Some assets are exempted to individuals filing in this manner. Many persons or corporations filing for bankruptcy choose to file under one of the chapters which are designed to aid him in recovery and settle his debts. The special cases covered by chapters 8 through 14 are as follows:

Chapter 8:   Railroads. Reorganizations and arrangements with creditors to settle debts.

Chapter 9:   Certain public authorities.

Chapter 10:   Business reorganizations. Management is replaced and trustees are appointed by the court to reorganize and recover business profitability.

Chapter 11:   Business. Court supervised arrangements worked out between debtor and creditors for eventual settlement of debts.

Chapter 12:   Real Estate. Unincorporated debtors with debts secured by real estate.

Chapter 13:   Personal. Court supervised arrangements worked out between debtor and creditors for eventual settlement of debts.

Chapter 14:   Maritime liens. Court supervised arrangements.

Bar chart

A graph drawn on any type of charting paper in which a vertical line represents a range of quantities. In stock charting it may represent the range from the high to the low for the period of time covered. There is frequently a small flag on the bar at the closing price for the reporting period. In reporting other types of statistics a wide bar may include the entire area from zero up to the quantity being reported. See Bar Charts on page 34. See STOCK CHARTS for other types of charts and graph paper used for them.

Barefoot pilgrim

A naive person who can be quickly disadvantaged by an unscrupulous sales person. Sometimes also called a lamb.

Barometer stock

A single stock which fluctuates in price approximately the same as economic conditions in general. It is therefore watched as an index to the whole market by varifying any reversal that the market makes. Also see STOCK for more information and listings of other types of stock.

Barron's confidence Index

An index which compares yield on high grade bonds with the yield on low grade bonds. An indicator which is interpreted to anticipate market moves. The theory is that "smart money" becomes confident before the general market shows any sign of bullishness. Bond yields tend to push up in times of uncertainty, because it takes more yield to attract investors in those times. Lower yields, then, on low grade bonds reflect a more confident position as investors are willing to accept lower quality with lower yield.

Base

In securities charting and forecasting, it is an area on a stock chart which shows a narrow range of trading

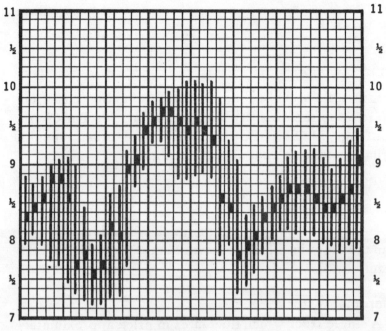

BAR CHART (stock prices)

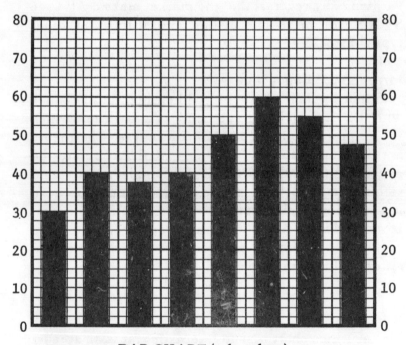

BAR CHART (other data)

prices over an extended time. The period of time involved is called a consolidation period if it follows a period of general decline. Any departure from this area is expected to be upward if the analyst interpreting the pattern is correct in his judgment. However, if the next departure is downward, the chart analyst will proclaim in his most sophisticated professionalism that it was a shelf, not a base. See PATTERNS for other chart formations.

Basis points

1914724

For bond pricing it is 1/100 of 1%. The quantity used in the measure of bond yields when calculating the difference between the original issue price and the current market price. For example, if a bond was planned to yield 6.10% interest when issued but recalculating the rate using current prices, interest rate, and years to maturity showed an actual yield of 6.25%, it is said to have an increase of 15 basis points.

Bear

A person who believes the stock market will decline. The opposite of a bull.

Bear market

A declining market. A period of time when stock prices are declining in general. Some stocks may move opposite to the general trend, but most of the averages, indicators and investor emotion is negative. A serious decline is referred to as a recession, while an extremely severe decline is called a depression. A short decline in a generally rising market is looked upon as a technical correction or a time of profit taking. If a temporary correction holds more than a few weeks during a longer upward trend the decline becomes a set back.

Bearer bonds

Bonds that are issued to the bearer; that is, they belong to the person who holds them. Bearer bonds are not registered in the name of the owner, but the ownership is determined by possession. See BONDS for other types of bonds and comparisons between them. Coupon bonds are bearer bonds.

Bearish

A term to describe negative influences on a security or the market itself. For example, rising interest rates usually cause market prices to decline, hence a rise in interest rates is bearish. The term is also used to describe any indexes or indicators that show a declining market or a pessimistic attitude by observers. A twist in this measurement of outlook is in commodity futures trading. Influences which are good for the farmer are bad for the commodity trader and vice versa. A drought damages crop output and prices rise accordingly, so a bearish report on commodities really reflects good conditions for producers.

Bell shaped curve

A curve on a graph which is formed by plotting the variables of a large number of happenings. Mathematical probabilities for variations show that the great bulk of cases fall near the center of the entire range and a diminishing number of cases occur toward the extremes. These probabilities, when charted, produce a line that roughly resembles a bell. Also called normal curve.

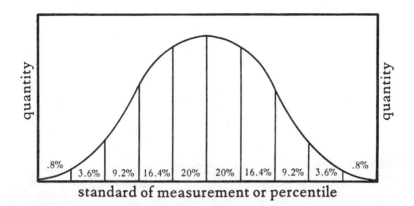

standard of measurement or percentile

BELL SHAPED CURVE

Reading horizontally across the bottom is the standard of measurement, or the level of achievement in any situation. This is the qualitative analysis of a study. Reading vertically determines the number of cases involved for the quantitative analysis. The areas enclosed within each segment of the curve represent the percentage of the total cases in each percentile bracket.

Beneficiary

A person who receives or is scheduled to receive something. For example, the person named to receive an insurance settlement at the death of the insured, or a person who is named as the owner in a trust agreement, even though someone else has the authority to manage the account for a specified time.

Best efforts

Investment bankers, instead of underwriting an issue of stock, or actually purchasing it themselves, then reselling it, may act as agents only, and declare that they will use their best efforts to sell the issue in a public offering. If the entire issue does not sell, the investment banker is under no obligation. Note the difference from UNDERWRITING or an ALL OR NONE OFFERING.

Bid

The price offered by a prospective buyer for a stock. If bid and asked prices are quoted by a broker, the bid represents the highest price anyone has offered to pay for that security at that time. The seller may choose to decline the offer if it is not high enough to suit him. The asked price then is the lowest price a seller will take for his security. Bid and asked prices are a firm quote for trading either way . . . buying or selling. A price given as "asking . . ." is a negotiable price that a seller is seeking. Bid price for a mutual fund is the liquidating value or net asset value of its shares. Also see FIRM and FIRM MARKET, INDICATED MARKET, and SUBJECT MARKET.

Bid wanted

A notation that a dealer has a security for sale and is seeking bids for it from anyone. The notation appears as BW in the *pink sheets* which are published daily by the National Quotation Bureau, and lists dealers for all over-the-counter stocks and the latest prices for those stocks.

Big board

A common term for the New York Stock Exchange, also often referred to as NYSE. See NEW YORK STOCK EXCHANGE for membership requirements, number of seats available, etc.

Block positioning

A move by an institutional brokerage house to buy all or part of a block of stock on which he has received an order to trade. For example, if a mutual fund places an order to sell 20,000 shares and the broker locates buyers for only 10,000 shares, he may buy the other

10,000 for his own account with the expectation of being able to sell them later on. In this case he has taken a position of 10,000 shares of that issue.

Blocks of stock

A large quantity of stock usually numbering more than 10,000 shares. It is not a unit of trading as is the round lot and may consist of an odd number, such as 72,425 shares. Blocks are usually traded under special handling because of the impact they could have on market prices. See SECONDARY DISTRIBUTION, EXCHANGE DISTRIBUTION, OVERHEAD SUPPLY, and CROSS for methods of trading in blocks. Also notice ROUND LOTS, ODD-LOTS, and UNIT OF TRADING.

Blue chips

Stocks which are considered to be leaders in their field and have a long record of good earnings, financial strength, and stable stock prices. Also see STOCK for more information and listings of other types of stock.

Blue laws

State laws which were based upon the religious convictions of law makers some years ago. Most often the term is applied to laws restricting commercial business activities on Sunday. They were called blue since their critics without such convictions considered them severely restrictive. Many such laws have been dropped and others are not being enforced. The appearance and disappearance of laws of this nature do not prove the value of the laws as much as the fickle mind of man and the fact that men choose to regulate others by their own likes and dislikes. Notice the differences from BLUE SKY LAWS.

Blue list

A daily trade paper of municipal bond offerings covering the entire country. It is printed on blue paper in blue ink, hence the name it bears.

Blue sky laws

A popular name for laws that various states have enacted to protect the public against securities frauds. The term is believed to have originated when a judge ruled that a particular stock being questioned had about the same value as a patch of blue sky.

Board

1. The term applied to any of the stock exchanges, but especially to the New York Stock Exchange. Sometimes preceded by the term "big" if referring to the NYSE. The term may apply to an electronic display of constantly changing ticker prices in a conspicuous location of a broker's office.

2. The term board is also applied to a group of directors elected by the stockholders of a corporation to guide the overall operation of the company. Their purpose is to look after the best interests of the stockholders they represent. The board elects these operating officers: the president, vice president, secretary, and treasurer. These officers are often selected from among the directors themselves, but they need not be. Neither is it necessary for a director to be a stockholder, but very often they are.

Board of directors

A group of people elected by the stockholders of a corporation to direct the affairs of a corporation. The highest authority in corporate planning and policy making. The board is made up of two or more individuals depending upon the size of the company. Very large international corporations may have 20 or more directors, but the number selected is determined by shareholder vote and written into the articles of incorporation. Directors are usually shareholders but do not have to be. They are also usually very knowledgeable and experienced business professionals chosen because of reputation and/or community standing. Besides making major policy decisions they also appoint these corporate officers: the president, vice president, secretary, and treasurer, along with any assistants for these four offices. Often the directors serve without compensation, and they may meet only once or twice a year for some smaller companies. In other companies they may meet more frequently and be paid on a per meeting basis. Most directors serve one year terms and may be re-elected.

Board room

1. The room set aside for meetings of the board of directors. Usually the focal point is a large conference table suitable for seating a sizeable group including all the directors plus appointed officers and any guests, such as accountants or attorneys who may give reports, or experts on some topic of discussion. The board room could also be any suitable place so designated if the meeting is to be held away from headquarters. Always, the term suggests the seat of power and final authority for a corporation.

2. Many brokerage offices have a large room, open to the public, where a large electronic display board occupies one wall and reports a constantly updated

flow of stock prices as they are printed out by the stock ticker.

Boiler room

An illegal brokerage firm characterized by high pressure selling of securities of questionable value. Often they make extensive use of telephone sales. Sometimes the term is applied half jokingly to aggressive brokers.

Bond

Basically an I O U or promissary note of a corporation usually issued in denominations of $1,000, although $100 and $50 have been used in the past. A bond is a debt, and the company usually promises to pay a specified amount of interest for a specified length of time, as well as to repay the loan by the expiration date. A bond represents *debt*, not *equity*. The holder of the bond is a creditor of the company, not an owner, as is a stockholder. Many different types of bonds have been issued for different purposes and with different benefits or limitations for the bond holder. Many of these are listed and described under the heading BONDS. See BOND PRICING for discussion of bond costs.

Bond funds

Mutual funds which invest mainly in bonds. Their objective is to achieve maximum income with safety of principal. These funds are very conservative and are of interest to retired people or others no longer able to work or unwilling to accept the risks of growth type investments. See INVESTMENT COMPANIES for other types of funds and descriptions of each. Also see INVESTMENT COMPANY ACT OF 1940 for definitions, purposes, and limitations.

Bond pricing

Nearly all bonds are issued at a par or face value of $1,000. A few years ago some companies tried issuing "baby bonds" at $100 or even less, but they proved to be more nuisance than help. Most of them are now out of circulation. After being issued, many bonds continue to be traded on the open market at prices that fluctuate with economic conditions. Market prices for bonds may range from 100% over par to 80% under par but most remain closer to par. Changes reflect variations in interest rates. If the price falls below par, it is said to be trading at a discount. This has the effect of raising the interest *yield*, since interest is always paid on the par value. If the market price rises above par, it is said to be trading at a premium; the effect then is a lower yield. The cause for this condition might be that the bond was issued at a high rate of interest while later issues carried lower coupon rates due to slower economic conditions. In the market for bonds, people will then be willing to pay a premium to get the better yield. There are some convertible bonds that have features so attractive that investors are willing to pay premiums high enough that *all* yield is cancelled. When this happens, the bond is said to be trading on a zero-yield basis or even a minus-yield basis. See BONDS for a list of different types of bonds and descriptions of each.

Bond ratings

A system for evaluating the financial strength behind a bond and also the desirability in terms of maturity, yield, or risk involved in a given bond. Ratings are made by numerous advisory firms, but the most widely known are *Standard and Poor's* and *Moody's*. The words ratings, rankings, and grading are practically synonymous. See RATINGS OF SECURITIES for a list of the letter gradings for bonds and stocks.

Bonds

There are more than 100 different types of bonds in use today. They can generally be divided into several categories for descriptions as follows:

1. Those which identify the issuer: government bonds, state bonds, municipal bonds, railroad bonds, industrial bonds, public utility bonds.

2. Those which identify the purpose of the issue: public works bond, school bond, highway bond, equipment bond, construction bond, dock and wharf bond, reorganization bond, terminal bond, refunding bond.

3. Those which indicate the type and extent of collateral backing the issue: revenue bond, special assessment bond, collateral trust bond, guaranteed bond, income bond, first mortgage bond, sinking fund bond, junior lien bond, first lien bond.

4. Those which include special privilege: convertible bond, profit sharing bond, continuing bond, optional bond, assented bond.

5. Those which describe certain features: coupon bond, registered bond, interchangeable bond, interim bond.

6. Those which describe the terms of repayment: callable bond, irredeemable bond, perpetual bond, annuity bond, extended bond.

7. Other bonds not pertaining to investment: bail bond, fidelity bond, performance bond.

Some of the different types of bonds in use are:

Annuity bond: A bond which bears no maturity date. It will continue drawing interest indefinitely. Also called continued bond, irredeemable bond and perpetual bond.

Assented bond: A bond which has been deposited by the owner pending the issuance of a more definitive bond resulting from a voluntary organizational change in the issuing company. It is also called an interim bond.

Assessment bond: Those bonds issued by a municipality which will be repaid by property assessment taxes.

Bail bond: One of several types of bonds which are not investment securities. This is money deposited to guarantee the appearance of a defendant in a trial. Often bail bonds are posted by an outside party who charges a fee for the loan. The bail bond is returned after appearance at the trial.

Bearer bond: A negotiable bond which is not registered in the name of the buyer but can be transferred simply by possession. Coupon bonds are a type of bearer bond. Whoever presents a coupon for interest payment may collect the payment.

Callable bond: A bond which may be called in before maturity for redemption or repayment. Also called a redeemable bond.

Collateral trust bond: A bond which represents a debt that is secured by depositing some other security with a trustee.

Construction bond: A bond issued by a state or local government agency for construction purposes. It will be repaid from tax levies.

Convertible bond: A bond which has a provision for exchange for a given number of shares of common stock by the same issuer at some specified date in the future. It not only gives the safety and income of a bond in the early years but it also gives the holder the benefit of participating in growth if the company does well.

Coupon bond: A bearer bond which is not recorded in the name of the owner. There are coupons attached with payment dates for interest payments. The owner clips and presents each coupon for payment at the appropriate time.

Debenture bond: A bond with no specific collateral pledged to guarantee payment other than the general credit rating of the issuer. Basically an I O U. Many government bonds are of this type, and they are considered to be the highest grade bonds available. This is also called a plain bond.

Discount bond: A bond which is sold at a discount from its face value. It usually does not earn interest during its life, but the interest is paid in a lump sum when the bond is redeemed. Savings bonds are of this type. Also called a non-interest bearing bond.

Equipment trust bond: Bonds secured by tangible property such as railroad equipment and passenger aircraft. The title to the equipment is held by a trustee while the equipment is leased to the issuer.

Estate tax bond: A special issue of long term treasury bonds that is sold at a discount but may be redeemed at par value for payment of estate taxes upon the death of the owner. Also called flower bonds since the special feature is usable only at the death of the owner.

Extended bond: A Bond which has had the maturity date postponed with the agreement of all the bondholders.

Fidelity bond: One of several types of bonds which are not investment securities. This is a contract in a form of insurance under which an outside firm guarantees a company or an individual against loss through the misconduct of another person who holds a position of trust. The contract becomes valid after an investigation of the bonded party and the payment of a fee by any interested party. The bonding fee is not returned after completion of the terms of the contract.

First lien bond: A bond that is backed by any asset whether real estate or other tangible or intangible assets and ranking ahead of any other liens on those assets.

First mortgage bond: A bond that is backed by a pledge of real estate that is not otherwise subject to any liens or other debts.

Flower bond: A special form of government bond sold during World War II which had a special provision whereby the bond, which was purchased at a discount, could be redeemed by the government at the full face value at any time before maturity for the purpose of paying estate taxes, in the event of the owner's premature death. It is the same as an estate bond.

Full faith and credit bond: A type of municipal bond which has no collateral to back it other than the pledge to repay. It is basically an I O U with the authority to levy taxes as the only strength to the pledge of faith.

Government bonds: Debt secutiries sold by the U. S. government. They are regarded as the highest grade in existence. There are seven categories distinguished by their time to maturity. Four of the bonds are true bonds and the other three are more properly called short term obligations. The longer the maturity time, the higher the interest earned.

1. Treasury bills: Also called T-bills. Mature in 13 to 26 weeks.

2. Treasury certificates: Mature in 6 months to one year.

3. Treasury notes: Mature in 1 to 5 years

4. Series E bonds: Also called a savings bond. Mature in 7 to 10 years, depending upon the time period in which they were issued. They may be retained for 10 years beyond maturity for additional growth in redemption value. This is a discount bond which receives interest in a lump sum at the time of redemption. War bonds were of this type. They are sold in denominations of $25 or larger.

5. Series H bonds: Mature in 10 years. Interest is paid semiannually. Sold in denominations of $500 or larger.

6. Treasury bonds: Also called treasuries. Mature in 5 to 28 years with the maximum interest rate set at 4½% by law. To make them attractive to the public, they are also sold at discounts which raise the effective yield to over 10% depending upon the economic conditions and bond market demand at the time.

7. Agency bonds: Bonds that are not truly issued by the government but by certain agencies of the government or sponsored by the government. They may issue securities backed by the credit of the U.S. government. Some of these agencies are:
Commodity Credit Corporation
Department of Housing and Urban Development

Federal Deposit Insurance Corporation
Housing Assistance Administration
Tennessee Valley Authority

Other federal agencies issuing securities that are not guaranteed by the U.S. government are:

Banks for Cooperatives
Export Import Bank
Federal Home Loan Bank System
Federal Intermediate Credit Bank
Federal Land Bank
Federal National Mortgage Association
Federal Savings and Loan Insurance Corporation

Guaranteed bond: Also called endorsed bonds, assumed bonds or joint bonds. Repayment is guaranteed by someone other than the issuer. For example, a parent company may guarantee the repayment of an issue by a subsidiary.

Income bond: A bond with the specifications that interest payments will be made from current earnings of the issuer.

Industrial bonds: Any of a broad range of bonds issued by business corporations except utilities and railroads. The bonds are sold to private investors who seek more safety than is commonly found to the owner. The issuing company uses the proceeds of the bond sales for capital expansion or operating expenses and promises to repay the face amount of the bond at some specified date that can be up to 100 years from issue. A few have been issued as perpetual bonds. Some will mature in as little as 10 years, and others can be converted into common stock if so designated at the time of sale. Some varieties of industrial bonds are:

1. Bearer bond: Bonds which are not registered in the name of the purchaser. Ownership is determined by possession. These usually have coupons attached which must be clipped and presented for interest payment. Also called a coupon bond.

2. Blanket bond: Those bonds which are backed by an overall second or third mortgage on all assets. They rank below mortgage bonds.

3. Convertible bond: Those bonds which have a special provision written into them whereby the holder may exchange them for common stock issued by the same company, at some future time, at the option of the holder.

4. Coupon bond: A bond which has coupons attached to the certificate which are dated for each interest payment date. The coupons must be clipped and presented by the owner of the bond to receive his interest payment. The bond is not registered in the name of the purchaser, but ownership is determined by possession. It is a bearer bond.

5. Debenture bond: Bonds which are backed only by the credit rating of the issuer. Basically an I O U or promissory note. Often called a plain bond.

6. Mortgage bond: A bond which is backed by a mortgage on real estate. These are considered to be the highest grade industrial bonds.

7. Participating bond: A bond which provides for the owner to share in the profits of the issuer as does a shareholder, and also to receive a guaranteed interest payment and the greater safety of a bond.

8. Serial bond: A single issue of bonds that are all sold on one date but mature at varying times.

9. Series bonds: A single issue of bonds that are sold at

varying intervals in order to provide a regular flow of operating funds and less burden at the time of redemption.

Industrial development bond: A tax-exempt municipal bond that is sold in a given community for the purpose of financing facilities for private business. It is a plan by the federal government to attract needed industry to areas in need of economic growth. The tax-free status attracts investors, and low cost financing, energetically promoted by local government, attracts new business, new jobs, and new tax receipts.

Interchangeable bond: A bond which can be exchanged for a different form of bond after purchase. As an example, a coupon bond, which is a bearer bond, may sometimes be exchanged for a registered bond which is registered in the name of the holder. Protection from loss is much better with the registered type. Any special features like this must be written into the bond at the time of issue.

Interim bond: A temporary certificate that is intended to be exchanged for a definitive bond at a later time.

Irredeemable bond: The same as an annuity bond or a perpetual bond which does not have a maturity date. The holder continues to earn interest indefinitely.

Joint bonds: A bond issue which is jointly issued by two or more companies and guaranteed by both. This proceedure may be used by two power companies to finance a new large facility. It may also be used by a parent-subsidiary effort.

Junior lien bond: A bond that is backed by a pledge of real estate but is in a subordinate position behind another mortgage.

Mortgage bonds: Bonds which are backed by a mortgage on real estate. Considered the best type of industrial bonds. They may be first mortgage, second mortgage, etc., indicating priority of claims against the property.

Municipal bond: Bond issued by states or local governments and other taxing agencies except the federal government. Generally, interest on municipals is wholly or partially tax-free to induce investment in local government projects. In some cities they are called corporate stock.

Optional bond: A bond which may be redeemed prior to the maturity date if the issuer so agrees.

Overlaying bond: A bond which ranks behind another issue by the same issuer in claims against some asset. It ranks behind the prior lien bonds.

Performance bond: One of several types of bonds that are not investment securities. This is money deposited by one party of a contract to guarantee to the other party that he will perform his part of the agreement. Construction contractors frequently must post performance bonds with cities to insure satisfactory completion of public works programs. An entertainer or other public figure may post such bonds when renting an auditorium. The bond is returned upon completion of the contract terms.

Pepetual bond: The same as an irredeemable bond or annuity bond which has no maturity date but continues earning interest indefinitely.

Plain bond: Another name for a debenture bond. It is a bond with no other specific collateral pledged than the credit of the issuer. It is an I O U. Many government bonds are of this type.

Prior lien bond: A bond which ranks ahead of another issue by the same issuer, in claims against some asset.

It ranks ahead of the overlaying bonds.

Registered bond: A bond which is registered in the name of the owner. It offers safety in the event of loss or damage.

Refunding bond: A bond issued to raise cash for the purpose of paying off an older issue or some other indebtedness.

Reorganizational bond: A bond issued to assist in the recapitalization of a corporation.

Revenue bond: A bond issued for special projects like toll roads, bridges, transit systems, and sewer projects, where the income generated by the facility is used to pay the interest.

Serial bonds: An issue of bonds which is broken into many groups maturing at periodic intervals. Note the difference from series bonds which are defined by the *date of issue.*

Series bonds: A single issue of bonds that is broken into many groups for issuance at regular intervals over a period of years. They all have the same backing but may have different terms according to the year of issue. Note the difference from serial bonds which are defined by *maturing dates.*

Sinking fund bond: A bond issue that has as one of its terms the requirement for a sinking fund to be established for bond redemption. This fund consists of money set aside yearly and perhaps invested until needed to pay off bonds.

Special assessment bond: A bond backed by the taxation powers of a local government to assess specific persons for the cost of a special project which will primarily benefit those being taxed. An example is a project to widen certain streets or install sidewalks in an area recently annexed into a city.

Subordinate debenture: A bond with the lowest rank in its claim on assets. No specific collateral is pledged to back the issue. Also called a plain bond.

Tax exempt bonds: Also called municipals. A form of bonds issued by local governments to finance city or county projects. Under federal authorization, the income received by bond holders from these bonds is exempt from federal income taxes. The purpose for the arrangement is to attract financing to many otherwise unglamorous municipal projects such as sewer systems, water treatment plants, highway departments, parks, etc. Generally, the interest paid on these bonds is lower than industrial bonds, but the tax-exempt status offsets the difference, especially to individuals in high tax brackets.

Book

A notebook used by an exchange floor specialist to keep a record of the buy and sell orders for stocks he deals in. Entries are made at specified prices in the order received from other brokers.

Book equity

The percentage of a company's book value to which a particular class of stock has claim. This figure may vary from time to time. For example, if a preferred stock has prior claim and the book value declines below the amount due preferred shareholders, then the common stock has no book equity at all. In practice, a company may assign almost any conditions to any class of stock prior to its issue so that many variations can exist. Notice the difference from BOOK VALUE.

Book value

The net worth of a company, or the value of its depreciated assets, as they are carried on the records. It is also called capital or shareholder's equity. The value may differ from true liquidating value because assets are carried on the books at their depreciated value, which may vary from the actual market value if the assets were sold. Book value is calculated by subtracting all liabilities . . . bank debt, current payables, taxes due, interest, depreciation, and bond or note redemption cost from the total assets . . . real estate, equipment, inventories, receivables, securities, cash, prepaid expenses and intangible assets. Notice the difference from LIQUIDATING VALUE. Also see DEPRECIATION, ALLOWED or ALLOWABLE.

Book value per share of common

Total tangible assets of a corporation as they are carried on the books less liabilities, less the liquidation value of the preferred stock outstanding, divided by the number of shares of common stock outstanding.

Boom

A period of rapid economic growth and expansion along with the usual rising stock prices.

Bottom

In stock charting it is a term used to describe the lowest point for any given period of time on that chart. It can only be said in retrospect and must be followed by a recovery. If a chart shows falling prices which the chartist believes will show a turnaround soon he may say that it appears to be bottoming. Occasionally a chart may show a bottom followed by recovery that fails and returns to another bottom in the same price level as the first. This double bottom is interpreted to be a sure sign that the market will go no lower. Chartists draw a line across the chart connecting the two low points and extended a few weeks or months ahead. This line is called a support line which is considered impervious to further price declines. If the price hits a bottom, then holds for any length of time at that level, it is called a base, which is interpreted as a sign of consolidation or gathering of strength for a strong push upward. See PATTERNS for a list of chart patterns that have meaning for chartists.

Bourse

A French word for stock exchange. The term is commonly used throughout Europe.

Box

A term of convenience when referring to the inventory in a particular stock of any investor's portfolio, whether an individual or a dealer. If an investor owns 500 shares of XYZ company among his other investments, he is said to have 500 XYZ in the box. It is the same as saying he has a long position of 500 XYZ. The term gets use when a person holds shares of a given stock which he expects to decline in price. He does not want to sell his stock but wants to take advantage of the decline. He will then sell against the box, or sell short while holding his long position. After the decline he will cover the short for a profit and he will still have his other shares intact. See SELLING AGAINST THE BOX for added information.

Box differences

Shortages or overages in the inventory of securities held by a broker. They may result from bookkeeping error, mistakes when making deliveries to customers, or possibly theft.

Brassage

A charge made by the government for converting bullion into coins. Sometimes it is used as synonymous with seigniorage. As an example, a 50¢ coin may be minted to contain only 25¢ worth of silver. When the metal value increases to the point where its intrinsic value is more than its face value, the coins tend to be hoarded and even melted down and sold for metal. Usually a government will recall the coins before that point is reached. They may then change the alloy of metal used in the coins. This tendency to be hoarded is defined in GRESHAM'S LAW.

Breadth

1. When referring to the market for a single security it means the distribution of *shares* in the hands of investors. A security with only a few shares in public hands is said to have a thin market. A broad market is one which has a large number of shares in public hands and it probably has heavy volume in trading, also. When referring to the entire securities market, breadth means the distribution of *trading*. A large number of shares being traded by a few institutions would not constitute a broad market, but a large number of smaller investors trading a few shares each would be greater breadth.

2. Breadth is also used to refer to a technical study of stocks listed on the New York Stock Exchange to determine the reliability of interpreting *any* market moves as a reflection of *all* investors. Certain indexes used to indicate market breadth are: ad-

vance-decline line, daily volume, volume momentum, and a composite breadth index.

Break

In stock charting it is a point on the chart where the prices begin a pronounced decline. At the time when the prices do break, it is also said that they top out. Also see REVERSAL, CORRECTION, PROFIT TAKING and DOWN SIDE for different views of a decline. See STOCK CHARTS for illustration.

Breakout

A term used in technical analysis to describe a decisive move with heavy volume upward from a consolidation area on a stock chart. It has also been applied to the same type move downward. For an example, if a stock has been trading for a number of weeks in the 16 to 18 area, a strong climb with heavy volume in trading up to 20 would be called a breakout. It may be called a breakout any time it passes through a resistance line or support line. Also see UP REVERSAL, RALLY, RECOVERY and TURN-AROUND for similar moves in varying degrees, and STOCK CHARTS for the illustrated chart patterns.

Broad tape

A teletype printout in brokerages throughout the country which continuously records updated financial news issued by the Dow Jones news ticker. Also see TICKER for additional information.

Broker

A person who acts as an agent, who buys or sells for a client's account from or to another broker or dealer, and earns commissions as compensation. The term differs from dealer in that a dealer buys for his own account and then will sell to a client from his account. The term is often applied to the person who handles security trading orders for investors. While that person may actually be a broker, or the licensed principal in that brokerage, more often he is a licensed representative of the broker. The representative is properly called an account representative, account executive, customer's man, or customer's broker. Still, he is loosely called "my broker" by most investors.

Brokerage house

Any firm whether acting as broker or dealer, which assists investors in securities trading. Most large brokerages are members of the New York Stock Exchange, as well as some of the other exchanges. These member firms may act as brokers when arranging trades on the exchange floor for their clients, or they may act as dealers when buying for their own accounts or selling from their own accounts to investors. See STOCK EXCHANGE, MEMBER FIRM, and EXCHANGE SEAT for more information on brokerages.

Broker's loan

Money borrowed by brokers from banks for a variety of uses. It may be used by specialists and odd-lot dealers to help finance inventories of stocks they deal in, by brokerage firms to finance the underwriting of new issues of corporate and municipal securities, to help finance a firms own investment, or to help finance the purchase of securities for customers who prefer to use the broker's credit (margin purchase) when they buy securities.

Bucket shop

An illegal operation in which a broker takes a

customer's money for an investment but does not actually buy the security ordered. The operator is betting that the market will go against the investor, so he holds back, thinking he can make delivery later with securities purchased at a lower price. The operator would keep the difference. This type scheme has disappeared from the industry since the formation of regulatory agencies and tight securities laws.

Bull

A person who believes the market will rise. Possibly so named because his four-legged counterpart is a stubborn, fearless creature that ponderously charges through any and all deterrents. Forward is the only direction he knows. Opposite of a bear.

Bull market

A rising market or an up market. A period of generally rising stock prices and optimistic outlook. Also called a strong market, advancing market, up market, up trend, and expansion period. These terms are usually used to describe the rising market after it has passed the level considered to be normal. If the market is recovering from a deep decline, the early stages of the up trend are called an up reversal, turnaround, rally, and recovery.

Bullish

An influence on the market which will tend to make prices rise, or an attitude of investors who believe the market will rise. The following are conditions that can normally be considered bullish influences: decreasing interest rates, increasing business expansion, increasing corporate profits, settling of labor strikes, settling of political unrest, expanding of international trade, or clearing up of *any kind* of uncertainty. A twist in this measurement of influences is in commodity futures trading. A favorable report for farmers would be good weather and bumper crops; however, this would tend to lower market prices for the produce, and it would become a bearish pressure on commodity prices. A bullish report for traders, then, is a bearish report for producers.

Bust
The opposite of a boom. Falling stock prices, slow down in industry, shrinking profits, lay offs, etc. It is also a period of economic recession or depression and a time when stock prices "fall out of bed".

Buttonwood tree
A tree on Wall Street under which securities trading was conducted two hundred years ago. In 1792 the activities were organized into a formal business which later on became the New York Stock Exchange. The oldest stock exchange in the world began in Germany about the middle of the 16th century. See CURB for the beginnings of the American Exchange.

Buy order
An authorization given by an investor for a broker to purchase a security. It can be issued at market, which would let the broker make the transaction at whatever price he is able to obtain; or it may stipulate a price lower than the current asked price, which would make it a limit order. The order will be held by the broker until the desired price is obtained or the order is cancelled. There are a number of different variations of orders that have special significance to investors and brokers. Each of the following are listed under

---

separate headings with definitions.

All or none	Immediate or cancel
Alternative order	Limit order
At market	Market order
At the close	Not held
At the opening only	Open order
Cancel order	Percentage order
Contingent order	Sell order
Day order	Stop limit
Discretionary order	Stop loss
Do not reduce	Stop order
Either/or	Switch order
Fill or kill	Time order
Firm order	Today order
Good until cancelled	When as and if
Hit the bid	

Buyer's market

A time when prices are weak and falling. The buyers are able to negotiate better terms for themselves. Opposite to seller's market, which is a time when demand is strong enough that the sellers can get nearly any price they want.

Buying power

In a margin account it is the amount of money you have available for additional purchases of securities. It is the difference between the amount of credit you are using and the amount available to you, based on the market value of securities in your account. It can be calculated by dividing the prevailing margin requirements (which can vary from 40% to 100%) into the current market value of your portfolio, then finding the difference between that result and the market value as the total margin available. If you currently have any debit balance owing, subtract that amount from the total margin available, and the remainder is your current buying power.

Buying range

An arbitrary area in a declining market price where an investor or analyst is forecasting a probable turnaround. Since the security price is expected to rise from that point, it would be the ideal time to buy. It can be used as a soft sell tactic by some brokers to suggest that you should buy at that time.

Buying signals

A progression of prices on a stock chart that exceeds what could be considered normal. It is read as an indication that self-stabilizing forces will soon take effect to cause a reversal in trend. Trading on such signals is moving with the odds. Several such conditions follow:

1. A sharp decline that continues for several days, following a longer period of slowly declining prices.
2. A leveling of prices following a period of unusually strong declining prices.
3. *Any* plunge, which is a sharp decline of 20 percent or more in a single day.
4. A low point on a wave pattern that appears to duplicate the duration and intensity of several preceding waves.

These signals should be interpreted in the light of *fundamental* conditions that can alter any normal patterns. Also see SELLING SIGNALS, CHARTING, TECHNICAL ANALYSIS, OPTIMAL ANALYSIS and TREND LINES for additional information on interpreting chart patterns. Samples of buying signals and other chart patterns are shown under heading of STOCK CHARTS.

Buying syndicate

A group of investment bankers formed to share the risk involved in underwriting an issue. They usually are assisted by a group of brokers and dealers called the participating brokers and dealers or selling group, which is not a part of the syndicate.

C

CBOE

The Chicago Board Options Exchange. An exchange set up by the Chicago Board of Trade and using facilities provided by the Board for open market trading of certain stock options. Previously, options had been used on an individually negotiated basis but still reached a volume of 320,000 trades, involving 32,000,000 shares during the one year period of 1972. The CBOE began operating in 1973, and within the first year the volume had reached an annual rate of 25,000,000 trades. It is expected that some 400 issues will eventually be traded with a volume 10 times as high.

An option is a contract to buy or sell a given security at a given price on or before a given date. The option to buy is called a call. The option to sell is called a put. A combination of put and call at the same time is called a straddle. Variations of a straddle are called strip and strap. These terms are described under separate headings. Also see STRIKING PRICE and EXERCISE for more information about options.

CBOT

The Chicago Board of Trade. The leading grain market in the United States, organized in 1848 as an association of grain dealers. The Board drafts and enforces facilities for trading in both spot prices and futures contracts. Its facilities are known as a commodities exchange. An offshoot from the Chicago Board of Trade is the Chicago Board Options Exchange (CBOE), which in mid-1973 began the first open market trading of security options.

C D's

Certificates of Deposit. Instruments which are used as savings deposits for larger amounts of cash. They are issued by banks for a specific period of time and are usually for larger amounts than ordinary savings deposits . . . $25,000, $100,000, or more. They earn slightly higher interest rates than other types of deposits. Since CD's are time deposits the money cannot be withdrawn early; however, the CD may be discounted to another individual, that is, sold at a discount.

Calculated risk

A venture which has uncertainities but the alternatives have been carefully studied in order to select the course with the highest probability of success. Also see RISK for an expanded discussion of types of risks and solutions to it.

Call

1. An option to buy a fixed amount of stock at a specified price within a specified time. It is a speculative device in which the purchaser of the call expects the market price of the stock to rise above his option price or striking price. If it does rise higher, he may exercise his option at the lower price, then immediately sell the security at the higher price. If, however, the market price falls or fails to reach the option price, the option holder forfeits the fee he paid for the option.

2. It is also a demand made upon holders of convertible bonds or convertible preferred stock to redeem the security or convert it into another type of security. Only those securities that are identified as callable at the time of issue may be called.

3. A margin call is a request by a broker for his client to put up additional cash in a margin account if the market value of the account has declined below the minimums required.

Call loans

A loan which is payable on demand. There is no specific due date assigned at the time of issue. See CALL MONEY MARKET for specific use of call loans.

Call money market

A special sector of the money market in which brokers and securities dealers borrow money to meet the needs of carrying margin accounts for their customers. The loans, which are due on demand by the banks, are secured by securities, and the interest rate is usually equal to the going prime rate. This money is used by brokers to re-loan to their customers for margin accounts. That is why margin accounts are said to provide the investor the use of the broker's credit to finance securities purchases. The rate of interest paid by the customer is usually a half percent above the prime rate or the rate paid by the broker. Most of these loans are made in New York, where many of the brokers have headquarters, so the demand for these loans has come to be called the New York call money market. In the same manner, the interest rate for the loans is often termed the New York call money rate.

Call money rate

Interest paid by brokers on loans obtained to finance their customer's margin accounts. The rates are usually the same as the going prime rate set by banks for their most credit-worthy customers. Collateral pledged to secure these loans is usually the stock certificates for street name accounts. That is why investors must use street name accounts for margin trading. In these accounts the stock certificates are actually in the broker's name, and the customer is identified by bookkeeping entry only. These loans are call loans with no specific due date. It is really an open credit line for the broker where the amount of the loan may vary from day to day, depending upon the need for credit to finance margin accounts.

Call price

The price at which a company will repurchase a callable security. The call is issued by the company at its option but all conditions of the call are stated before its issue.

Call protection
In a bond issue or callable preferred stock issue it is a clause which specifies a period of time during which the company cannot recall the security.

Callable bond
A bond which may be called in before maturity for repayment. The recall condition must be written into the bond at the time of issue. It is also called a redeemable bond. See BONDS for other types of bonds and comparisons between them.

Capital
The investment in business. It generally refers to the money or property used in business but can apply to cash in reserve, savings, securities, and other property of value, and a few economists even include special skills or talents because they can be used to produce income. On financial reports capital refers to the net worth of a company or the total of all assets less the total of all liabilities. In this sense it is also called the SHAREHOLDER'S EQUITY, BOOK VALUE, or CAPITAL OF BUSINESS.

Capital assets
The assets which represent a company's depreciable investment in business. It will include land, buildings, manufacturing equipment, office equipment, furniture, and other items used in business to produce income. Certain small items such as drills, wrenches, and desk calendars may be entered into the books as expenses. Often capital assets is synonymous with fixed assets. Notice the difference from CURRENT ASSETS, LIQUID ASSETS, QUICK ASSETS, and INTANGIBLE ASSETS.

Capital equipment

Equipment used in business in the performance of its operations and in the production of income. It excludes real estate or other investments but will include lathes, welders, trucks, bulldozers, cash registers, printing presses, and testing equipment. The term will apply to equipment used in the same condition as when purchased. Occasionally the term capital goods is used, but improperly so, to mean capital equipment. The distinction is that the term goods can apply to components of the finished product, such as motors, switches, hydraulic cylinders, valves, wheels, compressors, etc.

Capital gains

Profit that is received from the sale of some asset, either securities or other property, which has been held for more than six months since purchase. Certain types of royalties and some other forms of income are eligible for capital gains treatment by special tax law concessions, for lower tax rates than ordinary income. Also called long term gains. Notice that the words profit, growth and appreciation are usually applied to capital gains. By contrast, profit from property sold less than six months after it is purchased is called short term capital gains or ordinary income. Dividends and interest payments received from investments are also ordinary income.

Capital gains distributions

Payments made to shareholders of mutual funds which represent their proportional share of the net capital gains realized by the sale of securities from the fund's portfolio. These payments are carefully separated from income or dividend distributions because of the different tax rates that apply. See INVESTMENT COMPANY ACT OF 1940 for other limitations, purposes and definitions applying to mutual funds.

Capital gains dividends

The same thing as capital gains distributions. It is used only when speaking of distributions from mutual funds. The term dividend is used only because it represents money received from an investment, but it is clearly identified as the shareholder's proportional share of capital gains profits from the sale of securities. They are taxable as long term gains.

Capital gains funds

Mutual funds which have a policy of seeking profits through capital gains only. They will invest in growth stocks and some speculative issues. These funds will appeal to younger investors and professional people who have sufficient income but seek maximum growth for future years. Also see INVESTMENT COMPANIES for other types of funds and INVESTMENT COMPANY ACT OF 1940 for definitions, purposes and limitations.

Capital goods

Products and materials which are used in the manufacture of consumer products without themselves being consumed. Examples are as follows: electric motors, wood panelling, auto tires, and compressors. Products which are consumed or lose their identity in manufacturing processes such as chemicals, agricultural products, fuels, and textiles are called raw materials, supplies or commodities, as in the case of staples purchased in bulk form.

Capital loss deduction

Tax deductible loss received from securities or other properties that had been held more than six months since purchase. Individuals are allowed to deduct from taxable income, up to $1000 of net capital loss during the year in which it was reported. If the actual loss exceeds $1000, up to $1000 may be deducted as a short term capital loss in subsequent years, after adjusting for capital gains, until the loss is used up.

Capital statement

A brief report included in a company's financial statements which shows the capital or net worth, at the beginning of the reporting period, plus the additions to capital and the latest amount of capital at the end of the period. This report accompanies the balance sheet and the income statement in the periodic financial reports.

Capital stock

All stock of any class or type that is issued by a corporation. It represents ownership and is called equity. Bonds are not included, but are called debt securities, along with notes and commercial paper. See STOCK for distinctions and definitions with a list of different types being used.

Capital structure

The total capitalization of a company with reference to various types of securities it has issued. If it consists entirely of common stock it is said to be of a conservative structure. If bonds are also issued, it is then said to be leveraged, because the added capital can produce higher earnings for each dollar of equity. A highly leveraged company (with heavy debt capital) with a modest amount of common stock is said to be of a speculative structure. Notice that a speculative capital structure may even enhance the growth potential in its common stock. This would make it attractive to short term investors, but it could also be very risky in times of economic difficulty.

Capital surplus

The amount of value remaining from the original investment in a corporation. It is calculated by adding the net worth of the company (assets minus liabilities) to the stated value of the issued capital stock, then subtracting the earned surplus or retained earnings. The earned surplus represents profits from operations, so it is not counted as capital. Capital surplus is also called paid-in surplus.

Capitalism

An economic system under which the public is permitted to own property and operate any kind of business for its own benefit and profit. Under this system the government plays the roll of maintaining order, preventing abuses of the system whereby one enterprise infringes upon the rights of another, and operating such services as municipal services, highways, military forces, and other activities that could not be expected to be profitable for private business. Under capitalism individuals own privately or jointly, through corporations and partnerships, all manufacturing and service enterprises. They share the earnings of such companies through dividends, interest payments, and bonuses on an equal basis, according to their percentage of ownership. They may also hold, exchange, or sell their share of ownership at any time on the open market to any other private citizen. The profit incentive for investing in the business portion of national life is considered proper, desirable, and an open opportunity for everyone. It provides security for the investor as well as jobs, products, services, and income for many others. It is also from private business that a major portion of the tax money originates to support government services.

Frequently the term free enterprise is considered as synonymous with capitalism. Actually, capitalism pertains to the concept of individuals providing investment capital to operate the business system and receiving the profit in return. Free enterprise, in a narrow sense, pertains to the right of individuals to enter into any activity or contractual arrangement for their own well being through choice. Together, the terms maintain the rights of the people above the rights of government. Opposed to these concepts are socialism, communism, monarchism, fascism, military governments of various forms or the feudal systems of centuries ago. Also see FREE ENTERPRISE for some expanded information.

Capitalization
The total dollar amount of various securities issued by a corporation. It will include bonds as well as stock, whereas the term equity or equity capital includes only the value of stock issued. Capitalization, as carried on the books, may not represent either current market value or net worth but usually represents initial stated value or net proceeds received at the time securities are issued. Bonds may be listed at face value and stock can be listed at par value (a very arbitrary figure), stated value (another arbitrary value), or net proceeds, plus the paid-in surplus. See CAPITAL STRUCTURE and NET WORTH for differences from capitalization.

Capitalized expenses

Expenditures which are amortized over a period of time instead of being charged off as operating expenses, or "expensed off." They, therefore, receive the same treatment as machinery and tooling. Expenses which can be capitalized include some research and development costs, since the resulting product will produce income for many years ahead just as any other capital asset would. Patent costs, organizational expenses for a new venture, legal services, or other professional services leading up to the income producing stage of a product or service may be capitalized.

Carry forward

Business losses from prior years that are deducted from profits in current and subsequent years when filing tax returns. Also called loss carry forward, tax loss carry forward, tax credits, and tax loss credits. See TAX LOSS CARRY FORWARD for more information.

Cash

To most people it is just legal tender. To some it spells out the terms for a transaction . . . payment before taking delivery. It may suggest the action of submitting a demand for payment . . . cashing a check, or resignation from a venture . . . cashing in one's securities. It suggests financial strength, although most modern and prospering economies grow through credit. In inflationary times, cash is considered safer than securities, yet the securities could give growth, while cash is guaranteed to lose value through inflation. On a financial statement the heading cash is equated with negotiable securities, and, nearly always, the cash figure consists mainly of bookkeeping entries for bank deposits, while the actual money may be loaned out.

Cash account

An investment account with a broker in which trades are made only if the full payment will be made for each purchase. It contrasts with the margin account in which the investor may trade on partial credit. On a cash trade the investor still has four days after the trading date to make payment even though the record will show him as the true owner. The stock certificate may not be delivered for some time afterward. In margin trading there are no certificates delivered.

Cash equivalent

1. On a financial report the term refers to accounts receivable, securities, notes and other negotiable documents.
2. Certificates of deposit in units of $100,000 or more. It is a negotiable certificate giving evidence of deposit that cannot be withdrawn until the specified date. It is not a security which is subject to market demand but represents an exact amount of cash that will be paid to the owner on the specified date. Since certificates of deposit are time deposits, the bank can operate more safely without fear of having deposits withdrawn at awkward times. They will therefore pay higher interest rates on these CD's.

Cash equivalent fund

A mutual fund formed for the purpose of buying only high yield, large denomination certificates of deposit. CD's pay very high interest rates and are very low risk transactions but the large denominations ($100,000 for most) prevent most investors from participating. The cash equivalent funds permit the small investor to take advantage of the CD's with much less capital requirement. Such funds appeared as a solution to the ailing stock market of 1973 and 1974. Also see INVESTMENT COMPANY for other types of funds and INVESTMENT COMPANY ACT OF 1940 for definitions, purposes, and limitations.

Cash flow

A report showing the total of a corporation's revenues plus all bookkeeping entries for operating expenses, materials, services, depreciation, amortization of debt, and extraordinary charges to reserves, which are bookkeeping deductions but not actually paid out. Simply, it is a total of all receipts and expenditures. Cash flow has been used increasingly as a yardstick of a company's success because it gives a good indication of earning power.

Cash position

The ratio of a corporation's cash or easily cashed securities to other assets. An investment company which has sold a considerable amount of its securities and is holding cash while looking for other investments is said to have a strong cash position.

Cash sale

A transaction on the floor of the stock exchange which calls for both cash payment and delivery of the securities on that same day. By contrast, in "regular way" trades, the seller is allowed four business days after the day of the transaction for delivery, and the buyer has the same time for payment. See DELIVERY for other methods.

Cats and dogs

Highly questionable stocks. Usually low priced and quite speculative with little demand and small prospects for growth.

Caveat emptor

A Latin term meaning "let the buyer beware." It suggests that people still possess certain human traits that make some business deals suspect. There may be laws to protect consumers, but not all people abide by them. It is, therefore, the job of individuals to be cautious and avoid deals that are less than bargained for. In recent years there are new laws and new public attitudes that make it very necessary for the seller to beware as well, since some of our consumer protection efforts have made it possible and even popular to exploit corporations through legal pressure, public opinion and class action law suits.

Central certificate service of the N Y S E

A central depository for securities held by member brokers. Because of the immense job involved in physically transporting the millions of stock certificates representing daily trades, the CCS transfers many for street name accounts by simple entries on the books.

Certificate of deposit

A certificate issued by a bank for a single cash deposit which will be left on deposit for a specified length of time. Usually issued for larger amounts only: $25,000, $100,000, $500,000 or more. Recently some banks have offered some for as little as $500 in an attempt to attract more cash for working purposes. The certificates of deposit generally earn higher interest than ordinary savings deposits because the customer cannot withdraw his money before the specified date. Commonly called CD's. If a depositor needs his cash before the maturity date on the CD, he may sell the CD. The selling price in that case would be discounted from the face value by approximately the pro-rated interest to the date of maturity.

Chapter 8

One of the chapters of the Federal Bankruptcy Act under which an individual or business dissolves or reorganizes in order to settle debts. The Bankruptcy Act consists of 14 chapters in all. The first seven establish the structure of the system and the last seven define proceedings for specific cases. Some chapters pertain to individuals only and others to businesses only. Chapter 8 covers railroad reorganization and arrangements to settle debts. More information is given under the heading BANKRUPTCY.

Chapter 9

Another chapter under the Federal Bankruptcy Act described above. Chapter 9 deals with reorganization of certain public authorities. Also see BANKRUPTCY for more information.

Chapter 10

Another chapter under the Federal Bankruptcy Act described above which deals with business reorganizations. Under these proceedings, management is replaced and trustees are appointed by the court to reorganize and recover profitability of the business. Also see BANKRUPTCY for more information.

Chapter 11

One of the most commonly used portions of the

Chapter 12

Bankruptcy Act described above which deals with business. Under this chapter the business continues to operate with existing management under court supervised arrangements that are worked out between the debtor and creditors to settle all debts eventually. Also see BANKRUPTCY for more information.

Chapter 12
Another chapter of the Federal Bankruptcy Act described above. This chapter deals with unincorporated debtors whose debts are secured by real estate. Also see BANKRUPTCY for more information.

Chapter 13
Another chapter of the Federal Bankruptcy Act described above. This chapter deals with personal affairs. It is a court supervised arrangement worked out between debtor and creditors for eventual settlement of debts. Also see BANKRUPTCY for more information.

Chapter 14
Another chapter of the Federal Bankruptcy Act described above. This chapter deals with maritime liens. Also see BANKRUPTCY for more information.

Chartered financial analyst
A person who has met rigid requirements of knowledge and experience in the field of security analysis.

Charting
Recording of some variable quantity on some form of chart or graph. In investment circles many investors regularly chart selected stock prices for the purpose of

anticipating the most profitable time to buy or sell securities. A person who interprets charts is called a chartist and also a technical analyst and will rely on signals, shapes, and movements on the charts to indicate conditions or pending trends. Some terms that have special significance to a chartist are the following: Trend line, support line, resistance line, moving average, base, consolidation, sidewise market, divergence, breakout, turnaround, rally, recovery, spike, plunge, technical correction, line, saucer, head and shoulders, double bottom, double top, buying signal, selling signal, primary wave, secondary wave and fundamental wave. See separate headings for each term and see STOCK CHARTS for examples of some as they appear on charts.

Chartist

A person who records stock prices, averages, indicators, influencing factors or any other data on charts for the purpose of comparison and analysis to aid in making investment decisions. See CHARTING and STOCK CHARTS for more information and samples of charts.

Charts

A method of recording stock prices and other data which might influence the price so that analysis of an investment is made more mechanical and scientific. There are several types of charts being used, each with some advantages and some weak points. The proper chart for any person may depend upon his investment objective and opinions of the different systems. The different types of charts used are line charts, bar charts, and point and figure charts. They can employ arithmetic or logarithmic graph paper. One system of proportional charts uses specially designed graphs that translate price movements on any stock, regardless of price levels or volatility, into percentage of change and percentage of return. See STOCK CHARTS for more information and examples of various charts.

Chicago Board Of Trade

The leading grain market in the United States, organized in 1848 as an association of grain dealers. They draft and enforce rules under which commodities are traded and provide facilities for trading in both spot prices and futures contracts. Its facilities are known as a commodities exchange. An offshoot from the Chicago Board of Trade is the Chicago Board Options Exchange (CBOE), which in mid-1973 began the first open market trading of security options.

Chicago Board Options Exchange

An exchange set up by the Chicago Board of Trade and using the facilities provided by the Board for open market trading of certain stock options. Previously, options had been used on an individually negotiated basis but still reached a volume of 320,000 trades involving 32,000,000 shares during the one year period of 1972. The CBOE began operating in 1973 and within the first year the volume had reached an annual rate of 25,000,000 trades. It is expected that the volume will eventually reach 10 times that high on some 400 issues.

An option is a contract to buy or sell a given security at a given price on or before a given date. The option to buy is called a "call". The option to sell is called a "put". A combination of put and call at the same time is called a straddle. Variations of a straddle are called strip and strap. These terms are described under separate headings. Also see STRIKING PRICE and EXERCISE for more information about options.

Churning
The practice by a broker of making many trades or transactions in a customer's account in order to generate many commissions for himself. It is illegal and is seldom engaged in anymore.

Classified stocks
Any of the many categories of stock which can be issued by a corporation beyond the common stock. As a corporation grows, its need for money continues to grow, but problems compound because of the many people who must be dealt with. Some want to hold control and are willing to give up certain privileges to new investors if controlling interest is not lost. Others may settle for different concessions. As a result, many types and classes of securities are issued with varying privileges and limitations. Each is carefully and completely described before sale to the public. Some designations and classes which have appeared are Class A, Class B, or Class C common; Class A, Class B, or Class C preferred; prior preferred; second class preferred; convertible preferred; debenture stock; and even a phantom stock, which is not a real stock and is not actually issued, but the benefits to the holder are real. See STOCK for more information and a list of different types of stock that are commonly used.

Clean house
To take inventory of your investment portfolio and sell off all those securities which are not meeting your requirements.

Clearing Corporation
Facilities of the New York Stock Exchange set up to execute and clear stock transactions. *Execution* involves the use of facilities (including the trading floor) to locate buyers or sellers and complete a trade. *Clearance* involves delivery of certificates and payment for the trade. Other exchanges have similar facilities.

Clearing House
Another name for the clearing corporation above.

Climax
A buying or selling climax is said to have been reached when after an extended climb or decline in stock market prices there occurs a day of very heavy trading with little appreciable further advance or decline.

Close
The last price of a trading day in a given security. It is usually the price quoted by analysts, brokers and newspapers and is the price charted on most stock charts. Also called the closing price.

Close corporation
Also called a closed corporation. It is a corporation in which all shares are held by a small number of people, perhaps one family. Its shares are not available to the public and there is no trading over-the-counter. Notice a slight difference from a CLOSELY HELD CORPORATION in which most shares are held by a small group of people, and a small number are in public hands. Also see PUBLIC CORPORATION, PARTNERSHIP and PROPRIETORSHIP for differences.

Closed corporation

Also called a close corporation. It is a corporation with all its outstanding stock held by a very small number of people, perhaps a single family. There is no public market for the stock, it is not traded over-the-counter. Notice the difference from a CLOSELY HELD CORPORATION below, which does have some shares in public hands and which may have some infrequent trading. Most of the stock in a closely held corporation is owned by a single investor or a family. Also see PUBLIC CORPORATION, PARTNERSHIP, and PROPRIETORSHIP for differences.

Closed end funds

Investment companies, not truly mutual funds, which have only one offering of shares to the public. Those shares thereafter trade on the open market, as do the shares of any other public corporation. These companies comprise only a small portion of the total investment company market. Although often called funds, the term mutual fund is properly applied only to open end investment companies. Also see OPEN END FUNDS for contrast, INVESTMENT COMPANIES for other types of funds and descriptions, and INVESTMENT COMPANY ACT of 1940 for definitions, purposes, and limitations.

Closed end investment company

The same as a closed end investment trust or closed end fund above. It does not redeem its shares upon demand as does the mutual fund, but they are traded on the open market between individuals. They have been referred to as closed end mutual funds, but the name is not properly applied.

Closed end investment trust
The same thing as a closed investment company or closed end fund listed on page 85.

Closely held corporation
A corporation in which most of the shares and voting control are held by a small group, but some are in the hands of the public. There is a very limited market for closely held corporations so trading is infrequent. Notice a slight difference from a CLOSE COR- PORATION or a CLOSED CORPORATION, both of which mean the company is owned entirely by a small group of people or even by a single family. There is no market for the stock, it is not traded over-the-counter. Also see PUBLIC CORPORATION, PARTNERSHIP, and PROPRIETORSHIP.

Closing a sale
Getting a commitment from a customer after he has been given sufficient information to justify a purchase. There are times when a company places such an emphasis on the closing of a sale that they may act- ually employ a specially trained, highly experienced person to handle the closing exclusively. This person is called a closer. The preliminary work of the sale: educating the prospect with facts about the product and explaining how it meets the prospect's needs, is called the presentation.

Closing prices
The trading price of any security at the time of the last trade before the exchange closes for the day. Sometimes a figure is reported for the last trade of the week. Also called the closing sale or simply the close.

Cognovit note

A note giving evidence of debt and promising to pay to the named creditor a specified amount at a specified time. Usually signed by a debtor at the same time he signs other contracts for installment loans. The cognovit note obligates the debtor for the full amount of the contract until the last payment is made. It also waives the debtor's rights to legal process to defend his position, and very often it also pledges all of the debtor's other assets as security. The cognovit note is now becoming illegal in many states.

Coincident indicators

Indexes or indicators of economic or market activity that show changing trends at approximately the same time that overall conditions begin to change. They are studied as verification of any other indicators that show changing trends. Some coincident indicators that are published regularly and frequently followed are: personal income, gross national product, industrial production index, retail sales, manufacturing and trade sales, non-agricultural employment, and total employment. Also see LEADING INDICATORS and LAGGING INDICATORS.

Collateral

Securities or other property pledged by a borrower to secure or guarantee repayment of a loan.

Collateral trust bond

A bond secured by collateral deposited with a trustee. The collateral is often the stocks or bonds of other companies controlled by the issuing company, but they may be any other securities. See BONDS for other types of bonds and comparisons between them.

Collateral trust certificates
Bonds that are backed by other securities as collateral. The same as a collateral trust bond on page 87. See BONDS for other types of bonds and comparisons between them.

Combination
Any of several transactions involving simultaneous purchases of puts, calls, or futures contracts. The purpose of combinations is to hedge ones position when speculating. For example, a person may buy a call if he is expecting the price of a stock to rise. The call gives him the right to buy the stock at any time within the specified time at a set price. If the market price does rise above the striking price of the call, the speculator may exercise his option and buy the stock at the striking price, then immediately sell the stock at the market price for a profit. If, however, the speculator is doubtful about the prospects for the stock, he may buy a put along with the call. The put will yield a profit only if the price declines, and the call makes a profit only if the price rises. The risks of the two positions are largely cancelled out, but the profit is also reduced. By carefully following trends and timing his moves, the speculator can realize profit through these combinations. Some combinations are called STRADDLES, STRIPS, STRAPS, or SPREADS. Also see SELLING AGAINST THE BOX for an example of gain from taking opposing positions.

Commercial paper
Documents created to transfer funds for short periods of time. Used by industry, banks, and other agencies for direct negotiations, operating much like a check. Often they take the form of a negotiable promissory

note. They typically mature in 90 to 180 days, but the time can be as short as two or three days. There is the beginning of a trend to use interest rates on commercial paper as the basis for establishing the prime rates charged by banks. This would be a swing away from the current practice of basing the prime rate on the federal discount rate.

Commission

A payment made to a broker, salesman, or other professional intermediary as compensation for his services, based upon the selling price of the product, or as a percentage of the transaction. Notice that a *dealer* does not get a commission, but a mark-up or a profit, since he has purchased the goods for his own account and is now selling them again.

Commission broker

An agent who executes the buying public's orders for the purchase or sale of securities or commodities. The broker differs from the *dealer* in that the broker represents his client in buying from or selling to another party, while the dealer buys securities for his own account and resells from his account to his clients. The term commission broker is not used or known to many investors, but *all* brokers are commission brokers unless the securities they sell to a client come from their own accounts. In that case they act as dealers. Most large brokerage houses carry an inventory on some stocks so they can act as dealers on some transactions and as brokers on others.

Commission house

A member firm of the New York Stock Exchange which acts as a broker or agent to transact securities trading for their customers. They are distinguished from specialists and dealers.

Commodities

Staple products which are basic to certain industries and traded in bulk form. Included are corn, wheat, oats, soybeans, soybean oil, coffee, cocoa, cotton, wool, beef, pork, eggs, poultry, frozen orange juice concentrate, copper, silver, lumber, and others. Frequently, in the investment world, people will speak of buying commodities when they actually mean commodity futures contracts. The contracts are discussed below.

Commodities futures contract

A contract to purchase or sell a given quantity of a given commodity on a certain date in the future. Futures contracts were originally developed to assist producers or processors of raw materials to stabilize their costs and profits by hedging against their needs for some months into the future. A typical contract may involve 5000 bushels of wheat or 100,000 board feet of lumber, calling for delivery in May of a certain year at a specific price that is determined by open market bidding. A processor may buy the contract to assure a known price when he is ready for delivery, or he may "short" the contract to protect the investment he has in current stocks of the item. A speculator finding the low margins attractive and the volatility enticing would buy the contract with the intention of selling it shortly afterward, making a few points of profit.

Commodity market

The market or public demand for commodity futures trading. The commodities themselves, or the raw materials, are sold in large quantities to processors with pricing on a bid and asked basis. The market also offers futures contracts, which are the only contact that many thousands of speculators have with the market. While processors try to protect their investment in inventories or their costs for future delivery, a great deal of the market involves futures trading by speculators. Margin requirements are very small (about 10%), and prices are volatile. The presence of speculators in the market is desirable and is encouraged because it makes the market liquid enough to serve the processor's purposes. From the speculator's side, the market is risky, yet exciting. Potential gain is great; the speed of trading is fast, as a position may be entered and closed out again within an hour. Market influences include: weather, international trade agreements, political developments, shipping strikes, and almost any shadow that falls across the quotation board. Emotional pressures are great, and it seems, at times, that there is no connection between the market trends and the fundamentals of the market. The largest commodity market is located in Chicago at the Chicago Board of Trade. Others are located in Minneapolis, Kansas City, New York and Winnepeg.

Commodity trading
Buying and selling contracts for future delivery of some commodity. Speculators trade the contracts with no concern about actually taking delivery on the physical product itself. Since the margin requirements are very low, a small price change means a large change in the value of a contract. This leverage makes it possible to gain 100% on investment in a single week

or *lose* the same amount. Since this market is more concerned with contracts than the physical commodity, the transactions involve short selling as much as long buying. Also, spreads are common practices where a long position is balanced by a short position. Timing is critical, as there are times that a $3000 investment can gain as much as $900 within a few minutes after the opening of the market, only to lose $1800 within an hour, then repeat those gyrations two more times during the day. Emotions are the strongest influences on the market, as traders attempt to interpret fundamental conditions and second guess other traders.

Common stock

Certificates representing an undivided interest in the assets of a corporation with no set rate of return. Dividends are determined by the board of directors. Voting rights of the corporation generally go only to the holders of common stock. The term shares is often a *quantitative* term used when discussing the number of shares owned by an investor or the number of shares involved in voting for various management policies. A certificate may be issued to represent any number of shares, or even a fraction of a share in some cases. The term stock is usually applied more to the *concept* of joint ownership than to a specific proportion of ownership or control. A person may say, "I own *stock* in XYZ Company," or he would say, "I own 100 *shares* of XYZ company." See STOCK for more information and list of different types of stock being used.

Common stock funds

Mutual funds which have a policy of investing

primarily in common stock for the growth and income they can provide. By contrast, some funds will buy preferred stock, bonds, or a mixture of all. See IN-VESTMENT COMPANIES for other types of funds and INVESTMENT COMPANY ACT OF 1940 for definitions, purposes and limitations.

Common trust fund

An arrangement with a bank for several parties to combine funds and invest them under the bank's management.

Compensating balance

A deposit made by one party so as to offer benefits for another. Interest on the deposit and the principal belong to the depositor, but an agreement is made to leave the deposit in the bank while a loan is being made to the second party. When the loan is repaid, the deposit may be withdrawn.

Competitive bidding

1. In the securities business it is bidding among buying syndicates for the right to underwrite all or part of an issue. In the trading of securities, prices are determined by the auction process of bidding. Prospective sellers ask their prices, and prospective buyers make their bids. Within seconds, traders make their decisions to accept or reject the quoted prices. If the selling pressure is strongest, the seller may "hit the bid" and accept what is offered. If the buying pressure is stronger, the buyer may accept the asking price.

2. In businesses such as construction, manufacturing, engineering services, and others where work is

done on a contract basis, competition between companies is by written bids. Each bid involves extensive studies and planning before prices can be quoted. Competing bids are then studied for various approaches to a job. Presumbly, cost is not the only basis for judgment in awarding the contract. Consideration is given to technical expertise of the bidder's staff, management quality, financial ratings, conceptual approach, delivery times, and, at times, political influences.

Composite tape

A new stock ticker printout which reports transactions in all national and regional stock exchanges as well as over-the-counter trading handled in thousands of offices across the country. It is a major advance from the traditional ticker tape which reports only the transactions on the national exchanges. The composite tape is also known as the unified tape.

Composites

Any set of data which combines information from different sources to yield some measurement of conditions in the securities industry. Some composites combine stock and bond prices. Others combine prices from different industries, and some use weighted multipliers to adjust results. Others will combine two or more other indexes to form a reading of confidence, optimism, breadth, or some other meaningful measurement of investor emotions and intentions.

Compound interest

Interest that is paid on an account which includes principal plus any previous interest payments which were added to the principal in prior interest periods. It is really a straight line interest which is made to increase the yield by shortening interest periods. Thus, an account paying interest compounded monthly will yield slightly more than if it is compounded quarterly. Also see INTEREST for other methods of calculating interest and several examples of calculations.

Computer hardware

The physical equipment used for computers. It contrasts to computer software, or the supporting supplies and services used to operate the computers.

Computer software

The product of an entire industry which supplies computer programming materials and services. The term originated out of a need to differentiate between the basic equipment and the supplies and services necessary in the operation of computers. The computers themselves are known as computer hardware. Note the difference from SOFTGOODS and HARD-GOODS.

Cone

The name given to a certain chart pattern on some stock charts. It is one of many patterns which have some significance to some chartists. Other patterns are listed separately under PATTERNS and some examples are shown under STOCK CHARTS.

Confidence index

An index promoted by *Barron's* which consists of the ratio between sales of high grade bonds and low grade bonds. The index is claimed to show general market confidence based on the reasoning that sophisticated investors will switch to higher grade bonds when they lack confidence in other market conditions. Increasing confidence, then, would lead them to purchase more speculative securities.

Confirmation slip

A form mailed to an investor by his broker which verifies a buying or selling transaction in a security. It lists the name of the security, the date of the transaction, the number of shares traded the price per share, commissions, and taxes, the amount due to the broker or to the customer, and, finally, the payment date or final date for making payment. It is also called a transaction slip. Traders on the commodity exchange may receive a similar document called a purchase and sale memorandum. These slips are sent out for each transaction, in addition to the monthly statement for the entire account.

Conglomerate

A corporation which is strongly committed to growth by acquisition with little concern for product relationships. It is also called a holding company, but some differences exist. Conglomerates often provide managerial assistance, even though the subsidiaries may vary widely in their products or services rendered. Holding companies usually restrict their acquisitions to a particular industry but are satisfied to participate in profits while the subsidiary must develop its own management.

Conglomerate merger

The joining of two companies in different lines of business into one corporate entity. Notice the differences between CONSOLIDATIONS, MERGERS and AMALGAMATIONS.

Consolidated accounting statements
The same as consolidated balance sheet. Accounting statements of a parent organization along with its divisions and subsidiaries combined in one report showing assets, liabilities, and net worth of the total organization.

Consolidated balance sheet
The same as consolidated accounting statements above.

Consolidation
1. In charting of securities it refers to a period of inactivity after a decline. Also called a base on the chart.
2. In corporate activities it is the combining of two or more separate businesses into one to form an entirely new corporation while the pre-existing companies cease to exist. Also called an amalgamation. Notice the differences from MERGER, CONGLOMERATE, HOLDING COMPANY and ACQUISITION.

See STOCK CHARTS for illustrated chart patterns.

Constant dollar, current dollar
Constant dollars represent current prices for some product compared to some base period in the past, while current dollars represent prices prevailing at any given time. For example, a certain product may have cost $1.00 in 1957. In 1975 that same product may have risen to $1.50 due to inflation. Both of these prices are stated in current dollars. Inflationary pressures which raise prices also raise wages, so a person may have earned his 1975 dollars for less labor than the 1957 dollar. If purchasing power of the dollar had been reduced by 50% between 1957 and 1975, the constant

dollar price for that $1.50 product would be only 75 cents in constant dollars based on 1957. The constant dollar concept is roughly the same as stating costs of goods or services in the buying power of a day's wages rather than in dollars.

Constant ratio investing

One type of plan for formula investing in which the ratio of value between two types of securities is held constant. For example, an investor wishing to maintain a 50/50 balance between common stock and bonds would sell off certain stocks if the market prices rose while bonds held steady. He would also buy additional stocks if market prices dropped while bonds held steady. Also called constant ratio plan. See FORMULA INVESTING for other plans.

Constant ratio plan

The same as constant ratio investing above.

Consumer goods

Any product sold to the ultimate consumer or user such as food, clothing, automobiles, furniture, television, etc.

Contingencies

The word means something incidental to a plan or something that depends on chance or uncertain conditions. When the word appears on a financial statement it refers to an amount of cash held in reserve or allotted for a reasonable amount of unforeseen expense that might occur after the original plans or estimates are made. It may also be a reserve set aside for possible losses.

Contingent order

An order issued by an investor to his broker for the purchase of one security and the sale of another security at a stipulated price difference. Also called a switch order. See BUY and SELL ORDERS for a list of other kinds or orders used in securities trading.

Continued bond

A bond that bears no maturity date. It will continue drawing interest indefinitely. Also called an annuity bond. See BONDS for other types of bonds and comparisons between them.

Contractual plan

A program offered by some mutual funds under which an investor may purchase additional shares at any time. Under these plans an investor agrees to purchase a fixed dollar amount at fixed time intervals. Notice the differences from VOLUNTARY PLANS which permit the investor to purchase any amount at any time or buy none at all as his circumstances dictate. Both plans are called periodic payment plans. Also see *special features* under the heading of INVESTMENT COMPANIES for other variations.

Conversion

1. Exchanging one security for another under conditions stipulated at the time the convertible security was issued. Normally, conversion privileges are given on preferred stock or bonds if there is a need to sweeten or enhance the offer for investors. The result is that in early years, the owner of the senior security enjoys the income and the preferential status of bonds or the preferred stock. Later, when growth is established, he may

convert his security or exchange it for common stock which might enjoy more growth, higher dividends and voting privileges.

2. In mutual funds conversion is switching from one fund to another fund which operates under the same management. It may be advisable for a younger person to invest in a growth seeking fund while he has other income and then convert to a more conservative type of fund at his retirement. It is sometimes called switching, although this term is usually applied to a change made at the urging of a salesman in order to earn commissions. In this latter sense it is an unethical practice by the salesman.

3. In law, conversion is an illegal type of activity with a meaning similar to embezzlement or theft. It is taking something that belongs to someone else and converting it for your own use.

Conversion charge

A fee charged to switch from one mutual fund to another which is operated by the same management. The fee is usually less than the regular sales charge. See CONVERSION above.

Conversion parity

The price at which a common stock is the equivalent of a convertible issue. The holder of a security which has the right of conversion or exchange for a common stock will usually not exercise the conversion privilege until the value of the common equals or exceeds the value of the convertible issue. The point of equality is the conversion parity price stated in terms of market value of the common stock.

Conversion price

The price set for a common stock for which a convertible preferred or convertible bond will be exchanged. Often it is stated as the conversion ratio, which is the number of shares of common stock that may be converted for each share of the convertible issue. Dividing that ratio into the price of the convertible issue gives the conversion price of the common stock. Usually conversion is not considered until the market price of the common rises to about the conversion price.

Conversion ratio

The number of shares of common stock that a convertible issue may be converted into. Conversion privileges and ratios are determined at the time of issue of the convertible security. On rare occasions a security may be issued without conversion privileges, then in later years be changed to a convertible by a special offer by the company. It is usually done only in preparation for mergers, acquisitions, or refinancing.

Convertible bond

A bond with a privilege of being exchanged for a specified number of common shares at some specified time at the option of the holder. See BONDS for other types of bonds and for comparisons between them.

Convertible preferred

A preferred stock which earns specified dividends and has superior rating to common in the event of liquidation, which can also be converted in later years for common stock which is the only class of stock to have voting rights. The common may also show greater growth and could have better dividends if the growth of the company is substantial. The company may even call the preferred stock, which forces the holders to convert them. See PREFERRED STOCK for other kinds of preferred, and STOCK for listings of other types of stock.

Corner

To have control of the supply of some security or commodity by buying on such large scale that the entire market is affected. It is an illegal practice which can strongly influence market prices either driving them up so that the person with the corner makes undue profit or forces others with a short position to cover at a loss. It is also said that a manufacturer who has a product that holds a major portion of the market has a corner on that market.

Corporate shell

A corporation which is no longer doing business but is still legally in existence. It may have some officers, a bank account, and a name. They have been used in acquisitions or other corporate level activities as a device for quick, easy profits, or as a way to shelter some income. Their use can be either legal or illegal, depending upon how they are used.

Corporate stock

Not actually a stock in the sense of representing equity. This is a name given to bonds in some states that are issued by the state or local governments for use in financing local public works projects. They can also be issued by certain other taxing agencies except the federal government. Generally the interest yield is tax-exempt to induce investment in the projects. In most states they are called municipal bonds. See

BONDS for comparison to other bonds and STOCKS for comparison to equity securities.

Corporation

A legal entity whose shareholders generally have limited liability (limited to their investment only). A corporation has all the legal qualities and rights of an individual. Ownership is represented by shares which are issued to persons or other companies in exchange for cash, physical assets, services or goodwill. The initial issue of stock is sold or distributed on a basis determined by the original incorporators. Subsequent resale or exchange of the shares is subject to market demand for that security. Shareholders are the owners of the corporation, and they elect a board of directors who, in turn, appoint operating officers to manage daily affairs. The board of directors is the highest authority of the company and is responsible for setting major policy and determining dividend payout or other matters of interest to and for the benefit of the shareholders. The board is often made up of major shareholders but it need not be. Also the board may appoint officers from their own members, but they do not have to. See BOARD OF DIRECTORS, BOND, BONDS and STOCK for more information.

Corporation charter

A document that gives evidence of the creation of a corporation. It may consist of a special document issued by a state or the federal government authorizing the corporation, or it may consist of little more than state approval and recording of the corporation's articles of incorporation.

Correction

A break in the trend of stock market prices. The term

is used to explain a change when there is no fundamental reason apparent for the change other than the whim of emotional trading. The term suggests that the market trend has passed a level in keeping with fundamental strength and that it is now adjusting toward real values. Also notice the term CONSOLIDATION, a related term with a similar suggestion that the market is adjusting itself. These terms give admission to the fact that fundamental strength and economic conditions are only partly responsible for market prices and trends. Human emotion or reactions to conditions cause market moves that may be counter to economic conditions at times. Most of the technical aspects of security analysis actually amount to recording, analyzing and forecasting *human reactions* to the interplay between economic conditions and political or social developments.

Correspondent

A securities firm, bank or other financial organization which regularly performs services for another in a place where the other firm does not have offices or direct access. Some NYSE member firms with offices in New York act as correspondents for out-of-town members who do not have New York offices. Some may also have correspondents in other exchanges, or even overseas.

Cost plus fixed fee (C P F F)

A basis for paying for some types of development programs, construction, research programs, and service contracts. The contractor agrees to perform certain duties for compensation that is based on the still unknown cost of completing the project. Expenses and profits are settled on a pay-as-you-go basis. Sometimes stated as a cost-plus contract.

Cost push inflation

Inflation that is induced by increased cost of supplies and labor. As costs of raw materials, facilities and labor rise, a manufacturer may be forced to raise his prices. This type of inflation usually is the result of some imbalance in the system such as government controls, import problems, or labor union greed. Also see DEMAND PULL INFLATION.

Coupon

The portion of a coupon bond or bearer bond which is clipped off and presented for interest payments. It is dated and may be presented to the issuer for payment at any time by any person after the marked date.

Coupon bond

A type of bond with interest due every 6 months. The bond has coupons attached which must be clipped off and presented for payment. This type bond is a bearer bond, which means that it is not registered in the name of the holder, but ownership is determined by possession. Anyone who presents the coupon may collect the interest. See BONDS for other types and comparisons between them.

Coupon rate

The interest rate that is specified for any bond. The term is applied to all bonds, even though most bonds do not have coupons attached.

Coupon yield

Bond interest on an annual basis divided by par value, stated in percentage. This yield is only the theoretical yield if the market price remains the same as par value. Notice the difference from CURRENT

YIELD, which is the actual yield calculated by dividing interest by the market price for the bond.

Coverage

The ratio between the pre-tax income of a corporation and its liability for bond interest payments. Analysts suggest that a safe coverage would be a pre-tax income four times the interest payout. Utilities are considered safe at only three times interest payout. Preferred stock dividends are paid on *after tax* income but the term coverage is still used in discussing the ratio compared to payout. For comparisons between bond coverage and preferred stock coverage, assume a hypothetical company:

Company XYZ has 3000 bonds out at $1000 par, paying 7%. It also has 20,000 shares of preferred stock out at $100 par, paying 5%. Then there are 1,000,000 shares of common at no par, earning dividends as voted by the board of directors. This year a $.10 per share dividend is voted. If the company earns $1,000,000 *before taxes*, the payout will be as follows:

Gross income before taxes	$1,000,000
Bond interest (3000 x $1000 x 7%)	-210,000
Pre-tax net	790,000
Federal taxes (approximate)	-380,000
After tax earnings	410,000
Preferred stock div. (20,000 x $100 x 5%)	-110,000
Balance	300,000
Common dividends (1,000,000 x $.10)	-100,000
Retained earnings	$ 200,000

The retained earnings are plowed back into the business for expansion.

Covering
1. Buying a security which was previously sold short in order to replace those shares which had been borrowed for the short sale.
2. The rate of return on investment to a bond holder. Notice the difference from COVERAGE, which applies to the ratio of a company's pre-tax earnings and its liabilities for payment of bond interest.

Crash
A sudden and severe decline in general stock market prices. A depression. Much more severe than a recession or a slump. It is accompanied by widespread economic decline or collapse affecting the entire nation.

Creditor
The one to whom a debtor owes money.

Cross
A privately arranged sale of a large amount of stock traded between two parties. The transaction does not reach the exchange floor but must have exchange permission. Where most security trades go through a broker from a dealer's account to the buyer's account or from the seller's account to a dealer's account, the cross goes directly from seller to buyer through the broker's help. It is similar to the EXCHANGE DISTRIBUTION, except that the cross is not handled on the exchange floor.

Crowd
The trading crowd. It consists of traders gathered around the perimeter of the various trading posts on the stock exchange floor.

Cumulative preferred

A preferred stock which has a provision that if any dividends are omitted because of profit declines or any other such reason, all of the omitted dividends will be paid later before any dividends can be paid on the common stock. Also see PREFERRED STOCK for other kinds of preferred and STOCK for a list of all types of stock.

Cumulative voting

In director's voting rights, each director is granted one vote for each seat on the board. In shareholder's voting each shareholder is granted one vote for each seat on the board for each share of stock held. Thus, a person with 100 shares of stock would have 1000 votes if the corporation structure called for 10 directors. He could cast all votes for one director or distribute his votes in any proportion he chose.

Curb exchange

The former name of the American Stock Exchange, the second largest exchange in the United States. The term comes from the exchange's origin which was actually on the sidewalk of downtown New York. See BUTTONWOOD TREE for the beginnings of the New York Stock Exchange.

Currency cocktail or Currency basket

Any of several trading units devised to compensate for fluctuations in currency values on foreign markets. Instead of trade transactions being handled in any given currency which could have a much different value a few days later, the composite units were devised to average out the values and serve as an international currency without actually forming a new currency to compete with existing currencies. Also see EURCO and B-UNIT for specific plans for averaging of currency values.

Currency support
An effort by some governments to maintain reasonably stable exchange rates for currency on the open market. If, due to some market influence or pressure by speculative money traders, the exchange rate for some currency begins abnormal declines, that nation will buy large quantities of the currency in order to maintain prices by artificial demand.

Current assets
Those assets which are in cash or which can readily be turned into cash, usually within a year. It will include cash on hand, marketable securities, notes receivable, accounts receivable, and inventory.

Current liabilities
Money owed by a corporation which is payable within a year. It will include trade payables for materials, supplies, services, wages, taxes, insurance, bank loan repayment, etc., but does not include bond retirement or dividend payout.

Current position
A comparison of current assets to current liabilities. It is a quick method of measuring a firm's financial health. A two to one ratio, when dividing liabilities into assets, is normally considered sound, or one to one in the case of utilities. Usually the position is referred to as the current ratio.

Current ratio
The current assets divided by the current liabilities. A

ratio used to quickly measure financial strength of a company. Occasionally this ratio is spoken of as the current position. There are informal standards for different industries by which companies may be compared. For example, a heavy equipment manufacturer may be considered sound with a ratio of 2 or higher. A utility may be acceptable with a ratio of 1. Most businesses average around 1.5 or more, depending on the nations economic condition.

Current returns

The amount of income that an investor can expect from interest or dividends from any given company. It is usually stated as a percent of the current market price of a security. Also see YIELD.

Current yield

Bond interest on an annual basis divided by current market price stated in percentage. Notice the difference from coupon yield which is the theoretical yield calculated by dividing the interest by the par value. The coupon yield will remain constant while this actual current yield will change, depending upon the market price at any time.

Cushion bond

A bond that pays unusually high interest rates. High rates are defined differently as time passes. At one time an extremely high rate was anything over 5%. In the 1970's rates rose so high that many bonds carrying coupons paying 11% are still not considered cushion bonds. See BONDS for other types of bonds and comparisons between them.

Custodian

1. Any person or organization who holds assets for another.
2. Any adult who agrees to be responsible for a minor who purchases securities.
3. A bank which acts as a depository for the assets of a mutual fund. It handles some records, but the purpose is for safekeeping with no management or supervision involved.

Custodian account

An investment account set up with a custodian which might be a bank or brokerage firm. The custodian will handle the details of record keeping, certificate safekeeping, and collection of dividends for the investor. Decisions about buying and selling securities are still made by the investor in contrast to the discretionary account.

Custodian fee

A charge by a custodian bank to mutual fund shareholders for its services of safekeeping and record keeping. The fee is relatively small and is deducted from the income before payment to the shareholder.

Customer's broker

The person who handles security trading orders for an investor. A registered representative of any broker or dealer. He is trained by the broker and licensed by the NASD, state agencies and usually by the stock exchanges to sell securities. He is also called an account executive, account representative, customer's man, and customer's broker. The preferred term today is registered representative. Although it is not

111

technically correct many people refer to him as just "my broker".

Customer's man

A term that is now losing popularity which means the same thing as customer's broker, listed above.

Customer's net debit balance

The amount of credit made available by a broker to his customer who has a margin account. In credit or margin purchases a broker loans a certain amount to his customer and in turn borrows the same amount from a bank, usually at the going prime rate, using securities held by the broker to secure the loan. The customer pays a slight premium over the prime rate to cover bookkeeping costs. See MARGIN for more information.

Cut a melon

Dividing up some newly acquired prize between partners in some venture. A corporation cutting a melon would be declaring an extra dividend, to be paid in stock, perhaps.

Cycle

A complete round of the up and down movements of stock prices. Market prices are continuously moving through these cycles, but since they are caused by a large number of influences, some of which are unrelated, the cycles may vary widely in intensity, duration, configuration, and price level between the start and termination of the cycle. The Optimal Analysis system for security analysis identifies three types of cycles called primary waves, secondary waves, and fundamental waves. They all play a part in evaluating market trends and potentials.

Cyclic Pattern

A general term that refers to the shape intensity or duration of a particular segment of the charted record of stock prices. The term is used whether discussing line charts or point and figure charts. These patterns carry meaning to persons interested in technical analysis of stock charts. Stock prices tend to undergo changes from time to time and the changes also tend to recur. The cyclic changes reflect investor's emotional interest much more than the true value of the stocks involved. This interest rises and declines with various influencing factors such as international developments, economic conditions, political changes, and, of course, profit potential. These influences occupy shifting priorities in the minds of investors and when they are tempered by mental inertia or other human traits, they cause roughly recognizable changes on stock charts. These changes are analyzed and used as a basis for forecasting and security trading.

Cyclic patterns as they appear on stock charts are different from *signal patterns*, but both are valuable for security analysis. The cyclic patterns reveal mood changes in investors and are really measuring sympathetic emotional diffusion among the investing public. The signal patterns, by contrast, indicate important events when a number of influencing conditions coincide to exert a strong pressure on a market price. The deviation from normal signals a time for decision for an investor, and particularly, for a short term trader. Also, see WAVE CYCLE and WAVE THEORY for discussion of different forms of cyclic patterns. Samples of some cyclic patterns and signal patterns are shown on charts under the heading STOCK CHARTS.

Cyclical

A characteristic of a stock or an industry which displays large swings in prices as a result of major shifts in government policy (military production), styles (textiles and clothing manufacturing), or economic conditions (housing industry). Some companies have short cycles that follow seasonal changes. In technical analysis a cyclical stock is any stock that demonstrates a repeating wave pattern on a stock chart.

Cylinder

The name given to a certain chart pattern appearing on some stock charts. It has meaning to only a few chartists. See PATTERNS for a list of others.

D

Day order

An order issued by an investor to his broker to buy or sell a security which is good only for the day in which it is written. It can be a limit order or a market order, or it may have other specifications, but it must be filled on the day received, or else it is cancelled. Also see BUY or SELL ORDERS for a list of other kinds of orders used in securities trading.

Day trading

Buying and selling stock or commodities or selling short and covering on the same day. If the stock is volatile and the number of shares is large, the profit potential is sometimes attractive. It is a purely speculative practice and is of interest only to very knowledgeable people.

Dealer

In securities trading "dealer" means a person or

company who buys for his own account from his cutomers or sells from his own inventory to his customers. He differs from the broker in that a broker does not buy for his own account but merely represents his client in negotiating a sale or purchase. A dealer is also called a principal. His compensation is not called a commission as would be the case with a broker but a mark up, since he owns any security that he offers and must make a profit to support his business. The same individual may act as a broker or dealer, but he must state under which status he has acted.

Debenture bonds
Promissory notes, one form of a bond, backed only by the general credit standing of the issuer. Other bonds are backed by mortgages or liens on other equipment or income from a specific service. Often called simply debentures. Also see BONDS for other types of bonds and comparisons between them.

Debentures
A brief way of referring to debenture bonds. See above.

Debit
In double-entry accounting a debit is any entry in the left hand column. Since any entry must be balanced by another entry in the other column, a debit will be balanced by a credit. Thus, a debit entry will show as an increase in assets and a decrease in both liabilities and capital. It does not mean a charge or negative figure, but it merely identifies the left hand column, whether it is an account of assets or liabilities. By contrast, the right hand column records credits, whether entered in assets or liabilities.

Debit balance

The amount of money borrowed from a broker by an investor who trades in a margin account. Margin requirements remain relatively steady, as determined by the Federal Reserve Board, but the debit balance can change from day to day, depending on the market value of the securities in the account. Also see MARGIN.

Debt financing

Obtaining funds for business expansion by selling bonds rather than stock. It is called debt because a bond is really a promise to repay the face amount on a specified date. Also interest is paid to the creditor or investor, at regular intervals. By contrast, selling stock is called equity financing. See BONDS for various types of bonds being used.

Debt security

A bond. Unlike stock, bonds are debts that must be repaid at a certain time with interest. Stocks, on the other hand, are equity securities and represent ownership. See BONDS for comparisons between different types of debt securities and STOCK for different types of equity securities.

Default

1. In investment the term is applied to bonds when the issuer is unable to meet an interest payment. A preferred stock is also said to be in default if the issuer missed a dividend payment. The term may be applied to the issuer as well as to the security.
2. In finance it is failure to make any payment required or failure to perform some duty.

Defensive industry
An industry which can sustain good earnings, during bad times. Securities of these industries are sought out by some investors when a market decline threatens investment losses. Utilities are an example.

Defensive investing
Buying securities with attention to the stability of market prices and consistent income produced rather than growth of the security. The aim is to be less vulnerable during market declines and to avoid as much risk as possible. Defensive issues usually include bonds and utility stocks. Defensive tactics will include dollar cost averaging or other formula investing plans to stabilize any market fluctuations.

Defensive issue
Securities which are stable and low in risk, suitable for investment during a downturn in the economy. These include high-grade industrial bonds, government bonds, commercial paper, and stocks of utilites. A security which moves counter to the gencral market moves is sometimes called a trend bucker.

Deferred expenses
Also called "deferred charges". They are expenses shown on financial reports that are paid out for services not yet received. Examples would include insurance premiums, advanced payments on a contract, or development costs for a new product. It is important to notice that *deferred expenses* involve benefits which may not be received for a year or more and will appear on the asset side of the balance sheet. By contrast, *prepaid expenses*, which is a similar term, applies to benefits which will be received in less than a

year. Both deferred and prepaid expenses are listed as assets on the balance sheet.

Deferred income

Income that has been received before it is actually earned, such as rent which is collected in advance of the period of occupancy. It is also called unearned income and for accounting purposes is carried as a liability, since it is really owed to the payer until the earning period is complete.

Deflation

Economic conditions in which the purchasing power of money increases. Prices shrink or deflate so a dollar will buy more. The condition rarely exists, but it can occur when hard times hit and unemployment goes up. Wages usually drop, so manufacturer's costs are lowered, and prices can drop accordingly. Hard competition also lowers prices. People complain about inflation but prefer to live in inflationary times.

Delayed opening

Delaying the beginning of trading on a specific stock on some stock exchange. It may result from a heavy pile up of trading orders from the previous day, so the specialist dealing in that stock asks for the delay to permit a sorting out of orders before establishing a fair opening price. Sometimes a delay is due to critical timing of a momentous government announcement or a news break announcing a major bank failure. These delays are considered soaking periods during which investors can digest the news before making disruptive panic decisions.

Delist

An action taken by a stock exchange to remove a

company from the privileges of being traded on the exchange floor. It is a prestige loss for the company, because it emphatically announces that the company's financial strength has declined seriously. The cause of delisting is a shrinking of the market for the stock or deteriorating financial conditions that are expected not to meet the exchange requirements for a considerable time into the future. It is possible for a company to be delisted for improper financial reporting, but most often it is only a matter of falling below certain requirements for sales volume, profitability, market breadth for the stock, etc.

The delisted company reverts to trading over-the-counter. There have been cases of delisting at the request of the issuing company. This would occur when a major portion or even all of the outstanding stock is acquired by a single investor. See LISTED STOCK for requirements for listing.

Delivery

Any of several specific standards regulating the time limitations for delivering security certificates or the transfer of funds involved in the transactions:

1. Regular way: gives five days for delivery of a security certificate to the purchaser's broker for a transaction.
2. Seller's option: permits a delay of up to 60 days, depending on the instructions from the seller. This may afford a lower price for the buyer if he will accept the delay.
3. Cash sale: calls for payment and delivery on the same day of the transaction.

Demand deposit

Bank deposits that can be withdrawn at any time without prior notice to the bank. Regular checking accounts are demand deposits. Normally these deposits do not earn interest.

Demand note

A promissory note that is not dated for maturity but can be called at any time for payment. They are often used when uncertainties exist about the length of time the money may be needed. An understanding may exist of approximate repayment date but no deadline is set or enforced.

Demand pull inflation

Inflation which results from the condition of demand exceeding the supply. In the competition to buy the limited supply available, buyers will bid prices up or offer to pay premiums. Also as consumer demand for products increases, the prices tend to increase. Rising prices create a demand for higher wages, so inflation spreads. This type of inflation is typical of recovery periods after wars or after economic declines. It can also result from rapid population growth and political revolution. Also see COST PUSH INFLATION.

Depletion

The reduction in value of an asset due to its actual decrease in quantity available, such as mining ore reserves, timber, oil, etc. It is an accounting practice allowed by law to compensate for reduced reserves.

Depreciation

In accounting terms, it is the loss in value of an asset due to wear and tear or obsolescence. It is charged off against income as a business expense. This reduction in value is carefully calculated for all types of machinery, equipment, buildings and other assets for business planning and for tax purposes. In securities, depreciation is a loss in market value since purchase by reason of market demand. Opposite to appreciation. See PAPER LOSSES and REALIZED LOSSES for security depreciation.

There are several methods for calculating depreciation on equipment or other business assets.

1. Straight line depreciation: Assigning a given life to a piece of equipment and reducing its value by a set amount each year until the entire cost (less salvage value) is written off. For example, a $15,000 lathe could be depreciated in 7 years and end up with a $1,000 salvage value. The owner would write off $2,000 each year for 7 years.

2. Accelerated depreciation: There are several methods of increasing the deductions or write-offs during the early years, as follows:

   a. Double deduction for the first year, then straight line deduction thereafter.

   b. An extra 20% for the first year, then straight line deductions thereafter.

   c. Declining balance method . . . charging off a given percent of the remaining value each year. For example, 30% of the value remaining from the previous year would be written off each year.

   d. Sum-of-the-digits . . . charging off diminishing fractions of the value each year. The fraction is arrived at by assigning successive numbers to each year then totaling the digits. Thus, for a 7 year depreciation life the years are numbered 1,

2, 3, 4, 5, 6 and 7 which totals 28. On the first year 7/28 of the purchase price is written off. On the second year 6/28, the third 5/28 and so on.

There are other considerations that should not be forgotten when depreciation plays a part in planning. Depreciation can be allowed or allowable.

Allowed depreciation: The actual amount of depreciation claimed as deductions from income if it is within accepted accounting practices that are recognized by the IRS.

Allowable depreciation; In the absence of any actual depreciation claimed, it is the amount that *could have been* claimed. This is *added* to the value carried on the books until depreciation is claimed at a later time.

Depressed prices

Market prices for a security which have been forced lower than would be expected when considering the financial strength or other fundamental conditions within the company. This downward pressure on the prices results from the influence of general market conditions and investor gloom that carries over from other stocks to affect investor interest in even the best stocks.

Depression

A severe economic decline precipitating widespread business failure, unemployment, and personal hardship. Much more severe than a recession.

Devaluation

An official action by the government to lower the value of its currencies in relation to all other national currencies in international exchanges. Causes leading to a need for devaluation are the reckless cycles of inflationary price and wage hikes. It distorts the value of domestic goods in relation to foreign goods so badly that trade deficits drain money from the country. The devaluation does not have a serious effect on the domestic economy except where exports and imports are concerned. The main effect is the increase in the relative cost of imported goods and a reduction in the cost of goods exported to other countries. International debts are adjusted, and the imbalance in the flow of currency is corrected. Opposite of revaluation.

Differential

An additional charge made by a broker for a transaction in odd-lots. The charge is necessary because a broker handling the order must buy or sell the odd-lot through a special dealer who deals in odd-lots. The differential compensates that dealer.

Dilution

The condition which exists when the equity represented by a shareholder's investment is reduced. It can happen in several ways and is usually the result of perfectly proper, ethical, and even desirable events. If a company issues new shares to raise more working capital, the existing shareholders may not be in a position to buy additional shares themselves. After the new issue, their own shares will represent a smaller portion of ownership, even though their shares will still have the same liquidation value per share. Their equity position is diluted but not the market value. This is good for the company and will increase its earning power.

If the company purchases patent rights to a new product the inventor may be partially compensated by stock. Since the company does not receive cash for the stock the actual liquidating value of the stock per share is diluted. It is still to the benefit of the shareholders, however, since the new product may substantially increase the profits.

Occasionally a company will issue a stock dividend. Since no capital is received for the stock, the actual book value is diluted. If the dividend is small (5% or so of each shareholder's holdings), the market price is unaffected, and the shareholder's portion of equity is unaltered, but the shareholder has an increase in market value of his holdings, plus the psychological benefit of knowing he has more shares.

Sometimes stock incentives will be used to attract high quality management which may again increase the company's ability to earn a profit. Stock options used this way have a very small effect on the overall equity position for other shareholders but may be a major factor on future earnings.

There have been a few cases where individuals in control of a company have managed to get unjustified quantities of stock for themselves at unreasonably low cost, or even at no cost. This type of dilution is called WATERED STOCK.

Director

A person elected by shareholders at the annual meeting of a corporation to establish company policies and look after the best interests of the shareholders. The directors decide if and when dividends shall be paid and will appoint the operating officers, usually a president, vice president, secretary, treasurer, and any assistants required. The number of seats to be filled on any board of directors is determined by vote of the shareholders and written in the articles of incorporation. They very often serve without compensation, even though they are the highest authority within the company. Directors are usually selected from among the shareholders, although they need not be, but they are always selected because of their reputation as business professionals and their community standing. They often are elected for one year terms, but the terms can be decided by shareholder's vote. Re-election for many years is quite common.

Disburse
To pay out or distribute funds.

Disbursing agent
Usually a bank but may be a corporation or an individual who handles the mechanics of distributing dividends of a mutual fund to its shareholders.

Discount

1. Investment analysis: To evaluate news of market conditions and consider that some normally strongly influential news has already been calculated into any investment plans of investors. For example, a major political development will usually affect the market. However, if it is discussed or anticipated strongly for some time before the actual announcement, it may have already made its impact before being announced. There will then be no additional market reaction.

2. Loans: A method of charging interest. Interest for a given loan is calculated for the entire principal amount for the entire loan period. This amount is subtracted from the proceeds of the loan at the beginning. The borrower therefore receives less

cash than originally sought. This method has the effect of charging a higher effective rate than the stated amount of interest.

3. Retail trade: A reduction from a posted price. The product may never have sold at the posted price, but if it is at least listed, then any price less than the list price is called the discounted price. Different from a mark down in that the mark down is a reduction from the actual price at which the article was previously sold.

4. Securities: The amount a security is selling for below the par value (in the case of bonds) or below the asset value (preferred stock). If the market price rises above the par or asset value, the amount is called a premium.

Discount bonds

Bonds selling at below the face value. Almost any bond will fluctuate in market value according to economic conditions and market demand. If demand falls low enough, the bond will sell at less than the original issue price. The bond is then being discounted. See BONDS for other types of bonds and comparisons between them.

Discount loan

A loan in which the interest is deducted at the time the loan is made. The borrower will therefore repay more than he actually receives at the time the loan is made. There are no other interest payments to make. The interest paid is higher than the stated amount because of the way it is figured. The amount of interest is calculated on the full amount of the principal for the full term of the loan and deducted from the proceeds of the loan at the beginning. As an example, assume a need for a $1000 loan at 9 percent, for two years. If you seek a principal of $1000, the interest will be figured:

$1000 principal
x .18 interest at 9% x 2 years
180 interest deducted
$820 proceeds to you

In this case the true interest rate paid is 10.976% annually. If you need $1000 in proceeds, the figures will be:

$1219.51 principal
x .18 interest at 9% x 2 years
219.51 interest deducted
$1000.00 proceeds to you

The true interest rate is the same as above . . . 10.976% annually. Also for other methods of figuring interest, see INTEREST for add-on, straight line, and sum-of-the-digits methods.

Discount rate

The term often used in financial publications when referring to the rate that banks must pay for the funds they borrow from the Federal Reserve System. This rate has a strong influence on rates that the banks will charge their customers, and, therefore, the amount of credit in use across the nation. The prime rate does have an effect on economic expansion as a whole. The actual rates are determined by the Federal Reserve Board as they determine the need to tighten or loosen credit in an effort to control the economy. There is now a trend beginning to base the bank's prime rate on the interest rates charged for commercial paper rather than the discount rate.

Discounting the news

An expression used to explain why a piece of important news fails to have any impact on the stock market prices. The feeling is that the investing public had already made up its mind about the involved stocks and was even expecting the news announcement. It is the only way that analysts have found to explain some market reactions.

Discretionary account

An investment account in which the investor gives authority to a broker or some other professional manager to transact purchases and sales at his own discretion. Such an account may be completely discretionary, or it may specify certain limits or guidelines.

Discretionary income

Money left after expenses for essentials. This is the amount of money that an individual has to spend for leisure, travel, hobbies investments, or savings. It differs from disposable income, which is the total income left after meeting all tax obligations and is available for all living expenses.

Discretionary order

An order for a single transaction in which a customer gives his broker or other representative authority concerning the selection of a security, the amount of the order, and the decision whether to buy or sell. The authority given to the broker is limited to that one order only. If the investor wishes to extend the authority to cover all trades in the account, he must give written authority for a discretionary account. See BUY and SELL ORDERS for a list of other kinds of orders used in securities trading.

Disintermediation
The practice of individuals bypassing the banks with their surplus cash and buying bonds for savings. The formidable term originates in what is considered a normal condition when individuals deposit their cash in banks for savings and the banks in turn act as intermediaries by investing those deposits in some other phase of business. Disintermediation, then, is breaking the normal pattern. The practice becomes a factor in national economics during times of strong inflation.

Disposable income
An individual's total remaining income after meeting all tax obligations. It is the total money available for living expenses. Notice the difference from SURPLUS, EXCESS or DISCRETIONARY INCOME which apply to the cash left after providing for normal and necessary living expenses.

Distress sale
The sale of products or equipment at very low prices in order to move them out at any cost. The purpose of the sale may be to settle a bankruptcy case, to reduce a burdensome inventory, eliminate damaged goods, or to obtain cash for another emergency. Also called a panic sale, dumping, bail out, and unloading.

Distressed goods
Products being disposed of at greatly reduced prices for the purpose of a quick conversion to cash. The merchandise being sold at a distress sale listed above.

Distribution

An offering of some security to the public. Selling a large block of stock to a large number of investors without using the trading floor of an exchange. Also, distributing additional shares to shareholders of record following a stock dividend, split or spin off. There are several types of distributions:

Primary distribution: the original offering of a security to the public.

Secondary distribution: A special way of disposing of a very large block of any security held by an investor. It is registered with the SEC just as an original issue and sold in the same manner through a number of brokers.

Exchange distribution: A method of disposing of a large block of stock on an exchange floor, but not by the normal bidding. If the block is considered too small for a secondary offering but too large for routine trading, a member broker may facilitate the sale by soliciting and getting other member brokers to solicit orders to buy. These orders are lumped together and crossed with the sell order in the regular auction market. The solicitation may be at slightly below the market in order to attract buyers. The total commission is paid by the seller only. Also see CROSS for a variation of the floor distribution.

Distributions

Cash or securities paid out to shareholders. In mutual funds the term is carefully distinguished from dividend payments as a distribution of capital gains. They are profits received only from the sale of securities held in the portfolio of the fund. Other terms used having the same meaning, are securities profits distributuions or capital gains distributions. Occasionally the improperly used term capital gains dividends is used.

These distributions are taxed as long term capital gains, whereas dividends are taxed as ordinary income. Mutual funds will carefully identify the two classes of payments to shareholders.

Distributor

1. In securities the term is applied to an underwriter or an investment banker who purchases an entire issue of stock from the issuing company and then resells it to the public. Sometimes the term prinicpal underwriter is used.
2. In retail trade a distributor is an intermediary who buys large quantities of given products and in turn sells to retail outlets. He may be independent or factory owned. His purpose is to simplify the task of reaching a large number of retail outlets for a manufacturer who may be located far from the market and is not equipped for retail operations.

Divergence
Occasions when the Dow Jones Industrial Average and the Dow Jones Transportation Average do not show similar patterns. According to the Dow Theory, this divergence indicates that when a change occurs in the Industrial Average or Transportation Average it does *not* indicate a trend in the overall economy. By contrast, the theory claims that when the two indexes *do* show similar action, it signals the trend for the general market.

Diversification
Spreading investments among numerous different companies, sometimes in different fields, or purchasing different types of investments so that any

effects of weakening or failure in one area will not be overly serious to the total of the investments in the portfolio. It is called spreading the risks.

Diversified holding company

A corporation whose major purpose is controlling other companies. Holding companies are often created by a prosperous operating corporation in order to prevent controlling interest of the company from passing to outside interests. The newly created holding company acquires all or a major part of the outstanding stock of the original corporation. As the new parent company prospers, it often begins to acquire other companies. If the businesses acquired are unrelated, the name diversified holding company is applied. These holding companies are intersted only in the financial management of its subsidiaries. All operations are left in the hands of the original management team. Notice the difference from a conglomerate, which will take a part in management.

Diversified investment company

A broad term including most mutual funds. The term refers to compliance with the Investment Company Act of 1940. Similar in meaning to a regulated investment company. They combine the investment capital of many investors for the purpose of using professional management to invest in various types of securities purchased on the open market. See INVESTMENT COMPANY for other types of mutual funds or investment companies and INVESTMENT COMPANY ACT OF 1940 for definitions, purposes, and limitations.

Divest

To sell off or dispose of an asset or investment. The term is usually used to describe the action by a company that is under pressure or orders by the government to dispose of a subsidiary or product line to avoid anti-trust violations.

Dividend on

A way of quoting a stock price which means that a recently declared dividend will go to the buyer. Notice the contrast to the term ex-dividend which means that the dividend has already been declared and will go to the owner as of that date.

Dividend reinvestment plan

An arrangement under which mutual fund shareholders have their dividends automatically reinvested in additional shares. Also called accumulation plans. See INVESTMENT COMPANIES for more information about funds. See the sub heading of *special features* under INVESTMENT COMPANIES for other types of reinvestment plans, both contractual and voluntary.

Dividend tax credit and exclusion

The first $100 of dividend income which is excluded from income taxes for the individual.

Dividends

Payments by a corporation made to its shareholders that represent earnings of the company. In the case of mutual funds there will be two types of payments carefully separated:

1. Dividends are payments made only from interest

and dividend payments received from securities held in the portfolio of the fund. These are taxed at ordinary income rates.

2. Capital gains distributions are made only from the profits on sales of securities held in the portfolio.

Capital gains distributions are taxed at the long term rate.

Do not reduce order (D N R order)

A special designation for a transaction to be made by a broker for his customer. It is a limited order to buy, a stop order to sell, or a stop limit order to sell which is not to be reduced by the amount of an ordinary cash dividend on the ex-dividend date. A do not reduce order applies only to ordinary cash dividends. It is reduced for other distributions such as a stock dividend or rights. Also see BUY or SELL ORDERS for a list of other kinds of orders used in securities trading.

Dog

A derisive term in almost any field of endeavor. In securities it is a stock which suffers continuing public disdain and resulting price declines. It is not applied to securities which sustain temporary slumps, but to those with extended periods of losses and inactivity.

Dollar cost averaging

A system of buying securities at regular intervals with a fixed dollar amount rather than by the number of shares. The object is to reduce the average cost per share. This is accomplished by the fact that for a given dollar amount you receive fewer shares when the price is high and a larger amount when the price is low.

Notice the difference from AVERAGING DOWN. Also
see FORMULA INVESTING.

Double bottom

A "W" shaped pattern that may appear on a stock
chart. The double bottom is believed to give a strong
indication that an up-trend will begin. That interpretation is arrived at by the belief that the first
rally following a long decline establishes a support
level for the prices. If the price again drops to that level
and reverses upward a second time, it is taken as
verification that true support exists and that prices
must begin to move upward for some period of time.
Also see SUPPORT LINE or PATTERNS for more
information. Samples of charts showing some chart
patterns appear under the heading STOCK CHARTS.

Double taxation

The condition which exists in taxing corporation
dividends. A corporation pays income tax once on its
earnings before making dividend payments. Then,
when dividends are paid out, each shareholder must
pay additional tax on his portion of the profits.

Double top

An "M" shaped pattern that may appear on a stock
chart. One of the many patterns which have
significance to some chartists and security analysts. It
is interpreted as a strong indication that the market
has reached a peak and is now due to begin a long
decline. The interpretation comes from the belief that
the first decline from the peak was establishing a
resistance line beyond which prices are unlikely to rise.
The second approach to that resistance and subsequent retreat establishes verification that true
resistance exists, so prices must begin to decline. Also

see RESISTANCE LINE and PATTERNS for more information. Samples of charts showing some patterns appear under the heading STOCK CHARTS.

Dow (the)
A brief but incorrect way of referring to the Dow Jones Industrial Averages.

Dow Jones Average
A slight misnomer that is usually taken to be the Dow Jones Industrial Average. This index is composed of the cumulative total market prices of 30 leading industrial corporations that are listed on the New York Stock Exchange. The complete list is given under the heading DOW JONES INDUSTRIALS below. Other names are used for the DJIA, all with the same inaccuracy but with common understanding: The Dow, Dow Jones, The Industrials, the Market and Market Averages. They are inaccurate because the Dow Jones Company prepares other indexes to report certain segments of the market. See TRANSPORTATION AVERAGE, UTILITIES, DOW JONES COMPOSITE OF 65 STOCKS and DOW JONES BOND AVERAGE.

Dow Jones Bond Average
An index made up of the average prices of six bond groups. It indicates bond market strength and is taken as a measurement of the conservative side of the securities market.

Dow Jones closing
The final figure for the Dow Jones Industrial Average on each trading day. This Industrial Average is continuously calculated and followed as an indicator of market strength. It may show wide swings throughout

the day, but it is usually the closing price that is quoted and charted by analysts.

Dow Jones Composite Average

A composite index which combines market prices of all 65 stocks monitored by the Dow Jones Industrials, Transportation, and Utilities stocks. It is considered more indicative of the general market than the other averages separately. It is often referred to as the 65 stocks index. Also see AVERAGES, COMPOSITES and INDEXES for other indexes that are used in measuring market conditions.

Dow Jones Industrial Average

A composite of 30 large industrial stock prices. The most widely followed of market indicators for general market conditions. The group of companies composing this list are chosen because of their size and importance in various segments of the economy. Although the 30 industrials may sometimes differ from the market and their stability is better than the average company, they still reflect general attitudes of investors. The entire list of 30 companies composing this index is shown under the heading DOW JONES INDUSTRIALS below. The term is frequently shortened to Dow Jones index, DJI, the Dow index, the Dow, the industrials, the Dow Averages, the market report, and the market. Some of the terms are incorrect, but they are well understood.

Dow Jones Industrials

The list of 30 large industrial corporations that make up the Dow Jones Industrial Average index. The stock prices of these companies are combined into a single figure and are interpreted as an indication of general market interest. The companies making up the list may change from time to time, but as of January 1, 1975, the list included the following companies:

Allied Chemical	Goodyear
Aluminum C. of America	International Harvestor
American Brands	International Nickel
American Can	International Paper
American Tel. & Tel.	Johns-Manville
Anaconda	Owens-Illinois
Bethlehem Steel	Proctor & Gamble
Chrysler	Sears Roebuck
DuPont	Standard Oil (Calif.)
Eastman Kodak	Texaco
Esmark	Union Carbide
Exxon	United Aircraft
General Electric	U. S. Steel
General Foods	Westinghouse Electric
General Motors	Woolworth

Dow Jones Transportation Averages

A composite of 20 railroad, trucking and shipline stocks. An indicator of the conservative side of the stock market. While this average usually moves together with the industrial average, a strong divergent move is sometimes interpreted as an indication that a trend reversal is beginning. This index was originally called the Railroad Average, or simply the rails. As railroads began to decline and trucking expanded, the index was also expanded to include other forms of shipping to be more representative of all transportation systems.

Dow Jones Utilities

A composite of the market prices of 15 major utility

stocks. This is used as an indicator of strength in the defensive portion of the stock market.

Dow Theory

A theory of anaylsis based upon the performance of the Dow Jones Industrial and Transportation averages. The theory says that the market is in a basic upward trend if one of these indexes advances above a previous important high, accompanied or followed by a similar advance in the other index. When the indexes both dip below previous important lows it is regarded as confirmation of a basic downtrend. The theory also holds that if the Industrials indicate a reversal in market trend while the transportation or utilities indexes move in the other direction, that no change is expected to occur. This is called the divergence theory. The theory does not attempt to predict how long either trend will continue, although it is widely misinterpreted as a way to forecast future action. Whatever its merits, the theory is sometimes a factor in the market because many people believe in it or believe that others do.

Down market

A period of generally falling stock market prices. Also called a bear market, buyer's market, soft market, receding market, and shrinking market.

Down reversal

A sudden decline in market prices following a rising trend. The term reversal is only applied during the early stage of the decline. If a decline continues, it may be called a sell off, and later, after more decline, a soft market. If the decline continues many months and prices drop significantly, it will be called a down market. If the decline persists so that large losses are sustained by many investors, it will be called a bear market. In a severe bear market some observers may say that the market has collapsed, although it is an exaggeration.

Downside
A period of time when stock prices are declining. The term is usually used with the understood reference to a wave cycle which has both rising and falling portions. The downside, then, refers to the declining half of the cycle.

Downside risk
A likelihood for a stock price to drop.

Downside trend
The portion of a fundamental wave that shows declining prices. It may continue for several months while permitting several smaller up reversals to occur during the decline. The term is often shortened to down trend if the downward movement becomes larger than just the back side of a cycle.

Down stroke
A down payment. The term is usually confined to retail trade and automobile sales in particular.

Down tick
A term used to designate a transaction on a stock exchange made at a price lower than the preceding trade. The expression arises from the stock ticker which reports the trades in sequence. A zero minus tick is a transaction made at the same price as the previous trade, but lower than the last preceding

different price. Also see UP TICK and ZERO PLUS TICK.

Drilling fund

Investment companies which are organized specifically to take advantage of certain tax breaks available to oil prospectors. Since the tax advantage is substantial, the drilling funds seek investors to pool resources for the financing of drilling operations. By having sufficient cash to drill numerous wells, they are certain to get some producing wells for profit. Also see INVESTMENT COMPANIES for other kinds of specialty funds and INVESTMENT COMPANY ACT OF 1940 for definitions, purposes, and limitations.

Dual funds

Closed end investment company which is similar to, but not truly, a mutual fund. They have two classes of stock. One class is called income shares and receives interest and dividends that are paid by the fund's investments. The other class receives capital gains distributions that are derived from growth of the investments. Also called dual purpose funds, split funds, or leverage funds. Also see INVESTMENT COMPANIES for other types of funds and INVESTMENT COMPANY ACT OF 1940 for definitions, purposes, and limitations.

Dual listing

The listing of stock of any single company on more than one stock exchange. The request for listing is made by the issuing company. Notice the difference from UNLISTED TRADING PRIVILEGES which pertain to the granting of trading privileges on one exchange to a stock which is listed on another exchange. In this case the company does not apply but the request is made by the exchange to the SEC.

Dual purpose fund

The same thing as a dual fund listed on previous page.

Due bill

An I O U or a written statement that the issuer of the statement will forward to the holder something that has not yet been received by him. For example, if a stock is sold after a dividend is declared but before the payable date, the buyer will receive a due bill stating when the dividend will be forwarded to him.

Due date

The date on which an investor must pay for a purchase of some security, or the date when a selling broker must make delivery to the buying broker of the stock certificates. The so-called good delivery allows 5 trading days from the date of the transaction.

E

Earned surplus

An accounting term to describe the money earned by a company after taxes and plowed back into the business instead of being paid out as dividends. It will appear on the liability side of the balance sheet because it represents money owed to the stockholders. It is also called retained earnings or accumulated earnings. Notice the difference from CAPITAL SURPLUS or PAID-IN SURPLUS which represent invested capital rather than earnings.

Earnings

Net profit left after all expenses and taxes. In referring to the profit of a corporation, it is usually expressed in dollars per share. When speaking of the total amount of earnings, it is called income, or sometimes net income, or simply net. It differs from yield to an investor or dividend income in that not all of the company's earnings are paid out to shareholders. A company will pay out only a portion or perhaps none to shareholders. The retained earnings are plowed back into the business for growth. For contrasts, refer to NET PROFIT, MARK UP and PROFIT MARGIN.

Earnings multiple
The same as earnings ratio below.

Earnings ratio
A shortening of the term price-earnings ratio. It is the ratio formed by dividing the market price of a stock by the earnings for the most recent 12 month period. Also called P-E ratio, P-E multiple, earnings multiple and times earnings. See PRICE-EARNINGS RATIO for information about its use and average ratings.

Earnings report
A statement issued by a company to show operating expenses and earnings or losses over a given period. Also called the profit-loss statement, P & L sheet, earnings statement and income statement. It is one of the reports included in the financial statements of a corporation to its shareholders that are sent out quarterly or annually.

Econometrics
The branch of economics which expresses economic theory in mathematical terms and seeks to verify it by statistical methods. Its practitioners make economic forecasts and suggest economic policy by measuring the impact of one economic variable on another.

Economic analysis
Examining fundamental economic conditions (in-

dustrial production, unemployment, gross national product, capital equipment orders, wholesale price index, and other indicators) as a basis for forecasting future economic trends and stock market prices. Also called ECONOMETRICS.

Economist

A social scientist, a professional who studies the production, distribution, and consumption of wealth. His studies encompass the interlocking areas of labor, finance and taxation. To some critics he is a theoretician who can expound in great detail about what caused our past social and economic ills, while differing widely and vocally from other economists on the causes and effects of our present problems, and he has no idea of how to avoid our future problems.

Efficient market theory

A misnomer which means the opposite of accuracy and effectiveness that the word efficiency suggests. It is a theory that claims that since the stock market is an auction, the bidders base their judgment upon all knowledge available. Supposedly, this complete knowledge then discounts all influences of any activity of previous trading and makes each trading day a complete economic island by itself. Adherents to the theory are trying to say that all price movements and all market influences that have occured in the past have no influence at all on the market prices of today. The theory also goes by the name of Random Walk Theory, because it explains all market prices as random happenings in which we all have the same miniscule chance. Such theories are formulated by theoreticians who have little else to do but hypothesize and fabricate means to discredit other theoreticians whom they can not accept. In this case they were attacking chartists, who were attempting to analyze stock charts in an effort to find common denominators that would assist in anticipating future trends.

Either-or order
An order issued by an investor to his broker to do either or two alternatives, such as either buy a particular stock at a limited price, or buy on a stop order. If the conditions lead to executing one of the alternatives, then the other is cancelled. Also called an alternative order. See BUY and SELL ORDERS for a list of different kinds of orders used in securities trading.

Either way
A term used when requesting bid and asked prices, or firm quotes for buying and selling prices on an over-the-counter stock. A potential investor would ask for prices "either way." Compare FIRM QUOTES to INDICATED MARKET or SUBJECT MARKET prices.

Eligible list
The same thing as approved list and very similar to legal list. It is a list of securities from which a financial institution may select investments. The eligible list or approved list is prepared by authorities of some institutions who are free to set their own investment goals. Many financial institutions such as banks, insurance companies, and most investment companies are closely regulated in all their activities. State authorities will prepare a list of acceptable securities from which they may select. These state-prepared lists are called the legal list. In the absence of a legal list,

and sometimes in addition to it, there is a prudent man rule imposed upon the institutions to maintain professional caution among fiduciaries.

Endorsed bond

Another name for a guaranteed bond, which is a bond that is guaranteed by someone other than the issuer. For example, a parent company may guarantee the repayment of an issue by a subsidiary. See BONDS for other types of bonds and comparisons between them.

Enterprise

A project or undertaking, usually applied in a business sense, which requires serious effort to overcome difficult or risky obstacles. A bold venture. It is also applied as a characteristic of highly motivated people. The willingness to face challenge and endure self-sacrifice to accomplish a goal. Creativity with determination. Also see FREE ENTERPRISE and RISK.

Entrepreneur

A person who organizes and manages a business venture, assuming the risks for the sake of the potential gains. He is not the hired manager or the one who works up through the ranks, but is the founder and generally has risked all he had to build a business around a product or an idea he has developed.

Equipment trust certificates

Certificates which use equipment as security for financial needs such as the rolling stock of a railroad. A type of bond. Also see BONDS for other types and comparisons between them.

Equity

1. The net worth of a corporation or proportional ownership of a corporation by a shareholder. The money invested in the company represented by shares of stock. It is contrasted to the term security in that securities include bonds with stock. Bonds by themselves are not equity, but represent debt of the company to the bond holder.
2. The paid-up portion of some property which is being purchased on the installment plan.

Equity capital

Money used to purchase stock. It represents ownership of the company as opposed to bonds, which represent debt by the company to the bondholder. Equity capital is also referred to as risk capital. Raising money by selling stock is called equity financing in contrast to debt financing for selling bonds.

Equity financing

Selling stock to obtain capital for business expansion. This is one form of outside financing. Internal financing would consist of using retained earnings. Also contrasted to debt financing, which is selling bonds.

Equity security

A security which gives evidence of ownership of the company such as common stocks and preferred stocks. Bonds are not equity, but debt securities. See STOCK for a list of different types of equity securities.

Escalator clause

A clause in a loan contract which permits the lender to

increase or decrease the rate of interest charged if there is a substantial change in general conditions during the life of the contract.

Estate tax bond

A special issue of long term treasury bonds that is sold at a discount, but may be redeemed at par value for payment of estate taxes in the event of the premature death of the owner. Also called flower bonds or flowers, since its special feature is useful only upon the death of the buyer. See BONDS for other types of bonds and comparisons between them.

Estimated market

An approximate market price for a certain security. At times an investor wants a price for an over-the-counter stock when his broker knows that the customer is not likely to buy the stock. Rather than make a long distance phone call to get a current price, he may use a recent price as an estimate. He will state it to his customer as an estimated market, a subject market or an indicated market. If the customer is still interested, he will then place the call for a firm quote.

Eurco

A unit of trading for international transactions of very large proportions. Its value varies from day to day, but to a lesser degree than individual currencies. It is composed of many individual currencies in proportion to each nation's gross national product. It was devised to ease the problem of fluctuating currency values which complicated world trade and to be a substitute for the weakening dollar during the 1960's. Until that time the dollar had been a standard for much of the world's trade. The Eurco, in effect, averages out the many currencies involved to give a more stable unit of trade. The Eurco is one of the so-called currency baskets or currency cocktails Also see B-UNIT for differences.

Eurodollars

Credits or claims held by Europeans for U.S. dollars. These credits arise through international trade.

Euromart

A shortening of European Ecomonic Community but better known as the Common Market. An association of European countries which has as its purpose the complete phase-out of tariff barriers between their members. This would also increase duties on goods produced elsewhere.

Ex-dividend or ex-d

An expression that means without dividend. Every dividend is payable on a fixed date called the payable date to all shareholders as of a previous date, called the record date.Anyone buying the stock on or after the record date would not be entitled to that dividend. On stock market reports, an "x" or "ex" will preceed the reported data on such a stock. The person buying the stock does not lose out, however, because the price of the stock is automatically reduced by the amount of the dividend. Also called ex-distribution date since the dividend is to be distributed to shareholders of record on that date.

Ex-interest

A notation made with the quoted market prices of some bonds which means that the buyer of the bond is not entitled to an interest payment which is about to be paid. The buyer does not lose, however, since bond prices are adjusted accordingly.

Ex-rights

An expression which means without rights. When a public corporation offers a new issue of shares, it will issue additional documents to existing shareholders which give them pre-emptive right to purchase additional shares at a price somewhat below the market in order to maintain their proportional share of ownership. These rights may be sold on the open market if the holder of the rights does not care to exercise them by buying his alloted number of shares. The value of such rights equals the difference between the market price of the shares and the discounted price available to the owner of the right. If a person wishes to sell his existing shares but retain the rights for possible future investment, he will offer them without the rights, or ex-rights.

Excess profits

Profits that have been determined by the government to be abnormal, due to some condition such as war time mobilization. Such profits have from time to time been taxed heavily for two reasons: to help pay for heavy war time expenses, and to stabilize conditions in the business community.

Excess reserves

Deposits maintained by member banks of the Federal Reserve System which exceed the minimum required by the Federal Reserve Board.

Exchange

A place where brokers and dealers transact securities

trading for their customers. There are two national stock exchanges: the New York Stock Exchange and the American Exchange, both are located in New York. There are also a number of regional exchanges located in other major cities of the United States. Some are:

Boston Stock Exchange
Chicago Board of Trade
Cincinnati Stock Exchange
Detroit Stock Exchange
Midwest Stock Exchange (in Chicago)
National Stock Exchange (in New York)
Pacific Coast Stock Exchange (Los Angeles
    and San Francisco)
Philadelphia-Baltimore-Washington
    Stock Exchange
Pittsburgh Stock Exchange
San Francisco Mining Exchange
Spokane Stock Exchange

In addition there are foreign stock exchanges located in major cities around the world. All exchanges admit only their members to use the facilities. All trading is conducted on an auction basis, or matching bid and asked prices for securities. 86 percent of all U.S. trading takes place on the New York Stock Exchange. The American Exchange does more than all the regional exchanges combined, so trading in the regional exchanges amounts to very little of the overall trading. See EXCHANGE SEAT for requirements for membership in an exchange.

Exchange acquisition
A method of filling an order to buy a large block of stock on the floor of the exchange. Under certain circumstances, a member-broker can facilitate the

purchase of a block by soliciting orders to sell. All orders to sell the security are lumped together and crossed with the buy order in the regular auction market, which means he may offer a price slightly above the market to attract sellers. The price to the seller may be on a net basis (without commission) or on a commission basis. See CROSS for differences.

Exchange distribution

A method of disposing of large blocks of stock on the floor of an exchange if the order is too large for routine trading, but too small for a secondary offering. Under certain circumstances a member-broker can facilitate the sale of a block of stock by solicitations and getting other member-brokers to solicit orders to buy. Individual buy orders are lumped together and crossed with the sell order in the regular auction market. He may offer the sale at slightly below the market to attract buyers. A special commission is usually paid by the seller. Ordinarily the buyer pays no commission. Similar to the CROSS except that the cross occurs off the exchange floor. Also see BLOCK POSITIONING.

Exchange floor

A large area at a stock exchange where the actual trading is conducted between brokers and dealers. At the New York Stock Exchange the floor is about a half acre in size. There are 18 trading posts located around the floor. Each post is a horseshoe shaped counter around which the floor brokers gather to bid for securities. The post itself is about 10 feet across and is occupied by clerks who handle the records for trading. The specialists conduct the trading on the floor area outside the post. Each specialist makes a market in about 75 stocks or so. A floor broker with an order for a round lot of XYZ stock must go to the appropriate post to make his bid. If he has an order for an odd lot, he must work through a special dealer who adds an extra charge for the investor. If the order is for one of a number of inactively traded stocks, he goes to post 30, or the inactive post, which consists of numerous filing cabinets containing records for hundreds of different issues that have very low trading volume.

Exchange rates

The rate of exchange between national currencies, or the price of one currency stated in terms of another currency. Usually there are official rates established by the governments but unofficial rates fluctuate slightly due to political and economic conditions. Speculators prosper on these variations and cause the rates to swing even more by their anticipation of world developments.

Exchange seat

A membership in a stock exchange. The memberships are sold on the open market to brokers and dealers. Membership is required in order to transact business in the exchange. Your local broker will either own a seat himself or must deal through another broker who does have a seat when you purchase listed securities. Memberships are not required for over-the-counter transactions. There are a limited number of seats available in each exchange, so a prospective new member must find another departing member who is willing to sell his seat. Membership also requires licensing by the National Association of Security Dealers, state security authorities, and by the exchange as well. Licensing involves requirements for experience, training, and passing scores on extensive examinations. The applicants are also subjected to character investigations. The New York Stock Exchange has 1366 seats available, the American Exchange has 650 seats, and the Chicago Mercantile Exchange has 500 seats available.

Execute

To perform a duty or fill an order. In a typical transaction, you can call your broker to buy a given stock, and he phones the order to a floor broker in one of the exchanges. When the floor broker obtains the security, it is called executed or filled. The entire process can take place within minutes from the time you place your call.

Exercise

To complete the terms of some contract. For example:

1. Rights: To exchange your rights for their equivalent in stock, paying the price allowed by the right.
2. Options: To sell a stock in which you have purchased a put, or buy a stock in which you have purchased a call.

Also see EXPIRE for the opposite to exercise.

Expense ratio

The ratio between a mutual fund's average net assets and its operating expenses for the year. Also applied to the ratio between its net income for the year and the expenses for the year.

Expire

To lapse or become worthless. Since most rights, warrants and other options are good only for specific periods of time, you must either exercise them before the stated date or let them run out to become worthless. See EXERCISE for the alternative. Also see PUTS, CALLS, OPTIONS, RIGHTS and WARRANTS for assets that have value for a limited time only.

Exposure

The amount of risk an investor is subject to. If a person is trading on margin in volatile securities, he is exposed to greater risk than a person trading in a cash account or one buying bonds or high grade stocks. Likewise, commodities and options trading increase the risks considerably because margins are small and movements are difficult to forecast or anticipate. At the same time the person exposed to greater risk is also in a position of potentially greater gain.

Extra

The short form of extra dividend. It is a dividend in either cash or in the form of stock in addition to the regular dividend that the company customarily pays.

Extraordinary expense

In financial reports the term means the listing of expenses that are not normal to ordinary operations. Examples would be the cost of a major law suit, unreimbursed costs of flood or fire clean up costs, the write-off of unamortized development costs of an unprofitable product, or losses from discontinued operations. These expenses are deducted from income before taxes just as operating expenses are, but they are listed separately so that interested parties may compare normal expenses with prior years.

Extraordinary income

In financial reports this is the listing of income that

does not result from ordinary operations. Examples would include proceeds from the sale of some capital assets, settlement of law suits, and federal grants.

FDIC

The Federal Deposit Insurance Corporation. A federally sponsored corporation that insures savings deposits in national banks and certain other qualifying financial institutions. The maximum insurable amount is $40,000 per account, but there are efforts underway to raise the limits considerably higher.

FIFO

First-in-first-out. One of several bookkeeping techniques used to assign value to inventory. The FIFO method tends to keep the books in line with current prices for materials. Since goods are charged off in the order in which they were acquired, remaining inventory consists of the most recently purchased goods. See LIFO and WEIGHTED AVERAGE for other methods for keeping inventory records.

F O B

Literally, it means free on board. Actually its meaning originally meant that ownership and responsibility for transportation charges and insurance changed from supplier to purchaser once the product was on board a shipping medium. Today the meaning has changed slightly to require the use of clearly specified points or time for the transfer of legal title and responsibility. It may now be stated *FOB destination*, which means the seller will pay shipping charges and insure the item until it is received by the buyer. At other times the designation *FOB shipping point* may be used which means that ownership changes when it leaves the plant of the supplier, and the buyer must pay shipping charges and is responsible for any insurance. Variations in methods of stating the designations are FOB our plant, FOB factory, and FOB your plant.

Face value

The value of a bond that appears printed on the face of a bond. It is also called the par value. It represents the amount the bond may be redeemed for at maturity. The face value will have very little relation to the market value, which will vary with economic conditions. Interest payments are based on the face value, so the actual yield to the holder of a bond may be above or below the coupon rate stated on the bond.

Factory representative

An employee of a given manufacturer who is charged with selling the company's products or services to its customers, or he will represent the company in negotiations, adjustments, or product improvements. His customers are retail dealers, other manufacturers, or contractors of various types. There are several major distinctions between the *factory* representative and the *manufacturer's* representative, who is an independent agent:

Factory representative:

1. The factory rep is on the payroll of the manufacturer and is not an independent.

2. The factory rep is more of a liaison engineer or customer relations expert than salesman.

3. The factory rep does not operate a separate place of business, but works from company offices.

Manfacturer's representative:

1. He is an independent agent.

2. He may represent several manufacturers for different products.

3. He operates his own place of business independently from any of the companies he represents.

4. His compensation is from commissions, credits and overrides from the manufacturers instead of a salary.

5. His primary concern is distribution of products instead of improving products or customer relations.

Fall out of bed

Said of a person who loses heavily on securities. Also it is said of a stock price which suddenly plummets far below the price paid for it by a given investor.

Fannie Mae

One of a series of government sponsored corporations which were established to provide funds for low income home financing when other sources of such funds

dry up. The name is really a nickname, commonly used
by investors, that is shortened from its full official title . . . Federal National Mortgage Association.
Fannie Mae was chartered in 1938 as a public corporation, and in 1968 became a government sponsored
corporation under the Department of Housing and
Urban Affairs. Fannie Mae borrows money from the
U.S. Treasury and, in turn, buys mortgages or commits funds to buy future mortgages from lending
institutions, primarily banks.

By contrast, Ginnie Mae (for Government National
Mortgage Association) was organized to support
government housing programs and buys low rate FHA
or VA loans. It is a deficit program that buys the
mortgages from lenders at higher than market rates,
then re-sells them at the going rates to investors.The
plan is tax supported to maintain consumer financing
during slow times.

Another member of the group is Freddie Mac (for
Federal Home Loan Mortgage Corporation). It
operates like Fannie Mae, except that it serves only the
Savings and Loan associations which operate under
different regulations from banks. It is also a deficit
operation that uses federal funds to promote investment in mortgage markets.

Fed

A shortening for the Federal Reserve System, particularly the Federal Reserve Board which initiates the
policy by which the banking system operates and the
policy by which monetary controls are administered.
See FEDERAL RESERVE SYSTEM, FEDERAL
RESERVE BOARD, FEDERAL RESERVE
REQUIREMENTS, FEDERAL FUNDS, and FED'S
WINDOW for explanations of various facets of the
banking system.

Federal Deposit Insurance Corporation (F D I C)

A federally sponsored corporation that insures savings deposits in national banks and certain other qualifying financial institutions. The maximum insurable amount is now $40,000 per account, but there are efforts underway to raise the limits considerably higher.

Federal discount rate

Interest charged on federal funds, which are uncommitted reserves that banks may lend each other. The interest is charged on a discount basis, which is taking the interest out before the transfer of possession of the funds. Traditionally, the discount rate has been a key factor in determining the prime rate charged for commercial loans, and it has a strong influence on economic trends. The discount rate is determined by the Federal Reserve Board.

Federal funds

The money belonging to private individuals or corporations on deposit and held in reserve by banks to meet Federal Reserve requirements. It is called federal funds only because it is in reserve to meet the requirements imposed upon the banks by the regulations of the Federal Reserve System. It is moved constantly between banks to stabilize surplusses and deficiencies. Any bank borrowing those funds to meet its requirements will pay the federal discount rate for the few days it uses the money.

Federal Reserve Board

More properly called the Board of Governors of the Federal Reserve System. The governing body of our banking system which controls domestic monetary policy. Its purpose is generally to preserve the country's economic stability. The board is composed of seven members who are appointed by the President of the United States for terms of fourteen years each. They set the federal discount rate and the reserve requirements. The Board, along with five presidents of Federal Reserve banks, make up the Federal Open Market Committee, which regulates the open market operations (buying and selling government securities to stabilize the money market and credit).

Federal Reserve requirements

It is the amount of money that member banks of the Federal Reserve System must have in cash or on deposit with the Federal Reserve to back up their outstanding loans. The amount required is stated as a percentage of the bank's demand deposits and may vary from time to time, as the Federal Reserve Board determines the need. If the Board decides to restrict credit in an effort to slow economic growth, it may decree that banks must have higher reserves. The banks then would have less money to loan, and the interest rates would rise to cool the demand.

Federal Reserve System

A federally created system born of the Federal Reserve Act of 1913 by Congress to draw the nation's banking into a relatively centralized and controlled system. It consists of 12 Federal Reserve Banks located in 12 Federal Reserve Districts, plus 24 Reserve Branch Banks, plus all national banks and any state chartered commercial banks and trust companies which have sought and been granted membership. Its policies are set by the Board of Governors, commonly called the Federal Reserve Board. The Board consists of 7 individuals appointed by the President of the

United States for 14 year terms. The Board establishes reserve requirements (deposits) for member banks, the federal discount rate, and securities trading margin requirements. The board, along with the presidents of 5 reserve banks, make up the Federal Open Market Committee which determines official policy for open market operations. These operations amount to buying and selling government securities to increase or decrease the money supply and thus influence economic conditions. The Federal Reserve System, and particularly its Board of Governors, is frequently referred to as the Fed.

Fed's window

A brief way of referring to the Federal Reserve discount window. The window is really a plan under which member banks may go to the Federal Reserve to borrow money while using promissory notes of their own customers as collateral. The discount rate charged at this window affects the national money supply. The Fed may close the window to cause a sudden shortage of funds and thereby tighten the reins of the economy.

Fidelity bond

One of several types of bonds that are not investment securities. This is a contract in a form of insurance, under which an outside firm guarantees a company or an individual against loss through the misconduct of another person who holds a position of trust. The contract becomes a valid after an investigation of the bonded party and the payment of a fee by any interested party. The bonding fee is not returned at the end of the coverage period. Also see BONDS for other types of bonds and the differences between them.

Fiduciary

A person or financial institution serving in a financial capacity for another, especially where he holds funds in trust for the other party.

Fill or kill order

A market order or limited price order given by an investor to his broker which must be executed entirely as soon as it reaches the trading floor. If it cannot be filled immediately it is cancelled. Also called immediate-or-cancel, at-the-opening-only or at-the-close-only orders. See BUY or SELL ORDERS for a list of other kinds of orders used in securities trading.

Financial reports

Another term for financial statements. See below.

Financial statements

A report issued periodically by corporations to their shareholders and security analysts which consists of the balance sheet, income statement, and statement of capital. The balance sheet reports assets and liabilities. The income statement reports all sources of income and all expenses. Usually costs are broken down into manufacturing costs, administrative expenses, depreciation, interest costs, dividends paid, taxes, etc. The capital statement is a brief report showing the net worth at the beginning of the reporting period, any changes during the period and the net worth at the end of the period. Publicly held corporations are required to make the financial statements public. Certain privately held corporations and even partnerships may publicize theirs for public relations purposes.

Firm
The term has several meanings in the business world.

1. As a noun it means a company of any type, either incorporated or unincorporated.
2. As an adjective it suggests that a price or an offer is not subject to negotiation or reduction. A firm listed price will not be discounted.
3. As a verb it suggests that prices are rising . . . prices are *firming up*.
4. In securities trading it means a verbal contract or a binding promise. A dealer asked for a quote on a certain stock may answer with "9 1/4 - 9 7/8 *firm*." As a dealer he is making a *bid* of 9 1/4 and *asking* 9 7/8. A firm bid is a valid commitment to buy a certain quantity at the specified price. The firm asking price is a valid commitment to sell at the specified price. He is obligating himself to buy at least one round lot at the prices quoted. The obligation to trade at the quoted prices continues only till the end of the conversation. Since most trades are handled by phone, it is easy to determine time limits. If a second phone call is made before the transaction is agreed upon, the dealer may quote different prices in keeping with market variations. By specific agreement, a dealer who is quoting prices by phone may extend the time limit for holding a price that is quoted. A case of this happening may be when the calling broker has to call his client back for approval, and the market is not too aggressively going against the quoting dealer. All verbal quotes by phone or in person are treated as binding contracts within the accepted time limits. See STOPPED STOCK for a special case of holding a price beyond the normal time.

Firm market

Firm prices quoted by a securities dealer for both bid and asked prices. The buyer is obligated to buy or sell at least 100 shares at the prices quoted and the trade must be in round lots. Notice the difference from SUBJECT MARKET or INDICATED MARKET. Also see *asking price* mentioned in point 4 on page 167.

Firm order

An order issued by an investor to his broker to buy or sell securities, given by an investor, for his broker to execute at a specified price or better. Also called a limit order, limited order, or limited price order. See BUY or SELL ORDERS for other kinds of orders used in securities trading.

First mortgage bonds

A debt security sold to investors which is backed up by a mortgage on facilities. They are considered the safest of industrial bonds. See BONDS for other types of bonds and comparisons between them.

Fiscal year

A corporation's accounting year, which may not coincide with the calendar year. It is a twelve month period chosen which will permit convenient bookkeeping activities. The practice is common to avoid the severe burden on accounting firms by choosing a period ending sometime during the calendar year. It may also be a convenience for some firms which have seasonal slack periods to end their fiscal year during this period to ease their own work load.

Fixed assets

On accounting records this term refers to facilities

such as land, buildings, and machinery. Called fixed because they are more or less permanent in nature and are not traded frequently or consumed in the operation of the company. There is depreciation or wear and tear to be considered, and certain standards have been accepted by the government for the gradual write-off of the cost of different types of fixed assets. These are also called capital assets. The term fixed assets may be identified as property, plant, and equipment on some financial statements.

Fixed charges

The same as FIXED EXPENSES below.

Fixed costs

The same as FIXED EXPENSES below.

Fixed dollar investment

An investment which returns the same principal amount when sold as when first purchased. Savings accounts, certain government securities, and most bonds are examples. They are also called fixed *income* investments because interest payments are set at the time of issue. Bonds are included in this category, although they may sell at discounts or premiums during their lifetimes. There are some differences from fixed income investments as explained below. A person buying a bond at a discount after the original issue will get a higher yield on his investment dollar than the original purchaser, but if a bond is held by the same person from original issue to maturity, he would receive the same principal in return that he originally paid. Exceptions are bonds which are converted to common or some other security, savings bonds or other discount bonds, estate tax bonds that are redeemed early because of the death of the owner, and defaulted bonds of a bankrupted company. also called fixed dollar *security*. See VARIABLE DOLLAR INVESTMENT.

Fixed expenses

A company's operating expenses which will not change from month to month in relation to the volume of sales of merchandise or services. Rent, mortgage payments, insurance, property taxes, and equipment leases will not vary appreciably as will material costs, labor, supplies, advertising, sales expenses, and shipping expenses, which are called variable expenses. Often the fixed expenses and variable expenses are combined in reporting operating expenses in a financial statement. They will be separated when used for planning purposes.

Fixed income investment

A bond or preferred stock which pays a stated rate of return. Notice a difference from fixed *dollar* investment above. The fixed dollar investment will return the same principal at redemption as the original price. This is applicable only to certain bonds, debentures, and savings. The fixed *income* investment will also include preferred stock because it pays a stated dividend throughout its life. It is not a fixed dollar investment however, because it is never redeemed, except by a special call made by the company. In such cases the call price may be intentionally made attractive to induce holders to make an exchange for whatever the company is offering. Such a call could be made in the event of a pending merger, recapitalization, and possibly as part of reorganization due to bankruptcy. A fixed *income* investment will include both preferred stocks and bonds, but a fixed *dollar* investment will not include preferred stocks. Fixed income investments are also called fixed income securities. Also see VARIABLE INCOME SECURITIES.

Fixed return dividend

A dividend that remains constant throughout the life of the investment. This is usually the case with preferred stock. It is also called an interest type dividend. By contrast, the dividend on common stock is variable and must be voted by the board of directors each year.

Fixed trust

A scheme to form a mutual fund with no appreciable management. Planned so that its assets are invested in a specified, fixed list of securities which are then deposited with trustees. Its effect is an absentee management. Its purpose is misleading and its success has been nearly zero.

Flag

The name given to a certain pattern that appears on some stock charts. It is one of the many patterns that have significance to some chartists. It seems to represent a plateau in prices but offers little meaning to most chartists. See PATTERNS for a list of other patterns that are commonly translated into meaning for technical analysis of securities.

Flat

A term meaning that the price at which a bond is traded is without consideration for accrued interest. Bonds that are in default of interest or principal are traded flat. Income bonds, which pay interest only to the extent earned are usually traded flat. All other bonds are usually sold as ''and interest'' or ''with interest'' which means that the buyer pays the market price, plus the accrued interest since the last payment. The interest accrued until the time of sale is paid to the seller.

Flier

A reckless venture in investing. Also called a plunge. Notice the difference from a "high-flier" which describes a stock with volatile prices, rapidly increasing income and high price-earnings ratios.

Float

1. An amount of money on hand that represents the overlap between a continous inflow and outflow of funds. In some cases a business is able to operate on the float of funds belonging to their customers without having to rely upon interest-bearing debt of their own. Banks always carry a substantial float of customer's money which is in the process of being transferred from one activity to another on behalf of the cutomer. Even the Internal Revenue Service carries a large amount of cash which is refunded to taxpayers each summer. During the time the money is held, it is put to use as if it were actually government money. No interest is paid on float.

2. It also means to issue something. For example, a company may float a bond offering to raise money. In this case the word is used as a verb. It can also be applied to the issue itself when used as a noun.

3. Sometimes the term is used to refer to the *quantity* of that particular security that is on the market. In this case the term is synonymous with BREADTH in discussing the market for a security.

Floating interest

A new type of bond that was devised in mid-1974 which offers an interest rate that is adjusted quarterly to be in line with market and economic conditions. This variable rate was put into effect to counteract some investor resistance at a time when interest rates were climbing to historical highs. Some investors did not want to get locked into a fixed interest rate if there were some chance that the rate would climb even higher in a few months. It also had the advantage for the issuer of permitting a reduction of rates in future years when general rates declined.

Floating supply

The amount of a given stock which is in the public's hands and is possibly available for another investor to buy. The floating supply is also called the float or the market breadth. There are many cases when all of the stock that has been issued is not available for other investors to buy. Some may be held by the founding family, so it is generally considered unavailable for the investing public. Also some foundations may hold certain securities almost permanently. Treaury stock, or stock that has been repurchased by the issuing company for acquisitions, stock options, or other purposes, is not considered part of the float.

Floor

The traveling floor of a stock exchange. The large area at a stock exchange where stocks and bonds are traded. At the New York Stock Exchange the floor covers about half an acre in area and provides space for 18 posts, which are horseshoe shaped counters around which the floor brokers gather to transact business with the specialists who man the posts. The specialists conduct the trading while standing on the floor outside the post. The floor brokers, who are called the trading crowd, communicate with the specialists by hand signals and shouts. The floor brokers in turn communicate by signals with other brokers who are located at telephones around the perimeter of the floor. These men are receiving trading orders from local brokerage offices around the country. The posts are occupied by clerks who handle the records of all transactions. Each specialist will carry 75 or so different securities, so any one wishing to purchase a certain security must go to the appropriate post to make his bid. See EXCHANGE SEAT, MEMBER FIRM, SPECIALIST, and NEW YORK STOCK EXCHANGE for more information.

Floor broker

A member of a stock exchange who executes trading orders on the floor of an exchange to buy or sell any listed securities. In his transactions he represents other parties. His clients may be customers of his own firm or other brokers in any part of the country. By contrast, there are also floor traders, who are members but are buying and selling for their own accounts.

Floor partner

An officer or partner of an exchange member firm whose duty is to represent his firm on the trading floor of a stock exchange.

Floor trader

A registered trader who is a member of a stock exchange and trades on the exchange floor for his own account rather than for other parties.

Flower bond

A special issue of long term treasury bonds sold during World War II which had a special provision whereby the bond, which was purchased at a discount, could be redeemed by the government at full face value at any time before maturity to pay estate taxes in the event of the owner's premature death. It is also called flowers and, more properly, estate tax bond. Also see BONDS for other types of bonds and comparisons between them.

Flowers
The same as flower bonds above.

Fluctuation
A variation on a stock price as reported from time to time. Market prices change constantly due to investors' emotional reactions to economic conditions, political conditions, and fundamental conditions within given industries or individual companies. These changes are reported in points and fractions of a point which represent dollars and fractions of dollars. Prices can fluctuate from minute to minute as various bits of news reach the public. These very short term changes are difficult to anticipate, but when the prices are charted over a period of weeks, there are patterns that develop and can give an experienced analyst clues of approaching trends. See CYCLIC PATTERN, CHARTS, CHARTING, STOCK CHARTS, OPTIMAL ANALYSIS, and TECHNICAL ANALYSIS for more information about price fluctuations and their meaning to investors.

Flurry
A sudden increase in trading volume in a given stock which usually results from a news report and is temporary in nature. It gives proof that market prices are not a reflection of value but of investor's feelings about what the values are or might become.

Foreign exchange

A process of settling international debts. Through international trade there are vast amounts of currency being either physically transported or being transferred through credit and accounting procedures, from one nation to another. Because of political conditions, fiscal policies, credit conditions, and other influences, the desire for various currencies will vary from time to time. Supply and demand will cause the exchange rate for various currencies to fluctuate. Speculators may buy a strong currency with a weaker one with the hope that the stronger one will gain further and thus yield a profit. The process for exchanging these currencies is called foreign exchange while the fluctuating demand for the various currencies is called the money market.

The term foreign exchange is sometimes used to refer to foreign stock exchanges, but the usual practice is to name the particular exchange by the city in which it is located, or, if referring to more than one, to say foreign stock exchanges. See INTERNATIONAL MONETARY FUND, PAPER GOLD, CURRENCY COCKTAIL, B-UNIT and EURCO for more information on the financing of international trade.

Foreign selling

The selling of securities in the United States by foreign investors.

Formula investing

Any of several investment techniques which call for following a precise plan which is intended to eliminate any need or usefulness for analyzing fundamental or technical conditions in the market. They are conservative in nature and can help an unsophisticated investor, but cannot approach the advantage of experience and skill in investing. Several plans are the following:

1. Constant ratio investing: A plan whereby the investor maintains a given ratio between common stock value and bonds or preferred stocks in his portfolio. Using this plan, an investor would buy additional stocks if the market value of the stocks he held should decline while the bonds held steady. In like manner, he would sell off some stocks if those stocks increased in value while the bonds held steady.

2. Dollar cost averaging: A plan whereby the investor buys securities at regular intervals with a fixed dollar amount rather than by the number of shares. The object is to reduce the average cost per share. This is accomplished by the fact that for a given dollar amount you will receive more shares when the price is low and fewer shares when the price rises. This is also called averaging. Notice a difference from AVERAGING DOWN, which is a more sophisticated technique of buying additional shares of any stock you own when the price is declining. This calls for active charting to reveal cyclic price patterns and buy signals for proper timing of the purchases. The purpose is the same as dollar cost averaging, but it does require considerable effort in analysis of market trends.

3. Formula timing: A plan that approaches the conventional investment techniques of buying and selling according to analysis of conditions and prices. This plan calls for purchases or sales on a regular basis, but the decision to buy or sell is based upon certain conditions, and subsequent trades continue until the conditions change.

4. Investing in an average: Not really a formula, but a philosophy of investing in all the stocks that make up an average like *Standard and Poor's 500*. It is more of a defeatist attitude than an investment practice and is typical of propositions that appear during bear markets. It is supported by statistics showing these averages outperforming investment managers during selected periods of bear markets. This proposal arises from proponents of the random walk theory or efficient market theory.

5. Variable ratio investing: A plan whereby an investor keeps both common stocks and bonds or preferred stocks in his portfolio but, varies the proportions between the common stocks and the more stable senior securities. The ratio varies with general market conditions. Usually the percentage of common stocks is kept higher during rising markets and smaller during bear markets.

Forward market

A term that is applied to the market for any kind of transaction which is negotiated at currently prevailing prices but calls for delivery at some future time. Commodity futures contracts and stock options are of this nature. There is also a little known but important forward market in currency. Using this technique, an international company may arrange payment for imported merchandise at prevailing prices in the currency of a nation which they consider economically strong. If that currency rises in value in the foreign exchange rates before the contractual delivery date, the company earns a profit on the currency exchange transaction aside from whatever profit it might make on the merchandise transaction. The forward market is also called forward exchange. See OPTIONS and

---

COMMODITY TRADING for more common uses of forward markets.

Freddie Mac

One of a series of government-sponsored private corporations which were established to provide funds for the consumer financing industry. Freddie Mac is actually a popular nickname for Federal Home Loan Mortgage Corporation, created to support the housing industry by buying mortgages from Savings and Loan Associations. It can also commit funds for future mortgages. It is a deficit operation that is tax supported and sells the mortgages to private investors at the going rates after having bought them at higher prices from the Savings and Loan Associations. The concept is one of support for the industry during slow times in the economy. Other related programs are Fannie Mae, Ginnie Mae and Sally Mae. Each has a different purpose. These are listed below:

Fannie Mae: (Federal National Mortgage Association) borrows money from the U. S. Treasury and buys mortgages from banks. It is similar to Freddie Mac, except that Fannie Mae serves only banks which operate under different regulations than the S & L's.

Ginnie Mae: (Government National Mortgage Association) buys low rate FHA and VA loans and supports government housing programs. It is a deficit operation like Freddie Mac.

Sally Mae: (Student Loan Marketing Association) loans money to universities or lending institutions for re-loan to students under government guarantees.

Each of these programs is listed under separate headings with expanded definitions.

Free and open market

A market in which supply and demand are expressed in terms of price. The greater the demand, the higher the prices will rise; and the weaker the demand, the lower the prices will fall. It contrasts with a controlled market in which supply, demand, and prices may all be regulated.

Free enterprise

The capitalistic system in which every individual has the right to own property and engage in economic activities of his own choice and for his own profit. Under this system government controls are minimized and are only intended as a means to protect the public and stabilize conditions. This is the ideal economy, but real life forces an increase in controls and regulations as the size of the system increases. When controls become excessive, the system does not work efficiently and results can be inflation, deflation, unemployment, shortages, economic stagnation, gyrations in interest rates, and investment capital, and disruption in the supply and demand in raw materials and manufacturing processes. The term free enterprise is often used as synonymous with capitalism. In a narrow sense, free enterprise pertains to the right of individuals to enter into any activity or contractual arrangement for their own well being and choice. Capitalism, in a narrow sense, pertains to the concept of individuals providing the investment capital to operate a business system and then receiving the profit in return. Together, the terms capitalism and free enterprise maintain the rights of the people above the rights of the government. This is opposed to the concepts of Socialism, Communism, Monarchism, Fascism, military governments, and the feudal systems of the past. Also see CAPITALISM for more information.

Free rider

A speculator who places an order with his broker for shares in a new issue which he expects to be a hot new issue, and which he believes he can resell through a different broker at a profit before payment is due. This type of speculator is called a stag in the London Exchange.

Friday market

A tendency, considered to be normal, for stock market prices to slump on Friday. It is attributed to speculators balancing their accounts before a long weekend. The feeling is that during the two or three days the market may be closed, there could be adverse news announced, but there would be no way of making rapid transactions to protect the account. Speculators depend on timing for their profits and prefer to have minimum exposure to risk over the week end.

Friedman, Milton

An economist who perhaps originated the theory, but is at least credited with the promotion of the theory, that a nation's economy expands on contracts in a direct relation to the money supply. Since the money supply (defined as the nation's total bank deposits plus the currency in circulation) can be controlled by government sales or purchases of federal securities and by credit availability, it is, therefore, responsible for growth and contraction of economic conditions. Friedman's theory is called monetarism since monetary control is supposed to control economic conditions. Also see KEYNESIAN ECONOMICS which holds that economic growth and national income are controlled and determined by investment and a multiplier theory.

Front end load

Mutual funds which charge a sales fee to buy its shares. These fees can be as much as 8.5%. A small maintenance fee is also charged periodically. Although some funds have no sales charge (See NO LOAD FUNDS), the front end load type funds far outnumber the no load funds. Also see INVESTMENT COMPANIES for listing of different types of funds and features of each. Also see INVESTMENT COMPANY ACT OF 1940 for definitions, purposes, and limitations.

Full faith and credit bond

A type of municipal bond which has no collateral to back it other than pledges of faith to repay. Authority to levy taxes gives some strength to the pledge of faith. See BONDS for comparison to many other types of bonds.

Full service funds

Mutual funds which automatically re-invest capital gains and dividends for its shareholders. Generally the full service funds have higher sales charges (up to 8.5%) than other mutual funds, which can go up to 6.75%. Notice difference from FULLY MANAGED FUNDS. See INVESTMENT COMPANIES for other types of funds and INVESTMENT COMPANY ACT OF 1940 for definitions, purposes, and limitations.

Fully invested

The condition of a person or institution which has all

available cash invested and is unable to take advantage
of any new opportunity that may arise.

Fully managed funds
Investment companies or mutual funds which are not
restricted by their charters to any specific types of
investments. They may invest in common stocks,
preferred stocks, or bonds as the fund management
determines best for prevailing conditions. Notice the
difference from full service funds. Also see INVEST-
MENT COMPANIES for other types of funds and
INVESTMENT COMPANY ACT OF 1940 for definitions, purposes, and limitations.

Fund
1. A shortening of mutual fund. See INVESTMENT
   COMPANIES and INVESTMENT COMPANY ACT
   OF 1940 for definitions, purposes, and limitations.
2. The term is also used as a verb meaning to supply
   capital for some venture. A funded debt is capital
   raised by the issue of bonds.

Fundamental
A general term referring to the broad, underlying
economic conditions supporting the stock market, the
commodities markets or the economic and financial
conditions of a given security, futures contract or
company. The term *fundamental* opposes the term
technical. Comparing the two:
The *fundamentals* of a given stock pertain to the
issuer's earnings history, its ratio of earnings to net
worth, earnings to sales, assets to liabilities, inventory
turnover, cash position, its debt, interest coverage,
management experience, market penetration, competition, raw materials costs or availability, and a host

of other factors that can influence the future earnings prospects.

The *technical* conditions, for that same stock concern only the market price for the stock: stability of the market price, volatility, cyclic patterns, trend directions, similarity to market trends, moving average lines, earnings ratio lines, and other charted data.

Fundamental analysis

A study of economic conditions, market conditions, industry conditions, political conditions, financial conditions, and management capabilities that support or influence the future prospects for a single company, an industry, or nationwide business conditions. Research in this respect involves the study of massive quantities of statistics, news reports, financial reports, interviews, even rumors, then comparing with past performance, projecting future expectations for the subject of study. Investors seeking good quality, long term investments are much more concerned with the fundamentals than they are the current market price. If a shorter term objective is considered, a person will place more emphasis on the technical side of the security and will follow charts closely. See TECHNICAL ANALYSIS for a study of chart conditions as a guide to investment, and OPTIMAL ANALYSIS for a system that employs both fundamental and technical studies plus *statistical probabilities* to improve the odds for the investor.

Fundamental wave

The pattern on a stock chart using the Optimal Analysis system of investment management, which shows a major or fundamental trend of market prices. Fundamental waves are cycles which may span several years on a stock chart. See OPTIMAL ANALYSIS, PRIMARY WAVE, and CYCLIC PATTERN for comparison, and STOCK CHARTS for samples of each.

Fundamentalist

A person whose major concern in investment or investment analysis involves the fundamental conditions listed above. He has little interest in the current price of the stock or the appearance of the stock charts for the securities he selects. He will be a long term investor who is concerned with future potential only. Notice the difference from TECHNICIAN and OPTIMATICIAN.

Funded Debt

That portion of the indebtedness of a corporation which is represented by a bond issue rather than short term debt such as bank loans and notes. Note that bonds do not represent ownership or equity but make the bond purchaser a creditor. See BONDS for a listing of many kinds of bonds and comparisons between them.

Funding company

A new type company which offers a package of mutual fund shares and life insurance policies. One type sells its customer mutual fund shares, then borrows against those shares for money to buy a paid up insurance policy for the client. Another variation works in the reverse order, selling the client a paid up insurance policy, then borrowing against the policy to purchase mutual fund shares. The funding company acts in a brokerage or representative capacity and is not a mutual fund itself. See INVESTMENT COM-

PANIES for similarities and differences from mutual funds.

Futures

Contracts to buy or sell some commodity at a future date. The contract is purchased on a margin based upon prevailing commodity prices. If there is a change in actual market price any time before the contractual delivery time, it results in a profit or loss to the trader, depending on the type contract purchased. It is a speculative activity that can be lucrative or disastrous ...seldom anything in between. Most futures contracts are commodities futures, but there are also futures markets in stock options and even in international currencies. See COMMODITIES, OPTIONS, and FORWARD MARKET.

Futures market

Also called the forward market. The market of supply and demand for trading contracts for future delivery of any type asset.

1. One type futures market for food stuffs and metals in raw form is commonly called commodities trading. See COMMODITIES, COMMODITIES FUTURES, COMMODITIES MARKET, and COMMODITIES TRADING for more information.

2. There is also another futures market for securities where the contracts are called OPTIONS. See PUTS and CALLS for two types of options.

3. There is also a futures market for currencies. See FORWARD MARKET for the explanation.

G

GNP

Gross National Product. The total sales or output of goods and services at market prices for a full calendar year for the entire nation. The figure is used as an indicator of economic conditions or trends.

Gambling

Committing one's resources to the whim of chance with the hope that it will produce gain. Recognizing the risks, but either failing to exercise any protective measures or not caring to. See RISK for additional information.

General management investment company

A fully managed mutual fund which is not restricted by its charter to any specialized type of investment but has a policy of diversification with full freedom for management to use its own discretion in selecting

187

investments. Also see INVESTMENT COMPANIES for other types of funds and the INVESTMENT COMPANY ACT OF 1940 for definitions, purposes, and limitations.

General mortgage bond

A bond secured by a blanket mortgage on the company's property, but which is often outranked by one or more other mortgages. See BONDS for comparisons to many other types of bonds.

General obligation bonds

Municipal bonds backed by the full taxing authority of the issuer. See BONDS for other types of bonds and differences between them.

General partnership

A business formed by two or more individuals joining as co-owners. All partners are equally liable for all debts to the full extent of their personal assets. A general partnership does not pay taxes as a business, although it must file a return. Income taxes are paid by each partner individually on their share of the profits. Also see LIMITED PARTNERSHIP.

Gilt-edged

High grade bonds issued by a company that has demonstrated its ability to earn a comfortable profit over a period of years and to pay its bondholders their interest without interruption. This term has also been applied to stocks of high quality, but usually, the term BLUE CHIP is applied to the highest quality stocks. Also see STOCK for other terms used to define and classify stocks.

Ginnie Mae

One of a series of government-sponsored private corporations which were organized to support various segments of the consumer financing industry. Ginnie Mae is actually a popular nickname used by investors as a shortening of the official title, Government National Mortgage Association. The corporation was created to support government housing programs and to buy low rate FHA and VA loans. It is organized to operate at a deficit by buying mortgages from lenders at higher than the going market rates, then reselling them to investors at going rates. The program is tax supported to maintain consumer financing during slow periods in the economy. Other related programs are Fannie Mae, Sally Mae, and Freddie Mac. Each has specific purposes.

Fannie Mae: Federal National Mortgage Association, which borrows from the U. S. Treasury and buys mortgages from banks and certain other institutions.

Freddie Mac: Federal Home Loan Mortgage Corporation, which is similar to Fannie Mae except that it buys mortgages from Savings and Loan Associations since they must operate under different government regulations.

Sally Mae: Student Loan Marketing Association, which loans to universities or financial institutions who in turn make government guaranteed loans to students.

Each of these is listed separately with expanded definitions.

Give up

The passing of a portion of a commission to another broker when one broker, acting on behalf of his client, must work through a second broker to complete a transaction for his own client. The client pays only one commission, but both brokers are entitled to compensation, so they split the commission. It is a legitimate practice.

Glamour stock

A stock that has captured the public's collective fancy because of some real or imagined potential for fast growth or high earnings. These glamour stocks usually are in an industry with recently developed technology. Such stocks tend to have high price-earnings ratios because of the demand for the stock. They also tend to increase rapidly in value during bull markets, but decline disastrously in bear markets. See STOCK for more information and a list of other types of stock.

Go-go funds

Mutual funds which trade heavily in volatile stocks. Such stocks are often in the news because of public interest and the price swings make it possible to gain or lose heavily in a short time. The excitment accompanying such risk led to this comparison to the sensual dancer of a similar name. The term came into use in the late 1960's, and some of the funds showed growth over 200% per year. In the bear market of the early 1970's such funds became only historical memories. See INVESTMENT COMPANIES for other types of funds and descriptions of each. Also see INVESTMENT COMPANY ACT OF 1940 for definititions, purposes and limitations.

Go private

The reverse of going public. The process by which a corporation buys up its own stock which is in public hands, or a few large investors buy up the stock that is in the hands of many. It is not a complicated process as is going public, but rather a case of buying stock on the open market. A minimum of regulations must be complied with. The process is seldom used, but its purpose is simple. It facilitates an acquisition or merger with another company. It permits a change of management control, or it eliminates some abrasive federal regulations that public corporations are subject to.

Go public

To change a company from a privately held corporation (all shares owned by a family or few shareholders) to a public corporation (one which issues shares to sufficient people that the shares can develop a market for trading). The process generally involves registration with the SEC, the aid of an underwriting firm which handles the great mass of paper work, and assembling a group of participating brokers to assist in the offering. The cost of going public can amount to 10% to 15% of the entire proceeds of the sale of stock. Also see PUBLIC OFFERING, PRIVATELY OWNED CORPORATION, PRIVATE OFFERINGS, and GO PRIVATE.

Gold standard

A monetary system which is based upon a fixed price of gold. Under this system gold is not used for coins, but all forms of money can be redeemed in gold. Sometimes a nation will rule that money can be redeemed in gold bullion only for export purposes in which case the system is then referred to as the international gold standard.

Gong

A bell over the trading floor of the stock exchange

which signals the opening and closing of trading each day. It is also sounded to halt trading for announcements of important events and again sounded to resume trading. It may also be sounded to announce disciplinary action against a member.

Good delivery

Certain basic qualifications must be met before a security sold on the exchange may be delivered or used as collateral in margin buying. The security must be in proper form to comply with the contract of sale, and title must be transferred by the proper delivery date to the purchaser. Conditions required are:

1. Certificates must be in good condition.
2. They must belong to the person making the transactions.
3. They must be properly endorsed.
4. They must be accompanied by needed legal documents if any exist which are necessary to make them negotiable.

If an investor fails to make good delivery for a transaction his broker is permitted, after giving proper notice, to buy comparable securities for the transaction and charge them to the account of the investor.

Good till cancelled order (GTC order)

An order to buy or sell that remains in effect until it is either executed or cancelled. Also called an open order. See BUY or SELL ORDERS for a list of other types of orders used in securities trading.

Goodwill

For accounting purposes it is the value placed upon certain intangible assets such as: brand names, reputation, location, licenses, patent rights, etc. of a company. It is an important consideration in the event a business is sold. The established reputation of a product or company gives some assurance of continued business, whereas a new name would have to build consumer demand at considerable expense and effort. Goodwill is carried on the books as an asset and is used to help determine the value of the company in case of a merger or acquisition.

Government bonds

Debt securities sold by the U.S. Government, regarded as the highest grade issues in existence. There are six types, two of which are true bonds, and three are called short term obligations. They are distinguished primarily by time to maturity.

Treasury bills: mature in 13 to 26 weeks. Also called T-Bills.

Treasury certificates: mature in 6 months to 1 year.

Treasury notes: mature in 1 to 5 years.

Series E bonds: mature in 7 to 10 years, depending on date of issuance. They are sold at a discount in small denominations ($25, $50, and $100) and may be held up to 10 years beyond maturity for additional appreciation in redemption value. Called savings bonds or victory bonds during World War II.

Series H bonds: mature in 10 years. They are sold in $500 denominations or larger. Interest is paid semiannually.

Treasury bonds: commonly called treasuries. These mature in 5 to 28 years and bear a maximum 4.5% interest. To make them attractive to investors they are sold at a discount which raises the effective yield to between 6% and 10%.

Grading of securities

The classification of securities according to financial strength, stabilty, or risk. Several advisory firms provide rating services, but the best known are *Standard and Poor's* and *Moody's*. The actual ratings are listed under the heading RATINGS OF SECURITIES.

Gresham's Law

A principle formulated by Sir Thomas Gresham during the 16th century which states that if two or more kinds of money are in circulation, each of which are of equal face value but possessing unequal intrinsic value, the one with the highest intrinsic value will tend to be hoarded. It has been rephrased for popular quotation by saying that bad money will drive good money out of circulation.

Gross

A term most often used in reference to the total sales of a company, but which can refer to any total. If referring to gross sales, the simple expression gross is used. If referring to profits, expenses, shipping volume, or any other quantity, the term is so stated. Examples of this are gross profits or gross volume. Also see NET.

Gross national product

The total sales or national output of goods and services from all forms of business valued at market prices for a calendar year. The gross sales of all forms of business combined. It is a useful figure in evaluating economic conditions and trends. Often abbreviated to GNP.

Gross profits
Profits before allowing for taxes or other deductions.

Group averages
Indexes of stock market prices for a group of companies within a single industry.

Growth
Expansion, gains, increase in market value, or profit from a sale of a security. In securities, growth refers to market prices, which in turn are influenced by corporate earnings, but growth need not reflect corporate net worth or sales. In business operations, growth usually refers to the value of physical assets, sales volume, and marketing outreach. Companies with fast internal growth and profits can become glamour stocks until the growth rate peaks out.

Growth industry
An entire industry or segment of business which demonstrates steadily increasing sales and earnings. Stock prices of individual companies in the industry enjoy more popularity than other general industries. The interest may be generated by a few unusually strong companies in the group, while some of the popularity rubs off onto the weaker members within the industry. Heavy trading volume, rising market prices with some volatility, and high price-earnings ratios characterize the entire industry. Some industries which have enjoyed popularity at different times are Aerospace contractors, airlines, aluminum processors, containerized shipping, electronics, leisure time equipment, mobile homes, nursing homes, oil developing, pollution control businesses, research laboratories, and retirement community developers.

Growth stock

A common stock representing a company that has a record of steadily increasing earnings and sales. The growth can be achieved by internal expansion resulting from product success and management efficiency, or it can come from external expansion resulting from acquisition and merger. Growth stock is characterized by heavy trading volume, steadily increasing market prices, perhaps with volatile price swings and high price-earnings multiples. The difference from glamour stock is primarily one of degree. The glamour will be the highest growth and be a leader in public interest. Growth stocks usually do not pay dividends because the earnings are plowed back into the business to finance additional expansion. Investment in growth stocks is appropriate for individuals who are not concerned with income; that is, their retirement is some distance away, or else their other investments are substantial enough to meet all their needs. Also see INCOME STOCK for contrast and STOCK for additional information and a list of other types of stock.

Guaranteed bonds

Bonds guaranteed by someone other than the issuer, perhaps as in the case of a parent company guaranteeing a subsidiary. See BONDS for other types of bonds and comparisons between them.

H

Haircutting

The amount of reduction in the stated value of assets shown by New York Stock Exchange members when stating the condition of their capitalization and liquidity. It is intended as an effort toward conservative evaluation. The exchange permits stating 100% of cash, 80 to 99% of bond values, 70% of common stocks, and requires an extra 50% trimming if assets are more than 15% made up by securities from a single issuer. The cleanest haircut is in the value of the exchange membership seat which cannot be claimed at all, even though it may have cost the firm several hundred thousand dollars.

Hard goods

Manufactured products as a broad class. The term can apply to almost any manufactured product that is not handled in bulk quantities such as food products, chemicals, paper, textiles, rubber, fuels, metals, and printed materials. One definition lists products as hard goods if they are not consumed in use, or if the useful life can be expected to continue several years or more. It is applied to consumer goods or business equipment, and can include household appliances, sporting equipment, jewelry, tools, construction hardware, and a thousand other items.

Hard sell
Sales practices which depend upon repetition of slogans, imagery, showmanship, fast talk, and urgent decisions. Salesmen using the hard sell technique are aggressive and may use canned or memorized sales pitches. The prospect is intimidated, flattered, hurried, and sometimes overwhelmed so that he is compelled to buy. Also called high pressure selling.

Hardware
In industry it is the physical composition of an actual product as opposed to its earlier stages of engineering studies, design and planning. Industry frequently uses the term in reference to the beginning of the actual construction stage of a new product. After the product reaches the hardware stage it goes into the regular production and marketing stage. It is then said to be on stream. The computer industry has spawned another entire industry which supports computers with supplies and services. This is now referred to as software. The evolution of software has caused the term hardware, in computers at least, to be continuously applied to all the basic electronic equipment to differentiate from supporting products and services.

Head and shoulders
A pattern which appears on a stock chart in a series of

waves, with the central peak higher than the previous or the following high. Several generations ago, such patterns were more frequent and also more reliable in their meaning. Analysts then considered it a signal that an upward trend had come to an end, just as the same pattern inverted signaled the reversing of a downward trend to go upward. Market influences in recent years have caused the pattern to lose importance to analysts. It is similar to the double top pattern in formation and in its interpretation. See PATTERNS for a list of other patterns that are significant to chart analysts and STOCK CHARTS for some samples.

Hedge

An investment scheme to offset losses in one transaction by realizing a simultaneous gain on another. For an example, if a person owns 100 shares in a stock he expects to decline in price but does not wish to sell his stock, he may then sell short to take advantage of the decline. That means he will borrow someone elses stock to sell it. After the price declines he will cover the short which means he will buy 100 shares at the lower price to replace the 100 he borrowed. Since he sold at a higher price than he paid to buy the new shares, he earned a profit on the transaction. The loss on his own stock is offset by the gain from the short sale. The theory is simple, but the practice is financially risky. See PUTS and CALLS, SELLING AGAINST THE BOX, SHORT SALE, STRIPS, STRAPS, STRADDLES, and SPREADS for different techniques used to protect one type investment with another. Technically, the term hedging is not applied to speculative maneuvers, but rather to the practice of protecting a real investment with a short position on some futures contract to compensate for any loss in the event of weakening market demand or shortage of supplies. In other cases it is used as a speculative move to increase profits.

Hedge fund

An unregulated investment group of individuals who have pooled their funds to concentrate investment talent with professional guidance to seek maximum growth. The organization may use any speculative measures desired, such as margin purchases, short selling, futures trading, puts, calls, etc. to achieve its objective. It is not a mutual fund. See INVESTMENT COMPANIES for other types of funds and descriptions of each. Also see INVESTMENT COMPANY ACT OF 1940 for definitions, purposes, and limitations.

High

In stock prices high refers to the highest price reached during any designated period . . . a day, month, year, etc.

High flier

A security which has captured public interest so strongly that investors are willing to pay abnormally high prices for it. Generally it is also aggravated by speculator interest, so that prices far outweigh what is justified by expected earnings of the company. Because of strong interest, the stock will be trading at high multiples (many times its earnings per share) and will be quite volatile. The combination makes the risk higher than with more seasoned stocks.

High grade

A description applied to securities issued by a company whose financial condition is sound and whose ability to continue showing good earnings to meet its obligations is unquestioned. Many utilities have traditionally fit this category, since the demand for their services can not decline appreciably when other segments of industry fluctuate. During the mid 1970's inflation and fuel problems tended to tarnish many utility stocks when profitably rapidly faded.

High-low index

A dual line index showing new yearly highs and lows on a 10 week moving average basis. It is studied as a market breadth indicator which often confirms major trend changes where the two lines cross.

Hit the bid

A verbal instruction given by an investor to his broker to sell a security at the bid price (the highest anyone has offered), rather than try to negotiate a higher price. It is the same as selling at the market. See BUY and Sell orders for a list of other kinds of orders used in securities trading.

Hold

To own something such as stock or bonds. Usually the term also suggests that the owner intends to continue ownership for some long term period. For example, the expression buy and hold suggests long term investment as opposed to *trading*, which is buying and selling quickly to take advantage of market fluctuations.

Holding company

A corporation with a strong commitment to acquisition of other operating companies. Similar to a conglomerate except that the holding company is primarily interested only in participating in the profits of the subsidiary. The holding company usually will acquire other related companies in a particular industry. The conglomerate is usually less concerned with the industry or product, but it does often provide management assistance and an effort at blending operations in some fashion. Sometimes the term DIVERSIFIED HOLDING COMPANY is used for a conglomerate. Also see MERGER, AMALG-AMATION, CONSOLIDATION and ACQUISITION, for expanded information.

Hot issue
A new issue of stock which has a demand that exceeds the supply of stock available. Such issues usually begin trading at high premiums immediately after the initial offering is completed.

Hot money
Vast quantities of money which move quickly in international currency exchanges. Owned by corporations and foreign governments, it shifts with speculative buying of currency of different nations as economic climates change. It involves billions of dollars and can have very serious effects on international economics. It is legal in spite of the under world sounding name.

Hypothecation
The pledging of securities as collateral for a loan.

I

Immediate or cancel order

A market order or limited price order issued by an investor to his broker which is to be executed in whole or in part as soon as it is presented on the trading floor, and the portion not executed is cancelled. A stop is considered an execution. Also called a FILL OR KILL ORDER. Since these orders are usually issued at opening or closing time they are also known as AT THE OPENING ONLY or AT THE CLOSE ONLY ORDERS. See BUY or SELL ORDERS for a list of other kinds of orders used in securities trading.

Imputed interest

A device used by the Internal Revenue Service to help prevent hidden interest income. If a non-interest bearing loan is made by a person, the IRS will impose a tax on the theoretical interest that *could have been charged.*

In and out

Also called round trip. A complete cycle of buying and later selling a security. Often called a two way trade although sometimes this term means selling out of one security and at the same time buying into another. The terms in and out and round trip as used in the stock market are the equivalent of round turn as used in the commodities market.

In and out commissions

The total commission payable by an investor when he sells out of one security and at the same time buys into another. It differs slightly from two-way commission in that the in and out is the actual amount due by adding the proper selling commission to the proper buying commission. Since commission rates vary with the price of the security, the buying and selling commissions are usually different. By contrast the two way commission is an estimated figure calculated by doubling the buying commission. Also see TWO WAY COMMISSION.

Inactive post

A trading post on the floor of the New York Stock Exchange where infrequently traded securities are handled in units of 10, 25, or 50 shares instead of the usual 100 share lots. Better known in the business as Post 30. See UNIT OF TRADING for helpful information.

Inactive stock

An issue traded on an exchange or in the over-the-counter market in which there is a relatively low volume of transactions. Volume may be only a few hundred shares a week or even less. On the New York

Stock Exchange, inactive stocks may be traded in 10, 25, or 50 share units rather than the usual 100 share lots. See STOCK for a list of other terms used for different types of stock.

Income bonds

Bonds which have a set interest rate, but the payment of the interest is dependent upon earnings of the corporation. See BONDS for other types of bonds and comparisons between them.

Income statement

A statement of profit and loss, sometimes called a P&L sheet, or profit and loss statement; one of the three reports included in a corporation's financial statements. The other two are statement of capital and the balance sheet. The income statement shows total revenues, costs, taxes, and profits for a given period of time.

Income stock

A stock which has a record of high yield or dividend income. It is considered a conservative type investment suitable for retired people and those who need to supplement other earnings or protect the principal invested. Growth is not considered by investors seeking income type investments. Typical income stocks are public utilities, large food chains, steels, railroads or other large, well established corporations that consistently pay dividends and are relatively stable. Also see GROWTH STOCK for contrast and STOCK for listings of other types of stock.

Index

A statistical yardstick expressed in terms of per-

---

centages of a base period. It is not an average. For instance, the Federal Reserve Board's index of industrial production is based on the 1957-59 period as presenting 100. In 1968, the index stood at 165.5, which meant that industrial production at that point was 65.5% higher than in the base period. The base period chosen may be changed from time to time. Often the terms indexes, averages, and composites are used interchangeably, although incorrectly so. Some indexes are as follows:

AMEX price level
Barron's weekly confidence
Business failures inverted
Cost of living
Freight car loadings
High-low
Industrial materials
Industrial production
New business formation
NYSE composite
Short interest ratio
Short range oscillator
Trendlines odd-lot
Wholesale price
200 day moving average

See AVERAGES, INDEXES, INDICATORS, and COMPOSITES for differences and lists of other indexes.

Indenture

A written agreement under which debentures are issued setting forth maturity date, interest rate, security and other terms. So named because of its origin when two copies of the agreement were placed together and one edge torn off. Later, the copies being placed together would match on the irregular edge, verifying the authenticity.

Indicated market

A market price that is subject to confirmation. It is a qualification given by a dealer in securities when stating bid and asked prices that are *not firm*. Thus, prices stated as 9 1/2 to 10 *indicated* market mean that these are the approximate prices available, but if the inquirer wants to place an order, a more thorough check would be made before quoting firm prices. It is not a quote. Sometimes called workout market or subject market. Note differences from FIRM MARKET.

Indication of interest

A tentative offer to purchase a new security. Made on the basis of a preliminary or red herring prospectus and may become a firm offer to purchase upon delivery of a regular prospectus.

Indicators

Any quantity or effect, average, composite, or index which shows enough correlation to stock market trends or economic conditions that it is followed regularly, charted and quoted widely in attempts to forecast market trends. There are *leading indicators* . . . which shows movements preceding major market moves, *coincident indicators* . . . which help to verify market moves, *lagging indicators* . . . which follow market moves to verify the change in a trend, and other indicators which show significant trends in selected industries. See AVERAGES, INDEXES, and COMPOSITES for differences and examples of some commonly used indicators.

Industrial bond

Any of a broad range of bonds issued by business corporations except utilities and railroads. The bonds are sold to private investors who seek more safety than is commonly found in stocks, and they are guaranteed a regular interest income. The issuing company uses the proceeds of bond sales for capital expansion or operating expenses and promises to repay the face amount of the bond at some specified date that can be up to 100 years from issue. A few have been issued as perpetual bonds. A few mature in as little as 10 years, and others can be converted into common stock if so designated at the time of sale. Some varieties of industrial bonds are as follows:

Coupon bonds or *bearer bonds:* Bonds which authorize interest payments to any person presenting a coupon clipped from the bond.

Debenture bonds: Bonds which are backed only by the credit rating of the issuer.

Convertible bonds: Bonds which can be exchanged at some future time for common stock of the same issuer.

Participating bonds: Bonds which provide for the owner to share in the profits of the issuer and also to receive a guaranteed interest payment.

Serial bonds: Bonds which are sold all on one date, but mature at varying times.

Series bonds: Bonds which are issued at intervals, although they are all part of a single issue.

Mortgage bonds: Bonds which are those backed by a mortgage on real estate. These are considered the highest grade industrials.

Blanket bonds: Bonds which act as a second mortgage on all assets. They rank below mortgage bonds. See BONDS for listings of other types.

Industrial development bonds

A tax exempt municipal bond that is sold in a given community for the purpose of financing facilities for private business. It is a plan by the federal government to attract needed industry to areas in need of economic growth. The tax free status attracts investors and low cost financing; energetic promotion by local government attracts new business, new jobs, and new tax receipts. Also see BONDS for other types of bonds and descriptions of each.

Industrials

A shortening of Dow Jones Industrial Averages. A composite of the trading prices of 30 large industrial firms thought to be representative of the entire market. Widely followed as an indicator of market conditions and economic trends. Also see DOW JONES INDUSTRIAL AVERAGES. The entire list of 30 companies making up the list is shown under the heading DOW JONES INDUSTRIALS.

Industry

1. Manufacturing as a broad class. This would include auto manufacturers, plastic molders, textile manufacturers, food processors, printers, oil refineries, and an endless list of others.

2. Narrow groupings of related businesses such as auto manufacturing and primary suppliers of the auto makers. The drug industry includes the manufacturing of pharmaceutical products, related research laboratories, and retail drug stores, along with the distribution channels. The advertising field is not an industry in the sense of manufacturing, but it is an industry in the sense of being a clearly defined segment of business. Also, educational

services, insurance, banking, retailing, broadcasting, hotels and motels, restaurants, and the securities business are all considered to be separate industries.

Industry funds

Mutual funds which restrict their investments to senior securities (preferred stocks and bonds) which have high yield. These funds, like bond funds, seek income and preservation of capital and are of interest to retired individuals. See INVESTMENT COMPANIES for other types of funds and descriptions of each. Also see INVESTMENT COMPANY ACT OF 1940 for definitions, purposes, and limitations.

Inertia or market inertia

The tendency for a minor trend in market movement to continue for some time. This reflects the tendency of people to be reluctant to change. On an up reversal, there is a tendency to wait to verify the strength of the move before buying. In a down reversal, people wait again to see if the weakness is real before they sell. When market prices are charted, the inertia is evident in the length of time a trend continues before reversing direction.

Inflation

A decrease in the purchasing power of money due to the spiraling of increased prices, costs, and wages. Prices inflate so the dollar buys less. Labor, asking for higher wages, forces up costs, so manufacturers must raise prices. The higher prices starts the cycle again for wage increase demands. Also see COST PUSH INFLATION and DEMAND PULL INFLATION.

Inside information

True facts about conditions, actions and plans of a

company that should be known only to top management. Sometimes this vital information can leak out to some investors to give them some measure of investment advantage over others. The government generally tries to guard and regulate the handling of such information.

Insider
Officials within a company or organization who, by their position, have access to information not available to the general public. Some recent court decisions have extended the term to mean almost anyone who knows anything about a security before the *last* person hears about it.

Insolvent
The condition of a company or individual whose debts exceed assets or are so heavy that financial recovery is hopeless. Opposite to liquid.

Institutional house
Also called institutional brokerage. A brokerage firm which serves financial institutions such as banks, insurance companies, mutual funds, pension funds, and profit sharing plans rather than individual investors.

Institutional market
The demand for short term funds and commercial paper. The term has been applied to the professionals who handle commercial paper and short term funds. Their customers are corporations and financial institutions who need cash for short periods of time or have surplus funds that will not be needed for a short period of time, even over a weekend.

Institutions

In stock market jargon institutions refer to large financial organizations which are handling other people's money. They include mutual funds, insurance companies, pension funds, savings institutions, trust funds, etc. Their available cash is vast and their impact on the market is immense. It is calculated that institutions currently hold 70% of all securities being traded.

Insured deposits

Savings accounts which are guaranteed by the Federal Deposit Insurance Corporation against loss if the bank fails. Currently such accounts in qualifying institutions are insured up to $40,000. This limit may be raised by pending legislation.

Intangible assets or intangibles

An asset having no material substance. Services, skills, special rights, patents, copyrights, and special knowhow are considered intangible assets. Insurance, engineering, accounting, advertising, and many other professional services are considered intangibles as far as the sale of such services is concerned, since there is no physical product that can be touched, operated, or demonstrated.

Interest

A charge made for the use of someone else's money. It is usually calculated and stated as a percentage of the principal amount. Businesses which borrow public funds through the issuance of bonds generally pay interest on a relatively simple basis. However, most credit organizations who loan to the general public on installment payment accounts have devised numerous ways of charging interest so that the actual amount the borrower pays is considerably more than the stated rate of interest. Some of the various methods for charging interest are:

1. Add-on interest: The interest is calculated for the full amount of principal for the full period of the loan and added to the principal, then divided into monthly payments. The result is that more interest is actually paid out than would be the case with straight line interest because you are still paying interest on the full amount of principal right down to the last payment. Example: A $1,000 installment loan for two years at 8% add-on rate would cost $160 in interest by the time it is paid off. Monthly payments of $48.33 each except for one payment of $48. Also called a contract loan.

2. Discount interest: More properly called a discount loan. The interest is calculated for the full amount for the full period of the loan just as in the add-on method above; however, in this case the full payment for all the interest is subtracted from the amount of money given to the borrower. He must, therefore, borrow a larger amount than needed so that the interest deduction can be made and still provide sufficient cash. The effect of this system is to make the total interest paid even higher than the add-on method. Example: To receive the same $1,000 mentioned above for two years at 8%, you must borrow $1,190.40. The total interest paid out would be $190.40 and the monthly payments would be $49.60. This method calculates out to the same interest as add-on interest when figuring the same principal amount for the loan. However, since the borrower must borrow a larger amount in order to receive the same proceeds as in the other loans,

this results in a higher cost to the borrower than straight line or add-on interest.

3. Straight line interest: A straight percentage of the *unpaid balance* on an annual basis. Example: The same $1,000 installment loan for two years at 8% would cost $79.85 in interest by the time it is paid off. The monthly payments would vary from $48.33 on the first payment to $41.86 on the last payment. A variation to this method would be to set a fixed amount for each monthly payment. Interest is figured on the unpaid balance, so that for each successive month there is a larger amount of the payment applied to the principal and less for interest.

4. Prime interest rate: Usually called prime rate. It is the rate charged by banks to their top rated commercial customers. This is the lowest possible rate available at any time and forms the basis for determining rates for all other customers. Prime rate, in turn, is determined by the Federal Discount Rate, which is the amount the bank itself must pay to borrow federal funds.

5. Sum-of-the-digits or Rule of 78: Interest refunds or rebates, in case an add-on loan is paid off early, are often calculated on a different basis. The formula used frequently is the sum-of-the-digits or the rule of 78. The months in a year are numbered from the last month of the contract to the first then the numbers are added up for a total of 78 points for a year. The most recent month is given a value of 12 points, the next month 11 points, the next 10 points and so on. A refund would be calculated by dividing the total interest paid in by the total digits for the contract, then multiplying by the sum of the digits

for the remaining months. If, in the $1,000 loan example, the borrower desired to pay off the loan on the 20th month, the refund would be calculated as ...1 + 2 + 3 + 4 + 5 + 6 + 7 + 8 + 9 + 10 ... and so on up to 24 (for the total number of months). The sum of this equals 300 points total for the two years. The final 4 months of the contract would then be equal to 10 points. The refund would therefore be: $160 paid in interest, divided by 300 (total number of points) times 10 (the number of points for the last four months of the contract) or ... $160 divided by 300 times 10 equals a $5.33 refund.

6. Usury: Another term for interest. Modern interpretation of usury suggests excessive or unlawfully high interest rates.

Some other frequently used terms involving interest rates are:

1. Accrued interest: Interest payments due on bonds but unpaid for any reason. See separate heading for expanded definitions.

2. Compound interest: A method for calculating interest earned by paying interest on the total account which includes principal plus interest received for any previous payment periods. Interest can be compounded (or calculated and paid) on an annual, semiannual, monthly, or even daily basis.

3. Imputed interest: A device by the government to avoid unreported interest income. Where no interest payments are reported as being received for a loan, the IRS will charge tax on a theoretical interest at the rate of 6% (in 1974), even though no interest was actually received.

Interest coverage

The ratio between a company's pre-tax earnings and the annual amount of interest it must pay on bonds and bank financing. For example, if a company earns $1,000,000 in gross profits before taxes and must pay $200,000 in interest, it has coverage of 5 times. Analysts suggest that industrial companies should have coverage of at least 4 times. Utilities are considered safe with a coverage of 3 times. Interest coverage is figured against *pre-tax* income since it is an expense of doing business. Notice the difference from PREFERRED DIVIDEND COVERAGE listed separately, which is figured on *after tax* income, since dividends are distributions of profits. The example below shows breakdown of earnings and various amounts paid out for interest, dividends and taxes.

Assume a typical company with 3,000 bonds issued at $1,000 par, paying 7%. It also has 20,000 shares of preferred stock outstanding at $100 par, paying 5%. Then, there are 1,000,000 shares of common outstanding, no par, earning dividends as voted by the Board of Directors. This year a 10 cent per share dividend is voted. If the company earns $1,000,000 before taxes the payout will be as follows:

Gross income before taxes	$1,000,000
Bond interest (3000 x $1000 x 7%)	-210,000
Pre-tax net	790,000
Federal taxes (approximate)	-380,000
After tax earnings	410,000
Pref. stock div. (20,000 x $100 x 5½%)	-110,000
Balance	300,000
Common dividends (1,000,000 x $.10)	-100,000
Retained earnings	200,000

Interim bond

A temporary certificate that is intended to be exchanged for a more definitive bond at a later time. See ASSENTED BOND for a special case of the interim bond. Also see BONDS for other types of bonds and comparisons between them.

Interlocking directorates

A condition that exists if two competetive companies have some of the same men on their Board of Directors. It is considered illegal by federal anti-trust laws.

Internal financing

Paying for business expansion from retained earnings rather than by the sale of stock or bonds. By contrast, the sale of these securities to finance expansion is known as EQUITY FINANCING, DEBT FINANCING, or OUTSIDE FINANCING. See separate headings for differences between these methods.

International monetary fund

An agency of the United Nations organization which assists member organizations to maintain orderly economic development and to assist in establishing currency exchange rates. International trade deficits or surpluses are channeled through the IMF, which maintains a stock of gold deposited by member nations. In 1968, member nations voted to create additional credits called special drawing rights (SDR's) to simplify payment of trade debts and to extend the cash equivalent of gold on deposit. These SDR's are known as paper gold.

Interstate commerce

Transportation of products and securities across state lines for sale. Crossing state lines puts the activity under federal regulations.

Interstate Commerce Commission (I C C)

A federal agency which regulates the activities of railroads, water carriers, and trucking firms which cross state lines.

Intrinsic value

A value inherent in something. For example, silver dollars were recalled recently by the government because the actual silver content was worth more than a dollar. By contrast, a paper dollar is practically worthless for its paper content, yet it will buy the same amount of goods as the silver dollar. The intrinsic value of the silver dollar is, therefore, much greater than the paper dollar.

Inventory

An itemized list of a stock of goods and their worth. A manufacturing firm may carry an inventory of manufactured goods ready for sale and an inventory of raw materials and materials in the process of manufacturing. A retailer will carry an inventory of all goods on hand for sale. A broker will have an inventory of securities on hand in his own account for sale.

Inventory turnover

The number of times in a year that inventory must be replenished. It is measured approximately by dividing gross sales by the average inventory. Too slow a turnover is considered undesirable because it represents idle investment, but too high a turnover leads to scheduling difficulties and occasional down time which raises costs. Four times a year may be average for some industrial firms, while some heavy equipment manufacturers may be lower, and the retail food industry may go many times higher. Turnover in the securities business does not refer to inventory, but to trading volume or the number of shares that change hands in a day's time.

Investment

Putting anything to use for the purpose of gaining income or some other value for yourself. In the field of securities, investment is buying a security with the intention of holding it for a long term period for the income it will produce and to preserve the principal. Sometimes the term investment is used in a broad sense to include securities trading and speculating. Distinctions exist, however, between the terms and are generally accepted as follows:

Investing: Buying for the long term with the main considerations of income produced and preservation of capital. The investor characteristic most prominent is caution, with reliance upon the advice of some advisor for investment selection.

Trading: Buying with the intention of holding only until a reasonable profit can be realized. Little concern is given to income produced, but growth is sought. Trading requires a great deal of knowledge of securities markets, market influences and investor attitudes. Trading requires considerable time for study or research in economic conditions, industry trends, and even international politics and economics.

Speculating: Agressive trading that accepts greater risks for the prospect of greater return. Speculators generally deal in very short term trades and make considerable use of leverage devices such as margin buying, option buying, commodities trading, and special situations. A successful speculator is extremely knowledgeable. A person with limited knowledge who speculates in securities quickly becomes a loser.

Playing the market: Gambling with securities by buying and selling with no knowledge of the securities market or the fields of finance and economics. This type of speculator frequently follows tips and hunches and nearly always ends up losing and giving a bad name to the securities industry. The term is usually used by someone who neither has any investments nor understands anything about them.

Investment advisor

A person or firm, usually registered with the SEC, who provides investment guidance for sale to the investing public. Some advisors are hired by institutions to assist in supervising their portfolios. Also see INVESTMENT COUNSELOR.

Investment analysts

Individuals whose full time profession is the study and comparison of securities. They may serve brokerage houses or investment institutions. They have organized professional societies in many large cities and also have a national organization. See FUNDAMENTAL ANALYSIS, OPTIMAL ANALYSIS and TECHNICAL ANALYSIS.

Investment banker

A person or company who assists a corporation in getting its securities to the buying public, and who is also known as an underwriter. Very often a group of investment bankers form a syndicate to handle an issue. They will purchase the total offering outright, then along with participating dealers also called the selling group, will sell the security to the public. After this initial offering of a security, it will then be traded over-the-counter or on some exchange. Investment bankers may also be called upon to dispose of large blocks of securities to settle an estate or to aid a corporation divesting itself of large holdings of another corporation. Also see BEST EFFORTS for more information on the investment banker's activities.

Investment clubs

Small, informal groups of individuals who invest small amounts of money contributed by members. Their purpose is to educate members by exchange of ideas and shared experiences in investing. Clubs have more social value than economic impact.

Investment companies

A company which reinvests money which was obtained through issuance of its own securities. Also called investment trusts, mutual funds, or, simply funds. Most of these funds have chosen to meet the requirements of the Investment Company Act of 1940. Some of the major provisions of the Act of 1940 provide:

1. That more than 40% of the company's assets must must consist of investment type securities.

2. At least 75% of the company's assets must be so diversified that no more than 5% of its own assets are invested in the securities of any one issuer.

3. The company must not hold more than 10% of the outstanding voting stock of any one issuer.

4. At least 90% of the company's earnings must be paid out as dividends to its shareholders. If the 90% figure is maintained, the fund remains untaxed on those distributed earnings. Those companies meeting these requirements are referred to as regulated investment companies. Very few are not regulated.

Following are some of the different types of investment companies:

Balanced funds: Mutual funds which keep a balance between stocks and bonds in their portfolios. It is thought that the stocks can provide growth of capital, while bonds offer safety.

Bond funds: Mutual funds which invest mainly in bonds. Their objective is to achieve maximum income with safety of principal. These funds are of special interest to retired persons or others unable to work.

Capital gains funds: Mutual funds which have a policy of seeking profits through capital gains only. They will invest in growth stocks and some speculative issues. These funds will appeal to younger investors and professional people who have sufficient current income but seek maximum growth for future years.

Closed end funds: Investment companies not properly called mutual funds which have only one offering of shares to the public. Their shares thereafter trade on the open market as any other public corporation. These companies comprise only a small portion of the total investment company market. Although they are often called funds, the term mutual fund is properly applied only to open end investment companies. Also see OPEN END FUNDS.

Common stock funds: Mutual funds which have a policy of investing primarily in common stock for the growth they can provide.

Diversified investment company: A broad term including most mutual funds. The term refers to compliance with the Investment Company Act of 1940. Similar in meaning to a regulated investment company.

Dual purpose funds: Closed end investment companies which issue two classes of stock . . . income and capital shares. All income realized from the portfolio is distributed to the income shareholders, and all capital gains distributions are paid to the capital shareholders. Not a mutual fund.

Front end load: Mutual funds which charge a sales fee to buy their shares. These fees can be as much as 8 1/2%. A small maintenance fee is also charged periodically. Some funds have no sales charge (see NO LOAD FUNDS). The front end load is more popular.

Full service funds: Mutual funds which automatically reinvest capital gains and dividends for its shareholders. These funds generally charge higher sales charge (up to 8 1/2%) than other mutual funds (up to 6 3/4%). Notice difference from FULLY MANAGED FUNDS below.

Fully managed funds: Mutual funds which are not restricted by their charters to any specific types of investments. They may invest in common stock, preferred stocks, or bonds as the fund management determines best for prevailing conditions. Note difference from FULL SERVICE FUNDS above.

Funding company: A new type company which offers a package of mutual fund shares and life insurance policies. One type sells its customer mutual fund shares, then borrows against those shares for money to buy a paid up insurance policy for the client. Another variation works in reverse order, selling the client a paid up insurance policy, then borrowing against the policy to purchase mutual fund shares. The funding company acts in a brokerage capacity or representative capacity and is not a mutual fund itself.

Go-go funds: Mutual funds which have aggressive investment policies and show unusually high growth records. During the late 1960's several showed growth of over 200% a year. In the early 1970's such funds were only historical memories.

Hedge fund: An unregulated investment group of individuals which have pooled their funds to concentrate investment talent with professional guidance to seek maximum growth. The organization may use any speculative measures desired such as margin purchases, short selling, futures trading, puts, calls, etc., to achieve their objective. Not a mutual fund.

Industry funds: Mutual funds which restrict their investments to senior securities (preferred stocks and bonds) which have high yield. These funds, like bond funds, seek income and preservation of capital and are of interest to retired individuals.

Investment trust: Another word for an investment company or mutual fund.

Leverage funds: A mutual fund which has a policy of borrowing money for investment to increase the return for its shareholders.

Mutual fund: A broad term meaning an investment company or investment trust which is owned by many investors. It sells its shares to the public on a continuous basis and is obligated to redeem or repurchase those shares at any time at the net asset value. Since the number of shareholders may change from day to day, it is called an OPEN END INVESTMENT COMPANY. Also see CLOSED END INVESTMENT COMPANY. All mutual funds are investment companies, but not all investment companies are mutual funds.

No load fund: A mutual fund which does not have a sales charge for new shareholders. There is a maintenance charge made periodically to cover expenses of management. The no charge feature would seem attractive on the surface, but 95% of the money in mutual funds is in the front end load type.

Open end fund: A broad term applying to all mutual funds. This is an investment company which sells its shares to the public on a continuous basis and is obligated to redeem or repurchase those shares at any time at the net asset value. Thus, the number of shareholders may vary from day to day, which gives it the open end designation. Also see CLOSED END FUND.

Preferred stock funds: Mutual funds which have a policy of investment only in preferred stocks for income and safety of capital.

Regional funds: Mutual funds that have a policy of investing in securities of a specific geographical area such as the West Coast, Florida, the Midwest, etc.

Registered investment company: Another term for regulated investment company, mutual fund, or investment trust.

Regulated investment company; An investment company which has chosen to operate under the regulations of the Investment Company Act of 1940. The term covers all mutual funds. Most investment companies and investment trusts are mutual funds and, therefore, are regulated. While the terms are often synonymous there are a few investment companies that are not regulated. The hedge fund is an example of an unregulated investment company.

Split investment company: Another term for a leverage fund which may borrow money for investment in order to increase return for its shareholders.

Special features in some mutual funds: Many mutual funds offer plans for periodic investment to accumulate larger holdings in the fund. These plans can be *voluntary*, which means there is no obligation to make additional purchases, or *contractual*, which means that the investor commits himself to periodic purchases of more shares and pays the charges for it. Different funds have different names for the plans. Some are contractual plans, penalty plans, and prepaid plans. All of these plans are *contractual* agreements for the investor to purchase specific amounts of additional shares. All of the sales charges are deducted during the first year or two so the account shows little growth for several years. It may even show a loss for a time, hence the penalty name. These are definitely long term investments for unsophisticated investors.

Others are accumulation plan, cumulative plan, systematic investment plan, periodic payment plan, and continuous investment plan. The plans in this group are usually *voluntary*, which means the investor is not obligated to make regular payments or even to continue the plan. He may pay in any amount over a set minimum at any time. Voluntary plans usually have a sales charge for each installment equal to the rate paid when making the initial investment. Several other features are listed below.

Level charge plan: Accumulation plans for acquiring mutual fund shares over a period of time. The sales charges are levied at each time of purchase based on the size of investment. Voluntary plans are of this type.

Automatic dividend reinvestment: An optional feature in many mutual funds which provides for reinvestment of all income distributions for greater growth. Usually capital gains distributions are automatically reinvested unless the investor requests payment.

Withdrawal plan: A plan offered by some mutual funds by which an investor may receive monthly or quarterly payments for his living expenses. The payments may be limited to dividend or capital gains distributions, or it may be fixed at a rate higher than such distributions. In this event some shares are liquidated regularly to make the payments. The plan is suitable to elderly individuals.

Investment Company Act of 1940

An act of congress that resulted from certain investment abuses preceding and following the 1929 market crash. Its purposes are to protect investors, standardize investment company procedures, and promote professionalism in the industry. Some of the major provisions of the Act are shown below.

Limitations placed upon the investment companies:

1. More than 40% of the company's assets must consist of investment type securities.

2. At least 75% of the company's assets must be so diversified that no more than 5% of its own assets are invested in the securities of any one issuer.

3. The company must not hold more than 10% of the outstanding voting stock of any one issuer.

4. At least 90% of the company's earnings must be paid out as dividends to its shareholders. If this 90% figure is maintained, the fund remains untaxed on those distributed earnings. It must pay tax only on the 10% or less it retains. Companies meeting these requirements are called regulated investment companies. Very few are not regulated.

5. All mutual fund shares must be sold only at the regular public offering price (net asset value plus a fixed sales charge).

6. Mutual funds may not issue bonds, but they may borrow from banks if they provide 300% collateral for the loan.

7. Only voting stock may be issued with all shares entitled to equal voting rights.

Purposes of the Investment Company Act of 1940:

1. To insure that the public is provided with complete and accurate information about the company's policies, circumstances, and management.

2. Assure that the company is organized and operated in the interests of all shareholders rather than management, advisors, or special groups.

3. Maintain responsible and ethical management.

4. Assure proper accounting methods.

5. Prevent major changes in the organization without the consent of shareholders.

6. Require adequate reserves for the conduct of business.

Definition of an investment company:

1. An open end investment company (commonly called a mutual fund) is one which is continuously offering its shares to the public and will redeem those shares at any time at net asset value on the demand of the shareholder.

2. A closed end investment company is one which has a fixed number of shares outstanding. The company is not obligated to redeem the shares, but the shares are traded on the open market.

See STATEMENT OF POLICY for additional regulations placed upon investment companies concerning their operations.

Investment counselor

A person whose principal business consists of giving investment advice to individuals or institutions. He is usually registered with the Securities Exchange Commission (SEC) or state regulatory agencies. The difference between an investment counselor and an investment advisor is that the counselor serves individual accounts for a fee based on the size of the account. Fees often run from 1/4% to 1%, but can be much higher. Investment advisors, by contrast, may serve a mass clientele on a subscription basis. Subscriptions may cost from $50 a year up to $2,000 or $3,000 per year. In some cases the professional may serve in both capacities.

Investment fund

The same as investment company or mutual fund. See INVESTMENT COMPANIES for other types of funds and distinctions between them. Also see INVESTMENT COMPANY ACT of 1940 for definitions, purposes, and limitations.

Investment manager

Persons or companies that have the responsibility of investing money for institutions or individuals. Their purpose is to provide full time, professional attention to investment accounts for improved odds for success. Few individuals can manage personal accounts adequately while employed in other activities. The greater the wealth the greater the need for professional help.

Investment objective

The financial goals of an investor. There should properly be a difference in objectives for persons of different ages, family size, marital status, financial ability and personal termperament. For example, an unemployed widow would choose the safest type investment which produces regular income while a young, single professional person might seek rapid growth with no concern for income. He could well afford to speculate.

Investment policy

A stated plan used by an investment manager as a guide in his activities of investing funds entrusted to him.

Investment trust

A company that invests in other companies. There are two principal types: closed end and open end. Shares in closed end investment trusts are bought and sold like any other stock on the open market. Capitalization of these companies usually remains constant. Open end funds, which are called mutual funds, sell new shares directly to investors and stand ready to back their shares at any time. They are not listed on stock exchanges. Their capitalization is not fixed, but they may issue more shares as investors want them. See INVESTMENT COMPANIES for different types of investment companies and descriptions of each. Also see INVESTMENT COMPANY ACT OF 1940 for definitions, purposes, and limitations.

Investor

A person who buys a security or some other property for the purpose of obtaining an income from it while preserving the principal. His intentions are long term or buying and holding. Notice the difference from the terms TRADING, SPECULATING, and PLAYING THE MARKET, all listed under the heading INVEST-MENT.

Invoice

A bill calling for payment for merchandise or service. It is usually sent by a supplier to his customer after each business transaction and covers only that one transaction. For instance, a retailer may order from a certain manufacturer five times a month. An invoice is then sent to the retailer following each delivery. The invoice lists the quantities and description of each article delivered with individual prices. At the end of the month, the manufacturer may send a statement which lists only totals from each invoice. Payment policies vary widely and are also widely abused, but some variations include:

1. Payment due within 10 days after invoice mailed.

2. Payment due before the 10th of the month following invoice mailing date.

3. Payment due within 10 days after mailing of monthly statement.

4. Payment due within 30 days and with a 2% discount allowed if paid in less than 10 days.

5. Payment due on receipt of incoice and 1% interest added per month if over 30 days late.

Irredeemable bond

The same as an annuity bond. One that bears no maturity date. It will continue drawing interest in-definitely. See BONDS for other types and com-parisons between them.

Issue

Any of a company's securities that have been sold to the public, or the act of distributing such securities. It may include both stocks or bonds. Also called an offering.

Issuer

A company which offers shares of its stock or bonds to the public.

J

Jargon

Specialized terms used in some particular field of
activity. For example, a bull in the normal English
language is a large adult male animal, but in investment circles it is an optimistic market forecaster.
Then in standard English terminology, a pilgrim is an
early American settler, whereas in the hard driving
retail trade a pilgrim is a particularly vulnerable
customer who can be taken advantage of easily.

Joint account

An account in investing, banking, charge accounts,
etc., which lists two or more persons sharing equally in
the rights and liabilities associated with the account.
Most commonly used by husband and wife teams, but
occasionally found elsewhere. In the event of the death

of one party in the joint account, his portion of equity goes into his estate rather than to the other party, as in the case of JOINT TENANCY.

Joint bond

Another name for a guaranteed bond. A bond that is guaranteed by someone other than the issuer. For example, a parent corporation may guarantee the repayment of an issue by a subsidiary. Also see BONDS for other types of bonds and comparisons between them.

Joint tenancy

A legal term which means ownership shared equally by two or more persons, with each having full right of usage. Total rights of ownership or entire tenancy is conveyed to the surviving tenants at the decease of another. Notice the difference from a JOINT AC-COUNT, in which the equity of the deceased member goes into the estate of the deceased instead of to the surviving party.

Junior equity

Common stock. Contrasted to preferred stock, which is a senior security. The junior position refers to its standing in the event of liquidation and distribution to the shareholders. Although the common stock ranks lower than preferred stock in its claim on assets, it is usually the only class of stock that has voting rights. Notice the difference between equity and security. The term equity here includes both common and preferred stock, while the term security includes bonds with both kinds of stock. Bonds are a senior security. See STOCK for descriptions of different kinds of equity.

K

Key man

A person who is responsible in a large degree for the success of a company. He may or may not be in a position of primary authority, but, because of his skills or accomplishments, his presence is vital to the company. Key man insurance policies are common to protect a company from the loss of such a person. One example of a key man is an inventor who has developed a new product for a company. Since the inventor is the only one capable of steering the development up to the production stage, he may be covered by a large policy until the development costs of the project are recovered and the knowledge of how to continue the product has been gained by company engineers. The company pays the premium and is the beneficiary for such a policy. A special case of the key man is the entrepreneur who also organizes and manages the business.

Keynesian economic theory

A theory developed or at least attributed to John Maynard Keynes, a British economist. This theory holds that economic growth and national income are controlled and determined by investment capital and a multiplier theory. Under this theory investment capital produces income to investors which is recycled into buying more products. It also produces jobs, which then provide disposable income to buy more products. Since a known portion of income at any level is consumed, there is always a portion of the newly generated income which is recycled to produce more investment, products, and income. The multiplier theory has determined that every dollar invested returns $2.85 in disposable income through the various levels of the economy as it is continuously recycled. Also, a reduction in investment brings a similarly reduced cash flow in the economy. This theory is opposed to the monetarism theory developed by Milton Friedman which holds that the government controlled money supply is the fundamental stimulus for economic growth or contraction. Also see MONEY SUPPLY and MONETARISM.

Killing

To make a killing in the stock market is to realize spectacular profits as a result of careful study, perfect timing, and *fantastic luck*. It is the dream of all speculators and the ruin of many.

$$L$$

LIFO

Last-in, first-out. A technique used in accounting to assign value to inventory. This method tends to show a lower value to inventory than other methods. Normal inflation makes the most recent purchases more expensive and these are the ones moved out first, leaving the earlier, lower cost items. Also see FIFO and WEIGHTED AVERAGE.

Lagging indicator

An index of some quantity which generally shows a major change after a similar change has occurred in the stock market. Its value is in verifying that stock market movements are solid trends rather than temporary fluctuations. For instance, indexes of odd lot trading tend to follow major market trends. An analyst studying the indexes would interpret a heavy sell off by odd lotters as an indication that a market decline has already reached its bottom and is beginning a recovery. An upturn in the absence of the negative odd lot indication would be interpreted as merely a termporary adjustment. See LEADING INDICATOR.

The following indexes will either lag behind stock market trends or move simultaneously: Federal Reserve member bank free reserves inverted, disposable personal income, freight car loadings index, installment debt, long term unemployment inverted, wholesale price index, business expenditures for plant and equipment, book value of inventories, labor cost per unit of output, commercial loans outstanding, and consumer installment debt.

Lamb

An innocent, unsophisticated person who buys or sells a security with no knowledge of what he is doing. He is supposedly a sucker for a broker who may influence his trading to generate commissions. He is an investor who buys anything offered and may lose substantially on his investments. He is also called a barefoot pilgrim.

Leading indicator

An index of some quantity which tends to show a major change before a similar change occurs in the stock market in general. For instance, steel production, orders for capital goods, and expanding money supply generally are noticed well in advance of economic expansion and rising stock market prices. Opposite to lagging indicators. Some leading indicators are: employment rate (accession rate index), average work week, business failures inverted, business inventory changes, commercial and industrial building, corporate profits after taxes, housing starts, industrial materials, prices, layoff rate inverted, index of new business, new orders of durable goods, capital equipment orders. Also see LAGGING INDICATOR and COINCIDENT INDICATOR.

Leaseback

The practice of selling some asset such as plants, machinery, aircraft, or ships to an outside investor, then renting it back again under a long term lease. The purpose is to generate more cash which can be used to increase profit. The practice is profitable if a company can earn more money on its cash than it must pay in lease payments. One advantage of leasing is that leasing costs are 100% deductible, whereas purchase costs are not. This is a type of leverage.

Lectrascan

An electronic reporting system which displays stock market prices from the ticker tape. Instead of a moving tape, it displays prices in a stationary position momentarily, then advances to another price in the sequence.

Legal list

Also called legal investment. A list of investments specified by state authorities as being acceptable for investment by banks, insurance companies, and other financial institutions who handle money for the public while operating under state or federal regulations. Also called approved list or eligible list, especially when referring to mutual fund investments. There is a distinction between the two, however. If the list is prepared by state regulatory authorities, it is called a legal list. If the list is prepared by the management of the institution, it is called an approved list or eligible list. All institutions must use such a list, so if a state does not require a state-prepared list, then the institution provides its own. In addition, there is also a broadly defined Prudent Man Rule imposed upon these institutions and other fiduciaries. See separate heading for each term.

Letter stock

A common stock sold privately by corporations to certain individuals without the normal SEC registration. The purchaser must submit a letter stating his intention in buying the stock for investment and not for resale. The stock cannot be resold on the open market, so it gives the owner some liquidity problems. Also see STOCKS for more information and listings for other types of stock.

Level charge plans

Accumulation plans or periodic payment plans for acquiring mutual fund shares over a period of time. The sales charges are made at the time of each purchase and are based on the size of investment. Voluntary plans are of this type. See *special features* under INVESTMENT COMPANIES for more information. Also see INVESTMENT COMPANY ACT OF 1940 for definitions, purposes, and limitations of investment companies.

Leverage

The use of senior capital to increase the return of junior capital. That is, borrowing money through issuance of bonds for expansion of business which will result in greater return on the amount of equity capital involved. An investor can use leverage by using borrowed money to buy securities, as in the case of a margin account. In commodities trading where margin requirements are much smaller than for stock trading, the leverage is much greater. This expression means that for a small amount of cash you have the potential for much greater gains or losses.

Leverage fund

A mutual fund which can borrow money to increase its purchases of securities and hopefully increase its return. The Investment Company Act of 1940 prohibited the formation of any new leverage funds. Also see INVESTMENT COMPANIES for other kinds of funds and comparisons of each. See INVESTMENT COMPANY ACT OF 1940 for definitions, purposes, and limitations.

Liabilities

The claims against a corporation or individual including accounts payable, wages payable, dividends declared payable, accrued taxes, fixed or long term liabilities such as mortgage bonds, debentures, and bank loans. Opposite of ASSETS.

Lien

A claim against property, which has been pledged or mortgaged to secure or guarantee the performance of an obligation.

Lift a leg

To dispose of one side of a spread position. A person who has bought long on a commodity contract and sold short on another to reduce risks, is said to have a spread. If he believes the market to be rising he may cover, or buy another contract to repay the one which was sold short, in an effort to earn more profit on the long contract already held. Either covering the short position like this, or selling the long position while retaining the other half of the spread is called lifting one leg of the spread.

Limit, limited order, or limited price order
An order issued by an investor to his broker to buy or sell a stated amount of a security at a specified price, or at a better price if obtainable. Also see BUY ORDERS or SELL ORDERS for a list of other kinds of orders used in securities trading.

Limit move
In commodities futures trading, there are limits set on the amount of increase or decrease that is permitted on any given commodity for any one day. Since the commodities market is an auction market, prices would continue to rise or decline from previous prices until someone is willing to trade. If buying prices are so strong that bids reach the pre-determined limit and still no one offers to sell, the price holds steady until the next day, when it is permitted to rise again in search of a seller. The purpose of setting fixed limits is to stabilize the market to some degree. Without limits speculators become emotionally charged and bid prices up to unrealistic levels, then panic to sell out if any selling pressure sets in. The limits retard the strong movements to let people have more time to consider fundamental values and to evaluate news stories.

Limited partnership
A business formed by two or more individuals in which at least one partner is fully liable for all the

debts of the business. The other partners may have liability only to the extent of their investment. The purpose of such an arrangement is to attract some capital from individuals who are either unwilling or unable to participate in management, or perhaps who are retired from active participation but wish to keep the investment active. This type business is used for many brokerages, law firms, medical practices, advertising agencies, or other professional organizations. Also see GENERAL PARTNERSHIP.

Limited price order

An order placed by an investor with a broker or dealer to buy a security at a specific price, unlike a market order or open order which lets the broker bargain for a price. Also see BUY ORDER and SELL ORDER for other types of security trading orders.

Line

In manufacturing a line is a family of closely related products. In securities charting it is one of many patterns which have special significance to the chart reader. This pattern shows up as a period of three weeks or longer when the charted stock fluctuates very little, like a consolidation period, which is called a base by some analysts. See PATTERNS for a list of other chart formations used to indicate market trends and STOCK CHARTS for samples of some patterns.

Line chart

A graph which connects progressive recorded quantities by a single line. The graph resembles a jagged sawtoothed line across a graph. The technique can be used on any type of graph paper. See Line Chart on page 244. Also STOCK CHARTS for other types and samples of each type.

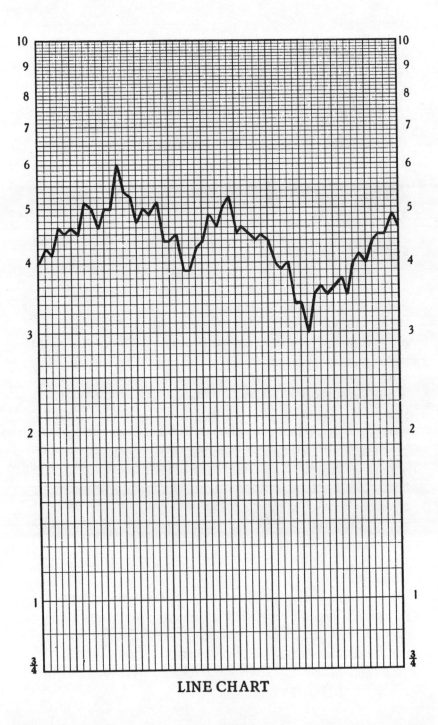

LINE CHART

Line management
Sometimes called operations management. The level of management most closely and directly associated with production or day-to-day operations. They are involved with labor, sales, service, and are responsible for the execution of schedules made by staff management. Also see STAFF MANAGEMENT and TOP MANAGEMENT.

Linear chart
A chart using arithmetic graph paper. Parallel lines on the chart are equally spaced and represent equal numerical value in a progression. Contrasted to logarithmic charts, proportional charts or ratio charts. Called linear because of the straight line arithmetical progression of chart divisions. See Linear Chart on page 246. Also STOCK CHARTS for other types of charts with samples of each kind of chart.

Liquid
The state of having sufficient cash or readily marketable securities to more than meet all obligations.

Liquid assets
Those assets of a company which could be converted into cash quickly. They include cash deposits, accounts immediately receivable, and readily marketable securities.

Liquidating value
The actual value left over from a company if it should cease operations, sell all assets and pay all creditors. This figure may differ from book value, since accounting records may carry real estate at acquisition

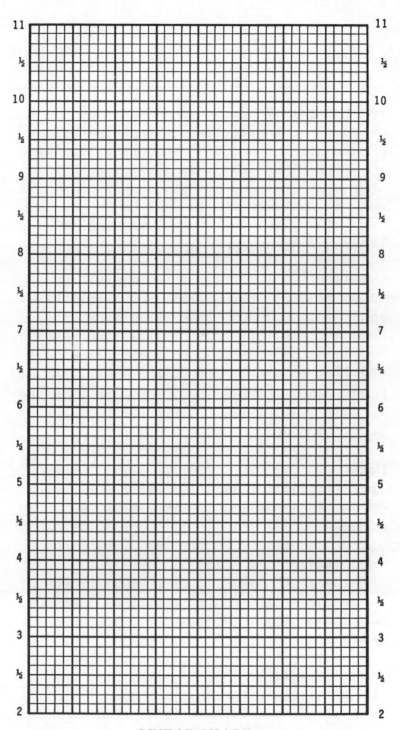

LINEAR CHART

value, which may be considerably less than current market value. Other capital equipment may be carried on the books at a fully depreciated value. Some items may have been charged off as expenses, yet still have value. Liquidating value may refer to the price that would be received if an investment portfolio were sold, as in the case of mutual funds where it is also called NET ASSET VALUE.

Liquidation

Exchanging assets for cash. Usually the term is applied to the process of going out of business. After the sale of assets, the proceeds are used to pay off creditors; then, if any cash remains, it is distributed among stockholders.

Liquidity

1. The ability of a company to meet all obligations or potential liabilities without endangering its financial condition. It reflects general strength without suggesting any quantitative measure of that strength.

2. The ability of the market in a particular security to absorb a reasonable amount of buying or selling at moderate price changes. It is one of the most important characteristics of a good market.

Listed stock

A security accepted by a stock exchange for trading on that exchange. On the initial request for listing on the New York Stock Exchange, the issuing company must pay a fee of $50,000 and meet the following requirements:

1. Have at least 1,000,000 shares outstanding in public hands.

2. Have at least 2,000 stockholders, each with 100 shares or more.

3. Have a current market value for publicly held shares of $16,000,000 or more.

4. Have at least $2,500,000 in pre-tax earnings in its latest year and $2,000,000 in each of the last two preceding years.

5. Agree to publish promptly all financial reports and maintain a transfer agent and a registrar to insure knowledge of stock transfers.

The company may decline from the above requirements after listing (due to market conditions), but there are certain minimums beyond which the exchange may delist the stock. Requirements may change from time to time as the exchange considers appropriate. Other exchanges have similar but less demanding requirements. See STOCK for other terms used to identify different kinds of stock.

Listing
The process of meeting requirements for having a security traded on a stock exchange. The requirements vary for different exchanges but include paying a substantial fee, plus maintaining specified levels of gross sales, net earnings, the number of shares of stock in public hands, and the number of shareholders owning the stock. See LISTED STOCK for additional information.

Litigation
A law suit. Legal controversy.

Little man
The small investor, odd-lot trader, average man,

unsophisticated investor, the person who, more than any other, needs protection and a hedge against the future through sound investment. But through ignorance, fear, or misinformation, he is the most frequent loser in the bewildering world of investment. 80% of the nation's investors are these small investors, even though 70% of the securities issued are held by or traded by institutions.

Living trust

A trust arrangement set up during the life time of its creator. An example would be a trust set up by parents for their children. Its purpose is to gain tax advantages over the ordinary transfer of assets by inheritance. It contrasts with a testamentary trust, which is created under a written will of a deceased person.

Load

The same as loading charge below. The load or sales charge can be calculated by subtracting the bid price or net asset value from the asked or current market price.

Loading charge

The sales charge on some types of mutual funds. It is also called the front end load, or simply load. It is the charge made at the time an investor first signs up with the fund and covers commissions and other distribution expenses. This charge is applied only at the time of purchase. Because of the charge, the amount of money actually committed to investment is less than the purchase price of the fund shares. Sales charges can vary from 6½% to 8½% depending on the type of fund. There are some that have no front end load at all. The amount of load can be computed by subtracting the bid price or net asset value from the

asked price or current market price. See NO LOAD
FUNDS for differences. Also see INVESTMENT
COMPANIES for other types of funds and descriptions
of each. See INVESTMENT COMPANY ACT OF 1940
for definitions, purposes, and limitations.

Locked in

An investor is said to be locked in when he has a profit
on a security he owns but does not sell because his
profit would immediately become subject to heavy
taxes. Another more serious case is found in commodity futures trading. When a commodity trader
purchases a contract, he expects the price to rise. If the
price drops, he will lose unless he sells. Often trading
will be so heavy that the price decline can reach a pre-
set limit and still not attract buyers. The trader is then
locked in to a declining situation that he can't get out
of. Since it is an auction market, a seller cannot sell
until someone becomes willing to buy. The same
problem can occur if a trader sells short on a commodity contract only to find the price rising. If the rise
reaches the daily limit, he is unable to cover the short
and must accept the loss.

Locked out

Being in a position where it is impossible to take
advantage of a situation. In commodities futures
trading if a person wants to buy a contract of a certain
commodity, he must find another person willing to sell.
If demand is strong and prices are rising sharply, there
are times when prices may move up the full amount of
a pre-set limit. If the limit is reached and no one is
willing to sell, the buyer is locked out. When owners of
contracts feel that they have gained as much profit as
they expect, they may then offer to sell, and trading

resumes. Also, if a person has a contract he wishes to sell, he faces the same bid-offer situation and may be locked in to a losing situation until buyers are willing to begin trading.

Logarithmic charts

Charts drawn on logarithmic type graph paper. Lines are parallel but progressively closer spaced in geometric proportions. One cycle of such a progression would represent quantities from 1 to 10. The second cycle represents 10 to 100. The third cycle would be from 100 to 1000. The progression follows a logarithmic formula. Each cycle covers exactly the same distance on a chart, even though the first cycle represents 9 points, and the second cycle represents the next 90 points. These charts are not as commonly used as arithmetical charts for stock charting, but they are preferred by the most sophisticated professionals. Proportional charts, which are a specially designed system of logarithmic charts, are the basic tool of the optimal analysis method of investment management. See STOCK CHARTS for comparisons to other types of charts and samples of each. The sample on page 252 shows a typical logarithmic chart used for securities records.

Long

The term signifies ownership of securities or commodities. For example, if you are long 100 shares of company XYZ, it means you currently *own* 100 shares. The term grew out from an opposing term SHORT, which means to sell a security which was borrowed from another investor. This practice is legal and quite common. Notice that there is no connection to the term

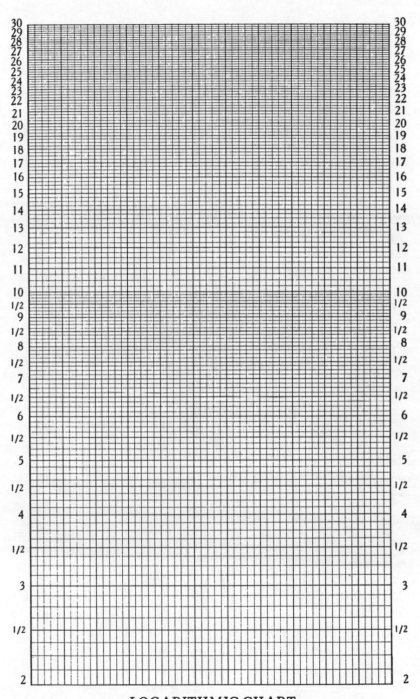

LOGARITHMIC CHART

LONG TERM, which pertains to the length of time a security is held.

Long term

Something that is planned for or expected to involve a *relatively* long period of time. A long term profit is realized from the sale of an asset that was held for more than six months before being sold. This designation is determined by tax laws. A long term market trend is one which continues a year or more. A long term market forecast may project from six months to several years. Long term business planning extends from two to five years. Some companies plan ten years ahead. A long term investment objective considers qualities and events for 5, 10, or, perhaps, more than 20 years. Notice the contrast to SHORT TERM, which suggests a short time span and SHORT TERM TRADING, which describes a philosophy of speculating with securities.

Long term capital gains

Profits on assets held more than six months. The income tax is not more than half that of ordinary income. Certain types of royalties and some other forms of income receive capital gains treatment by special tax law concessions for lower tax rates than ordinary income. Also called long term gains. Notice that the terms profit, capital gains, long term gains, growth and appreciation all apply to value gained by selling an asset if it has been held more than 6 months. If held less than 6 months, it is called short term capital gains or ordinary income, as are interest payments received or dividends, and is taxed at the same rate as salaries.

Long term debt

Debt owed for real estate and major assets which

generally are financed for longer than five years.

Long term gains

Profits received from the sale of some asset which was held for more than 6 months since purchase. Certain types of royalties and some other forms of income receive long term gains treatment for lower income tax rates than ordinary income. Also called capital gains.

Long term investment

A security or other asset that was purchased with the intention of holding it long enough that it can provide future income for you, or security and safe keeping for your surplus cash. As defined for tax purposes, a long term investment is one held more than six months. Profits realized from such an investment are taxed at a lower rate than regular income and are called long term capital gains. As defined for investment objectives it is an investment purchased for potential profit in the future or safety of principal during the present and the time in the future when the cash will be needed. Such investments are selected according to the financial strength of the issuer rather than according to market prices. Notice the difference from TRADING, which is a short term objective.

Loss carry forward

Business losses from prior years that are deducted from profits in current and subsequent years when filing business tax reports. Also called tax credits, tax loss credits or carry forward. See TAX LOSS CARRY FORWARD for more information.

Low

The lowest price reached by a stock during any

specified period. Also the lowest point reached by an indicator of market or economic conditions during any specified period.

Low grade

A classification of securities which indicates low investment quality. The grading is an opinion by analysts after studying the issuer's debt structure, earning power, sales volume, management strength, etc. Low grade securities usually offer higher yields to attract capital. Much of the meaning of grade or quality refers to a company's ability to maintain stable earnings and, therefore, the ability to repay all of its obligations. See RATING OF SECURITIES for fuller discussion of grades or rating and for the actual letter ratings used by several advisory services.

M

M I P
Monthly investment plan. A program designed for the small investor to permit regular investment at a set amount. For as little as $40 every three months, an individual may buy stock by the dollar's worth. In effect, it is a dollar cost averaging method of investment. Commissions on these plans may be higher than on normal transactions of larger dollar amounts.

Maintenance fee
In mutual funds which offer accumulation plans or systematic investment plans, it is a fee deducted quarterly from earnings to pay for the service of reinvesting those earnings and dividends.

Maintenance requirement
An amount of equity that you must keep in a margin

account to satisfy the rules of the brokerage house It is not regulated by the Federal Reserve Board, as is the original margin when buying the securities, but brokers generally set limits for their own protection. Generally, brokers require a customer to maintain at least 25% to 30% equity in the account. Should value drop sufficiently, a broker may issue a margin call for the customer to deposit more cash.

Major trend

The long term trend of the stock market, also called a fundamental trend. A general rising or declining of market prices which continues for a period of many months or years. See FUNDAMENTAL WAVE.

Making a market

This is said of a broker-dealer who maintains a quantity or inventory of a certain stock in his own account for sale to the public. He will also buy, within limits, any shares offered for sale. When he sells from his own account or buys for his own account, he is called a dealer. When he arranges transactions of other securities not in his own account, he is known as a broker.

Management

The group of people responsible for the operation and profitability of a company. Management can be divided several ways depending upon the purposes for definition. Outsiders, securities analysts, and news men may use two general distinctions:

Top management: The board of directors which are elected by the stock holders plus the operating officers, including the president, vice president, secretary, and treasurer, plus any vice presidents and assistants considered necessary. These operating officers are elected by the board of directors.

Middle management: Department managers and supervisory personnel.

There is also another way of categorizing management that is common among larger companies. These distinctions are more common among management personnel themselves.

Staff management: Vice presidents, divisional managers, and assistants who are responsible for implementation and coordination of policy and plans.

Line management: Department heads and supervisory personnel who are responsible for production, sales, and other phases of actual operations.

Management company

A company selected by a financial institution such as a mutual fund to act as its investment manager.

Management fee

A fee charged by investment managers for their services in supervising an investment portfolio. It is usually a set percentage of the net asset value of the account, although managers of some private portfolios may have other methods of determining the fee.

Management record

An expression which refers to measuring profits received or growth obtained under a given management. It is unfortunate that we measure skills in terms of dollars, and more unfortunate still that we fail to adjust the dollar figures for economic conditions. Good management may have a very difficult time showing profits during economic slumps, but even the most slipshod methods will be profitable in boom times. Still we continue to look at the record or the bottom line for profit in appraising management. The record is also called performance of management.

Managerial performance

Skills of management measured in terms of dollars or in ratios that can be compared with other companies. Some of these ratios are profit ratios, growth ratios, inventory turn over ratios, dividend pay out ratio, etc.

Manipulation

An illegal operation. Heavy buying or selling of a security for the purpose of creating false impressions of active trading in a security. The purpose of raising or depressing the price is to induce purchase or sale by others.

Manufacturer's representative

An independent agent operating his own place of business who has contracts with one or more manufacturers to sell their merchandise or services to various customers. Their customers may be retail dealers, other manufacturers, or contractors of various types. Manufacturers "reps" may or may not stock an inventory, but often they write orders for delivery from factory to the customer. Their compensation is usually a commission based on the selling price. Note the difference from FACTORY REPRESENTATIVE who is described as follows:

1. An employee of one manufacturer.
2. Operates from company offices.
3. Is paid a salary instead of commissions.
4. May be more a liaison engineer or customer

relations expert than salesman.

Margin

The amount paid by the customer when he uses credit to buy a security. In reality, the broker's credit is used, since the broker borrows the money from the bank and credits it to the customer's account for the purchase. The broker will hold the security and may even use it to secure his loan at the bank. Under Federal Reserve regulations the initial margin required in the past twenty years has ranged from 40% of the purchase price all the way to 100%. Margin requirements may be lowered at times to induce more trading in slow times or may be raised if overbuying or speculative fever appears.

In commodity futures trading, the margins normally range from 10% to 20% of the cash commodity price. Commodity margins are set by brokerage houses at some convenient, round figure and may change frequently, depending on market price levels and volatility. Notice the difference from PROFIT MARGIN.

Margin account

An account which permits the customer to use a broker's credit to purchase securities. To open a margin account the customer must sign a margin agreement which authorizes his broker to borrow any securities carried in the customer's account or to lend them to other brokers. In practice they are frequently used to secure loans from the bank, which provide cash for the margin accounts. Margin requirements, stated as a percent of a purchase price for a security, are established by the Securities Exchange Commission.

In commodity trading the principal is the same, but

margin requirements are much less and they are set by brokerage houses rather than by the Securities Exchange Commission. All margin accounts are set up in street name accounts to facilitate trading and to secure the broker. For the investor, the portfolio really consists of bookkeeping entries. See MARGIN and STREET NAME.

Margin call

A demand upon a customer to put up money or securities with the broker in order to cover margin requirements if market prices are falling. The call is made if a customer's equity in a margin account declines below a minimum standard set by the exchange or by the firm.

Mark down

A discount or price reduction from a former actual retail price. It is a frequent practice used to clear out seasonal goods at the end of a season, discounted styles and models, or damaged goods. Notice the difference from a DISCOUNT which is a reduction from a listed price whether or not the article ever was actually sold at the listed price.

Mark up

A certain amount added to cost by a dealer to arrive at a selling price that will pay for overhead and expenses and still allow some profit for his services. Depending on the type of product, mark ups can run 20% or 50%, or even 100% or higher. Although that may sound high to some people, the retailer typically makes only 3% to 10% clear profit after all expenses. Some make as low as 1%.

Market

A term used in many ways, but usually related to the supply and demand for some product or service. Following are some of the common usages with samples of each:

1. The price at which a security is currently selling . . . "The market for AT&T is currently 55½."
2. The number of shares of a given security which are in public hands . . . "General Motors has a broad market."
3. The demand for a given security . . . "There is no market for a new buggy whip issue."
4. The place where certain securities are sold, or a dealer who carries an inventory of a given security in his own account from which he sells to investors . . . "Merrill Lynch *makes a market* in Earth Sciences stock."
5. The stock exchanges . . . "The market is closed on weekends and all legal holidays."
6. All investors and potential investors grouped together as potential buyers for additional shares . . "The market is enthusiastic about new developments."
7. Availability of any investments to the public . . . "Several promising new issues will soon be on the market."
8. To actively promote securities or other products for sale . . . "We will market several new products this season."

The following are some other variations in the way the term market is used:

1. A broad market for stock means it is widely distributed, and it is heavily traded.

2. A narrow market means that a stock has few shares in public hands, and there is little demand for them.

3. Shares traded *at market* are sold at prevailing prices.

4. Market reaction is investor impulse following the announcement of some market influence.

5. Market inertia is the tendency for investor reaction to continue for a time after an economic adjustment disturbs the market prices.

Market average

A measure of price levels for some specific group of stocks. It is often used in reference to the Dow Jones Industrial Averages but can also be used to define any of a number of numerical indicators that are commonly used to analyze market conditions and forecast future trends. True averages total up the prices of a selected number of stocks, then divide the total by the number of stocks involved. The term average is often used to apply to an index or a composite price indicator, but, properly, an index applies to a measurement derived from plotting the relationship between certain variables to indicate some basic quality of the market. For instance, the ratio between sales of high grade bonds and low grade bonds is considered an index to indicate investor confidence. A composite, on the other hand may combine a number of actual market prices and be plotted as an aggregate number, or it may then be modified by a special formula to yield a usable quantity. See AVERAGES, INDEXES, and COMPOSITES for more information.

Market breadth

1. In general: The number of shares of any given

security in public hands and, to some extent, the volume of trading in that security.

2. Specifically: A study of technical conditions concerning the stocks listed on the New York Stock Exchange. Technicians use four principal breadth indexes: Advance-decline line, daily volume, volume-momentum, and composite breadth index. The comparison of these indexes is credited with indicating the total impact of market movements upon all investors. Thus, a market decline is considered unimportant if the number of people involved in the move or the amount of pressure involved in the move is small.

Market equity

The percentage of the total market value of a company's securities which is represented by each class of security. These percentages may change from time to time. For example, if the market prices are falling, the common may decline faster than the preferred stock. This is because the preferred may have a guaranteed dividend, while common dividends may be suspended for a time. The tendency would be for investors to hold the preferred and sell the common. Also, the senior standing of preferred, in its claim on assets in case of liquidation, would hold the market prices for perferred in a stronger position. Thus, common could represent a much smaller portion of the total market value of all issues by a given company in bear market times while it could increase dramatically in bull market times. Notice the difference from BOOK EQUITY, which compares the book value of assets to the claims of each class of stock.

Market letter

A short publication by a brokerage company or an

investment advisory service giving information about conditions and sometimes recommendations for buying and selling various securities.

Market order

Any order issued by an investor to his broker to buy or sell a security that is intended to be executed at the best price available at the soonest possible time. This will be transacted at the going market price in the order in which it is received by the floor broker. It can have a time limit placed upon it (today only, this week only, etc.), or it can be left open until filled, in case it is difficult to find buyers or sellers. See BUY ORDERS and SELL ORDERS for other types of trading orders used in securities trading.

Market price

The going price for a product or service. There are variables, however, that are considered for different types of marketables as follows:

1. In the case of securities, prices change constantly and rapidly with both bid and asked prices shifting positions of dominancy. The market price is then considered to be the actual trading price for the most recent trade. The last trade of the day is the price that is reported in newspapers and most often quoted among investors and analysts.

2. In many other large, infrequently traded articles like real estate, art works and collector's items, the market price is considered to be the highest recent price being offered, whether or not a trade actually takes place. Sometimes a professional appraisal will establish the value in the absence of an offer.

3. In numerous small retail products that are not

subject to negotiation, the market price is accepted
to be the price listed by the dealer or manufacturer.
Buyer resistance may force a change eventually,
but the price is actually set by the seller.

Market risk

The simple fact is that securities prices rise or fall
frequently, and there is no way to prevent a decline or
hold an increase. Sometimes a stronger degree of risk
(a greater chance for a decline) is suggested for certain
securities that are more likely to sustain selling
pressure during economic slumps.

Market studies

1. Securities markets: The study of data, news
   comments, conditions, and influences that might
   give any clue to the strength or weakness of any
   selected securities, industries, or even the entire
   market. The tools of this research are stock charts,
   indexes, statistical reports, financial periodicals,
   news letters, and interviews with business leaders,
   economists, or other key people in a position to have
   information.

2. Consumer products: The study of all conceivable
   variables that would influence buying habits or
   interests of consumers. See MARKETING
   STUDIES for expanded discussion and comparison
   to *sales* activities.

Market trend

The general direction of overall stock market prices
over a period of several months. Short term
movements are called cycles and may move contrary to
the major trend in short cycles lasting only a few days
or even in a series of short cycles extending several
months. The major trend is the major concern of

long term investors. Short term traders, on the other hand, are very much interested in the short cycles for timing their activities.

Market value
The actual price of a security on the open market. More precisely, the price at which the last trade took place. Usually the market value is considerably different from the book value that represents the net worth of the company. The ratio between the market value and book value is a fair representation of the company's ability to earn a profit. If the market price is considerably above the book value, it usually means that the company is earning good profits or good potential profits. A market value below book value indicates that the company or even the entire economy is having problems. All salable products and services have market values that may change somewhat more slowly than securities. Demand is the deciding factor, with prices rising when demand is higher. See MARKET PRICE for explanation of how determination of market prices may vary with different types of assets.

Market volume
1. The total number of shares of all stocks traded on a given day on a single stock exchange.
2. The total number of shares of a given stock which are traded on a given day.

Marketability
The ease with which something can be sold. It is a measure of public demand or potential demand for it.

Marketing
The phase of business which is concerned with

meeting the needs of the customer. It is more comprehensive than the term sales, which, being over simplified, is the effort to get more product out the back door. Conflicts arise in interpreting and applying the two terms, and some people use the terms interchangeably but there are important technical differences such as these:

1. Sales: a *product-oriented* activity which concentrates on convincing an ever-increasing number of people to purchase an ever-increasing quantity of products.

2. Marketing: a *customer-oriented* activity that begins by studying the needs and desires of the customer and then finds ways to meet that need economically. Marketing may include consumer studies, competition studies, product design, production costs, advertising, planning, distribution studies, sales programs, sales and service analysis, pricing, and profit studies. Marketing searches out and cultivates the market, then sales effort gets the product to the people, or the people to the product.

Marketing studies (consumer markets)
The study of potential markets for any product or service. It will investigate the demand for the product, determine the type customers most likely to use the product, geographical influences, distribution methods, advertising methods, competition, production costs, profitability, duration of market demand and nearly anything that a budget will allow to determine the advisability of taking a new product or service to the public. It is a study of customers or *people-oriented* influences and qualifications. Notice

the difference from SALES, which is a *product oriented* activity aimed at demonstrating, promoting, and writing orders for the merchandise.

Marking to the market

Making a cash deposit to make up a difference between the market value of a security and the value of a contract it is securing. Somewhat similar to a maintenance requirement in a margin account, except here the securities are serving as collateral for some other type contract.

Matched and lost

When two bids to buy the same stock are made on the trading floor simultaneously, and each bid is equal to or larger than the amount of stock offered, both bids are considered to be on an equal basis. So the two bidders flip a coin to decide who buys the stock. This term also applies to offers to sell.

Matched orders

A manipulative device which is intended to create the illusion of heavy trading volume in a given security. In it an investor would buy a security through one broker and sell it through another, or two brokers might work together to place simultaneous orders that would cancel out but still be recorded as transactions to boost volume of trading. It is also called wash sale. The practice is now illegal and rarely seen. Note the contrast to a CROSS, listed separately, which is a legal transaction in which buy and sell orders between two different parties are matched on the exchange floor.

Mathematical probabilities

Forecast probabilities for some occurrence based

upon mathematical computation of the laws of chance. Notice the difference from STATISTICAL PROBABILITIES, which are the forecast probabilities for some happening based upon analysis of the historical record. Here a large number of test cases are studied and all similarities are compared. The differences between the statistical record and the mathematical probabilities are due to human influence . . . emotional reactions by investors to day-to-day news and other stimuli. It is the reading of these human influences that makes statistical probabilities more useful to security analysts than mathematical calculations, since market prices and fluctuations are nothing more than measurements of investor emotion anyway.

Maturity
The date on which a loan or a bond or debenture comes due and is to be paid off or redeemed.

Member
1. In the field of investment a member is usually understood to be a broker or dealer who is a member of the New York Stock Exchange. They are usually called member firms. Many also hold memberships in other exchanges, but those memberships do not figure so prominently in the overall investment picture. Of the two national exchanges and eleven regional exchanges, approximately 85% of all trading is done on the New York Exchange. See SEAT, NEW YORK STOCK EXCHANGE, AMERICAN STOCK EXCHANGE, and REGIONAL EXCHANGES for more information about membership requirements and privileges.

2. In banking circles a member is usually understood to be a bank which is a member of the Federal Reserve System. They are usually called member banks. See FEDERAL RESERVE SYSTEM for explanation of this federal regulatory agency and its importance to the banking world.

Member bank

A bank which is qualified for, has applied for, and has received admission to the Federal Reserve System. Members own the capital of the Reserve banks and must be regulated by the policies of the Reserve System as interpreted and administered by the Reserve Board of Governors. Membership permits members to use the Reserve as a depository and to call upon it as a source of credit. All national banks are required to be members, and state banks may apply for membership at their own option. 45% of all commercial banks in the U.S. are members, and together they hold 80% of all deposits, both corporate and private. See FEDERAL RESERVE SYSTEM, FEDERAL RESERVE BOARD, FED'S WINDOW, and FEDERAL FUNDS for more information.

Member corporation

The same as member firm below. A member of a stock exchange.

Member firm

The same as a member corporation. A member firm is a brokerage firm which is a member of a stock exchange. Membership consists of the purchase of a seat on that exchange by at least one general partner of the firm, and meeting the requirements of the exchange. The seats are sold on the open market by other members who are leaving. Exchange requirements include certain financial standards and adherance to certain regulations. Membership permits the brokerage firm to buy or sell securities at the exchange for its own account or the account of a client. Non-members are not permitted the same privileges, but must deal over the counter or through members. Also see SEAT for requirements and other information.

Merger

The combining of formerly separate companies into one, where one loses its identity and the other receives all the assets and liabilities of the absorbed member. The merged company is acquired by the other. Notice differences from CONSOLIDATIONS and AMAL-GAMATIONS. Also see CONGLOMERATE and HOLDING COMPANY.

Mini account

The name applied to investment management services run by banks for their clients who are generally small investors and have accounts too small to interest the professional portfolio managers.

Minus yield

A condition that occurs when a convertible bond becomes so attractive to investors that they pay a premium for the bond that is higher than the interest yield on the bond. This is an unusual situation, but has arisen where a convertible bond has very attractive conversion privileges that offset the loss from yield. If the premium declines to the point where it exactly cancels out the interest yield, it is said to sell at a zero yield basis. Further market price reductions also reduce the premium so that yield to maturity increases. If the market price declines below the par value, it is said to be trading at a discount.

Monetarism

An economic theory originated by Milton Friedman, or credited to him, which claims that the money supply is the basic influence on a nation's economy. According to this theory, when the government puts more money into circulation, credit will tend to relax, interest rates will decline, and industrial expansion will follow to produce economic growth. This will increase available jobs, corporate profits, disposable income, and retail sales. The money supply is defined as the total of the nation's bank deposits plus the total amount of currency in circulation outside the U. S. Treasury. The government can control the money supply by purchases or sale of government securities on the open market. Purchasing these securities (bonds, bills, notes, and certificates) puts money into public hands. Selling the securities absorbs money from the public and leads to a slower economy. The theory is opposed to the Keynesian Economic Theory which attributes the basic stimulus to investment. Invested capital is said to eventually filter back to produce total income to the population about 2.85 times the original investment. See KEYNESIAN ECONOMIC THEORY and MONEY SUPPLY for more information; also notice the difference between MONEY SUPPLY and MONEY MARKET.

Money market

A term sometimes applied to international demand for exchange of various national currencies. Normal international trade of goods and services results in vast quantities of currency being either physically transported or transferred by credit and accounting procedures from one nation to another. Because of national political conditions, fiscal policies, credit conditions, and other influences, the desire for the various currencies will vary somewhat from time to time so the rates of exchange may be adjusted to continue the flow of money back to its own nation. The less desirable currencies will be exchanged at lower rates to keep them flowing. SPECULATORS then will anticipate the changing rates and buy a strong currency with a weaker one, expecting that the strong one will grow stronger and thereby yield a profit. This demand for various currencies is the money market, but the process by which it is handled is called FOREIGN EXCHANGE. Notice the difference from MONEY SUPPLY.

Money supply

The amount of money circulating outside the U. S. Treasury in public hands plus the total of the nation's bank deposits. This supply can be changed from time to time if the government desires by either selling short term securities which takes money out of circulation or buying short term securities which puts more money into circulation. The purpose is to control economic conditions sufficiently to prevent severe disruptions from frequent boom and bust cycles. Two other devices used by the government to control economic conditions are control of the federal discount rate and control of reserve deposits required. Also called money stock. Also see KEYNESIAN ECONOMIC THEORY and MONETARISM. Notice the difference from MONEY MARKET.

Monopoly

The condition of having exclusive, or at least

dominant control over the sale of a product or service. It violates certain federal anti-trust laws, since the lack of competition can lead to unfair prices or other consumer abuse. Certain industries such as utilities and transportation companies do operate under government sanctioned and regulated monopolies.

Monthly investment plan

Sometimes called MIP's. A program designed for the small investor to permit regular investment at a set amount. For as little as $40 every three months, an individual may buy stock by the dollar's worth. In effect it is a dollar cost averaging method of investment. Commissions on these plans may be higher than on normal transactions of larger dollar amounts.

Moody's

Short for Moody's Investor's Service. An investment analysis and advisory service widely used by professionals and sophisticated investors. Most libraries have their reference materials.

Moody's Investor's Service

A highly regarded company which sells its investment analysis and advisory service information and recommendations to brokers, investment analysts, and sophisticated investors. It also assembles financial data for publication and assigns ratings to various securities. Most libraries have these reference materials on their shelves. See RATINGS OF SECURITES.

Mortgage

A legal document which pledges all or part of the value of an asset as a security toward the repayment of a debt. Many bonds are backed by mortgages, and most real estate is purchased through the use of mortgages. The term is also used as a verb meaning to pledge an asset.

Mortgage bonds
Bonds which are backed by mortgages on specific property of the borrower. See BONDS for other types of bonds and comparisons between them.

Mover
A stock which undergoes dramatic market price changes. A highly volatile stock.

Moving average
Average prices of a stock calculated back 30 days, 90 days, 6 months, or 200 days, depending upon who is preparing the index. The average is recalculated daily and plotted on a graph with closing prices for each day. The average for the past period, compared to current price movements, is interpreted as an indicator of future trends. When the market price falls below this moving average, it is felt that an upturn is likely; or, if the market price is above the moving average, a decline is more likely.

Multinational
A company which has operations in many nations. Sometimes the term is used interchangeably with the term international. The main distinction between the terms is an imagined rank . . . the larger firms with foreign operations insisting that *they* are not just international, and the smaller firms insisting that *they* are multinational. Multinational seems to be in vogue now.

Multiple
The ratio obtained by dividing the market price of a

stock by its annual earnings per share for the previous twelve month period. High multiples are a reflection of popular expectation that the company can continue to earn a profit. It is also called the price-earnings multiple, price-earnings ratio, earnings ratio, and P-E ratio. See PRICE EARNINGS RATIO for average ratios and other information.

Multiple capital structure company

A company which has more than one class of securities outstanding. Any combination of common stock with preferred stock, warrants, bonds, debentures or long term bank loans, makes it a multiple capital structure.

Multiplier theory

A theory propounded by Keynesian economists that invested capital produces jobs, products, and income to cause economic growth. Then, since people have a propensity to consume, they will buy more products and invest more. This, in turn, produces more products, jobs, and income. This recycling of money has been calculated to return $2.85 to the economy for each dollar invested originally. Also see KEYNESIAN ECONOMIC THEORY and PROPENSITY TO CONSUME for related terms and MONETARISM for an opposed theory.

Municipal bonds

Bonds which are issued by public authorities (state, county, or city bond issues). Municipal bond interest payments are generally free from federal income taxes. State bonds, in addition, are usually free from state income tax when owned in the state of issue. The tax exempt status is a privilege afforded by the federal government in order to induce investors to assist in financing local government needs. Interest yield is considerably lower than industrial bonds, which are subject to ordinary income taxes, so the municipals are of interest to individuals who are in the high tax brackets. To someone who is in a high tax bracket the lower interest actually yields more than some high interest rates that are severely taxed.

Mutual fund

A broad term meaning an investment company or investment trust which is owned by many investors and is subject to regulations of the Investment Company Act of 1940. A mutual fund sells its shares to the public on a continuous basis and is obligated to redeem or repurchase them at any time at the net asset value. Since the number of shareholders may change from day to day, it is called an open end investment company. It must always provide a prospectus to any investor who is solicited for the purchase of its shares. This is in contrast to other corporations, who must provide a prospectus only at the time of the initial offering. All mutual funds are investment companies, but not all investment companies are mutual funds. See INVESTMENT COMPANIES for a list of many other kinds of investment companies and notice the difference from CLOSED END INVESTMENT COMPANY. Also see INVESTMENT COMPANY ACT OF 1940 for definitions, purposes, and limitations.

Mutual savings bank

A financial institution which accepts savings deposits which it then invests in real estate mortgages. It is not permitted to offer checking accounts as commercial banks do.

N

NASD

The National Association of Securities Dealers, which is a self-regulated organization of brokers and dealers who handle over-the-counter securities. It licenses qualified persons for the profession and has the power to expel members who fail to uphold ethical standards. Among its purposes it is organized to "adopt, administer and enforce rules of fair practice and rules to prevent fraudulent and manipulative acts and practices, and, in general, to promote just and equitable principles of trade for the protection of investors."

NASDAQ

The National Association of Securities Dealers Automatic Quotation. This is a system for reporting trading prices on certain over-the-counter securities just as are the listed stocks quoted by the exchanges.

These NASDAQ prices are reported electronically on the same equipment that brokers use to obtain data on the listed stocks. NASDAQ symbols for identifying various stocks are usually printed in small sized capital letters and will contain four or five letters. By contrast, the listed stocks are represented by larger sized capitals and the symbols usually consist of only three letters, and a few contain only one or two letters.

NAV

Net asset value. This is the same as the book value of a company and amounts to assets as they are carried on the books less all liabilities. It is the same thing as the net worth of the company. The term net worth is the common term when speaking of an industrial firm, but when speaking of investment companies the term net asset value is the preferred term. In this case the physical assets and liabilities are very small, but the securities in the portfolio are the largest part of assets. These securities are calculated at the current market values, so the assets can change from day to day. An investor purchasing mutual fund shares will pay the net asset value plus a sales charge (except for the closed end funds and the no load funds), and when selling he will receive the current net asset value.

The term is sometimes equated with liquidating value, although there may be a difference. In industrial companies and service companies assets will consist of many more physical assets, receivables, and inventory. These may be carried on the books at depreciated value which may be below the market value. In liquidation, then, these assets may be worth more than book value.

NSTA

The National Securities Traders Association. A

membership organization of brokers and dealers who
trade in over-the-counter markets. They may also be
members of stock exchanges and trade in listed
securities.

N Y S E
The New York Stock Exchange. Also called the big
board, or simply the board. See NEW YORK STOCK
EXCHANGE for more information about the NYSE,
including membership requirements and the operation
of the exchange. Also see STOCK EXCHANGE for a
list of other exchanges in the United States.

N Y S E common stock index
A composite index covering price movements of all
common stocks listed on the New York Stock Exchange. See AVERAGES, INDEXES, INDICATORS
and COMPOSITES for other common indexes and their
usages.

Naked option
An option to either buy or sell certain commodities
which are sold by a broker who does not actually own
either the physical inventory or futures contracts to
back up the option. A broker selling such options
operates on the principle that there will be enough
float of cash to keep his operation going. Such a broker
collapsed in 1973, leaving $50,000,000 in losses for
speculators and legal problems for himself. The
practice is still legal, but regulations are being considered which would eliminate it.

National Association of Securities Dealers
Commonly called the NASD. A self regulating

organization of brokers and dealers in the over-the-counter securities business. It licenses qualified persons for the profession and has the power to expel members for unethical practices. Among its purposes, it is organized to adopt, administer, and enforce rules of fair practice and rules to prevent fraudulent and manipulative acts and practices, and, in general, to promote just and equitable principles of trade for the protection of investors.

National Quotation Bureau

A company which publishes daily quotations (pink sheets) of over-the-counter securities. The pink sheets list all over-the-counter stocks and dealers who make a market in them. Also the latest bid and asked prices are shown. Some of these OTC prices are now available on electronic quotation machines along with the listed stocks. They are then called NASDAQ listings.

National securities exchange

1. A general term referring to the two largest stock exchanges which serve investors nationwide. They are membership institutions which provide facilities for their members to trade securities for their own accounts or the accounts of others. Non-members are not permitted to use the facilities, but may transact business through members. The New York Stock Exchange and American Stock Exchange are national securities exchanges.
2. The specific name of a small regional stock exchange located in New York.

Near term

The same basic meaning as short term. It is usually used in reference to forecasts of a market trend or reactions. *Short* term by contrast can be applied to past movements, or it can define a type of profit for tax purposes. On charts a near term forecast may apply only to the next cycle or to the first half of the next cycle to appear.

Negotiable

1. When referring to a security, its ownership is determined by possession. The holder may sell or transfer the security for his own account at any time. It is one which is not registered in the name of the owner.

2. When referring to terms of a contract or conditions of any relationship, negotiable terms are those which are open for discussion to reach mutual agreement.

Negotiate

To bargain for terms that are most agreeable to all concerned.

Net

The amount left after making deductions. Net profit is the profit after paying taxes and accounting for other expenses. Net sales are the figures left after accounting for warranty returns, merchandise damaged in shipment, merchandise stolen, given away in promotional efforts, etc. Sometimes the term net result is used to suggest the cancelling out of opposing influences, leaving some resulting effect or quality.

Net asset value (N A V)

True book value per share. Total assets minus total liabilities divided by total shares outstanding. In mutual fund investment, the shares are sold at the net asset value plus a sales charge (except for closed end funds) and are repurchased by the fund at the net asset value. It is the price an investor receives when he sells his shares in a mutual fund. Sometimes called the liquidating value, but this figure can actually be different. It is a common practice in accounting to carry assets on the books at the depreciated value. In several years the book value of many assets can be reduced to zero or a very low salvage value. In this case the liquidating value will be higher than the book value or net asset value.

Net change
The change in the price of a security from the closing price on one day and the closing price on the next day on which the stock is traded. The net change is ordinarily the last column in a stock price list. For example, the mark $+\frac{1}{2}$ means the price went up $\frac{1}{2}$ point or 50 cents a share from the last sale of the last previous day the stock traded.

Net income
The profit left after all costs of operations, taxes, bond interest, depreciation, leases, depletion allowances, and reserves for possible losses. Other nonrecurring expenses, such as proceeds of the sale of property or settlement of a major law suit, may be included in the reported income, but do not properly reflect the profit of doing business. In the analysis of a company's potential for producing profit, the analysts subtract such figures. It is the accepted practice to use the terms net income or income after taxes to mean the total dollar amount. Then the term earnings is used to refer to total net income divided by the number of shares outstanding. This is often called per share earnings or earnings.

Net investment income

The total income produced by an investment minus any expenses. In a mutual fund the net investment income is the total of dividends and interest received on its portfolio minus operating expenses.

Net position

In securities and commodities trading a person is said to hold a position in some stock or commodity if he has committed any amount of money to some transaction. He may buy for his account, in which case he has a long position in that stock or commodity. He may also sell borrowed stocks or commodities, in which case he has a short position. In commodities trading he may expect grain prices to differ from one month to another so he may buy a contract for one month, and, at the same time, sell for the other month. His position now becomes spread. If the person has any position, long or short, that is not opposed, then he has a net long or short position.

Net profit

In retail sales the term profit frequently is applied to the amount of money left after subtracting the cost of operations. Technically more correct is the term net income, which results after all costs of operations, plus additional expenses such as depreciation, bond interest, and reserves for probably losses are deducted. In many cases net profit and net income are used interchangeably; however, net income *after* taxes is the final, pure profit figure that is called earnings. Sometimes referred to simply as net.

Net sale

1. In securities trading: The amount of money

received from a security sale after deducting commissions, fees, taxes, and allowances for the individual transaction.

2. In business operations: The total sales figure or gross receipts minus shortages, allowances for prompt payment, returns, warranty costs, discounts, and uncollectable accounts. The net sales then amount to the final total of cash actually received for its sales before deducting its own expenses from operations. Other costs such as commissions, freight, insurance, advertising, and billing costs are considered cost of sales and are included in operating costs. When all operating costs are deducted, the result becomes pre-tax earnings.

Net unrealized appreciation or depreciation

The difference between the original cost and the current market value of your investment portfolio. Frequently called paper profits or paper losses. These become realized profits or losses when the securities are sold.

Net weight

The actual weight of some packaged product, not including the weight of the container or protective packing. Most bulk materials containers are marked with . . . total gross weight, tare weight (container weight), and net weight of the product. Most consumer products are marked only with the net weight of the product.

Net worth

The value remaining when subtracting all liabilities such as bond redemption cost, bank debt, all payables for wages, supplies, services, taxes, interest, depreciation, and loss carry forward from total assets like real estate, equipment, inventories, receivables, prepaid expenses, securities, cash, rents, and interest due. It is sometimes called the capital of business or capitalization, although capitalization to some people refers only to the original proceeds of the sale of securities and does not account for the additions to capital through profits. Book value and shareholders' equity are also used as synonymous with net worth, which may be shortened to worth.

New highs
The number of individual stock issues listed on an exchange which on a given day sold at their highest price for the year.

New issue
A stock or bond sold by a corporation for the first time. Proceeds may be issued to retire outstanding debt of the company, for new plant or equipment, or for additional working capital. There may have been previous issues made, but these particular shares were not previously offered.

New lows
The number of individual stock issues listed on an exchange which on a given day sold at their lowest price for the year.

New York call money
Money borrowed by brokers to meet the needs of margin accounts maintained by their customers. The brokers borrow from banks on open credit lines, then reloan to their own customers. The brokers, in turn, borrow the customers' securities to secure the loan

from the bank. Most of these loans are made in New York where a large number of brokerages have their headquarters, hence the name. The call money rate refers to the interest rates paid for such loans, usually at the going prime rates set by banks, and the call money market refers to the demand for the loans.

New York Stock Exchange

Often abreviated to NYSE in print. An exchange point for offers to buy or sell *listed* securities. A public corporation desiring to list its stock on the exchange is required to pay a substantial fee and also to maintain proof of substantial assets and earnings. Listing requirements may change but generally require publicly held shares of over one million shares outstanding, not less than 2000 shareholders and earnings over $1 million. See LISTED STOCK for other requirements. Brokers and dealers must hold memberships on the exchange in order to transact business there. Those memberships, or seats, are sold on the open market, just as securities are, to qualified applicants. There are only 1366 such seats available on the New York Stock Exchange. The New York Stock Exchange is a national exchange, as is the American Stock Exchange. There are also a number of regional exchanges in major cities around the U. S. See STOCK EXCHANGE for a list of other exchanges and SEATS for some requirements.

New York Stock Exchange composite index

A weighted average of all NYSE common stocks. A good indicator of general market conditions.

New York Stock Exchange volume

Total of all shares traded daily. An indicator of market

breadth which can also be plotted against other indicators to measure investor attitudes.

New York Times stock averages
An average of 25 industrial and railroad stocks. A
general market indicator.

News ticker
A teletype printer found in brokerage offices around
the country which prints out a broad tape with news
information about corporations and national economic
conditions which are published by Dow Jones. The
news ticker has a bell which is used to signal the
importance of some items being printed on the tape. A
signal of four bells may cause a broker to drop his
pencil and rush to see what the tape is receiving.
Notice the difference from the STOCK TICKER, which
prints out stock prices only. The output of the news
ticker is usually called the broad tape. The output from
the stock ticker is usually called ticker tape, or simply
the tape.

No load fund
A mutual fund which does not have a sales charge for
new shareholders. There is a maintenance charge
made periodically to cover expenses of management.
The no charge feature would seem attractive on the
surface, but 95% of the money in mutual funds goes
into the front end load type fund. Contrast to LOAD
FUNDS or FRONT END LOAD FUNDS. Also see
INVESTMENT COMPANY ACT OF 1940 for
definitions, purposes, and limitations.

Non-cumulative preferred
A preferred stock which stipulates that its dividends,
if not paid, do not accrue. That means that if for some

reason the company cannot meet the dividend payments on time, they will never be paid. See CUMULATIVE PREFERRED for contrast and STOCK for a list of other types of stock.

Non-cumulative voting

Shareholder's voting rights which authorize only one vote per share to a shareholder, regardless of the number of seats on the board of directors. Note differences from CUMULATIVE VOTING under separate listing.

Non-interest bearing bond

Another name for a discount bond. A bond which is sold at a discount from its face value. This bond usually does not earn interest during its life, but the interest is paid in a lump sum when the bond is redeemed. Savings bonds are of this type.

Non-taxable dividends

Dividends paid to shareholders which are specified as return of capital. This can be used when a company liquidates certain assets or sometimes to satisfy shareholders when earnings cannot justify dividends. Shareholders consider them welcome because of tax free handling; however, the cost basis of the security must be reduced by an equal amount, so in reality, these dividends are ordinary income being traded off for deferred capital gains for tax purposes.

Normal curve, normal distribution curve

A curve on a graph which is formed by plotting the variables of a large number of happenings. Mathematical probabilities for variations show that the great bulk of cases fall near the center of the entire range and that a diminishing number of cases occur toward the extremes. These probabilities, when charted, produce a line that roughly resembles a bell. See chart below.

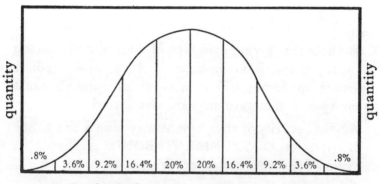

standard of measurement or percentile

NORMAL CURVE

Reading horizontally across the bottom is the standard of measurement, or the level of achievement in any situation. This is the qualitative analysis of a study. Reading vertically determines the number of cases involved for the quantitative analysis. The areas enclosed within each segment of the curve represent the percentage of the total cases in each percentile bracket.

Not held order

In securities trading this term applies to a market order or limited price order marked as . . . not held, disregard tape or take time. Any order which bears any other such qualifying notation. An order marked with "or better" is not a "not held" order. See BUY or SELL ORDERS for other kinds of orders used in securities trading.

Notary public

Individuals appointed under state laws to authenticate documents and signatures of principals to any document. They may also administer oaths.

Note

1. A document giving evidence of debt and promising to pay a specified amount to the named creditor either on demand or at a specified time. Interest charges, if there are any, are also stated.

2. A debt security of shorter maturity than a bond. See BONDS or GOVERNMENT BONDS for specific types of short term debt securities.

O

O T C
Abbreviation for over-the-counter. It is a negotiated market between brokers or dealers. There is no exchange floor for over-the-counter trading, so the trades are transacted wherever they can be negotiated. Usually there are several dealers who will carry an inventory of each issue. It is said that they "make a market" in the securities they handle. The over-the-counter market is where most new issues and the smaller corporations are traded. Some larger firms not choosing to be listed on an exchange also trade over-the-counter, as do many banks, insurance stocks, mutual funds, and utilities. The OTC trading volume is far heavier than exchange trading, and it is also the most volatile in prices.

Objective
1. The overall investment plan of any individual in-

vestor. This pertains to the nature of investments selected or their purpose, rather than dollar values that are being committed, or the expected returns. For example, a retired person with little or no other income will have a conservative objective . . . maximum safety of principal and income, with little or no concern for growth in the account. A younger person with adequate income but limited funds for investment would seek growth with good quality securities. If that young person has sizeable surplus income and generous investment funds he may be justified in seeking aggressive growth with no concern for income. He could accept much greater risks in seeking maximum growth.

2. The price that you expect a given stock to reach. An investor who trades securities frequently may form an opinion, either from chart analysis or from fundamental conditions about how far a security will rise or fall before he will make a decision to buy or sell. His decision price is his objective for that security at that period of time. His objective may change later.

Obligation

In the securities business this means a debt. Bonds and notes are called obligations since they are promises to repay a certain amount with interest. They are also called investments, since they are a means for using surplus money for gaining income and preserving the principal. Notice that while stock is also an investment, it is not an obligation with a promise of repayment, but rather an evidence of equity or ownership. The company does not promise to pay that money back. Equity is risked or ventured for the hope of profits.

Obsolescence

The process of becoming obsolete or useless because of newer developments. Usually the term is applied to equipment which becomes outdated by the fact that newer equipment is more efficient or serves the intended purpose better than the older item. In many consumer products the obsolescence is due to changing styles and trends rather than to efficiency. Notice that it is *not* a reduction of efficiency by wear and tear, which is depreciation. While depreciation can be deducted on a scheduled basis for tax purposes, obsolescence is generally claimed as a write off when the equipment is replaced. As an example, if a piece of equipment originally costs $27,000 and is expected to last 5 years and end up with a $2,000 salvage value, using a straight line depreciation method, the company would claim $5,000 each year for depreciation. If the equipment is outdated in three years because of new developments that provide much better speed in production the company may replace the machine earlier than planned. If the salvage price received is $4,000, and only $15,000 was claimed for depreciation, there is a difference of $8,000 that is written off due to obsolescence. Also see DEPRECIATION for several methods of calculating deductions due to wear and tear.

Obsolete securities

Issues for which no market can be found. The cost of such securities may be written off as a loss against income taxes if the holder obtains a letter from his broker stating that no market exists for the security. The write-off of such losses must conform to other IRS rules.

Odd lot

An amount of stock less than the established 100 share unit of trading. This will be from 1 to 99 shares for the great majority of issues. Odd lots are generally traded through certain special dealers at a premium of 1/8 point or more, depending on the breadth of the market for that stock. In certain stocks that are not traded frequently and even then in small quantities, the normal trading unit can be reduced to 10, 25, or 50 shares. In these inactive stocks an odd lot will be any number of shares less than the trading unit. See ROUND LOTS for more information.

Odd lot dealer

A member firm of an exchange that buys and sells odd lots of stocks. His customers are brokers acting on behalf of their customers. See ODD LOTS.

Odd lot index

A composite of odd lot sales. An indicator of small investor attitudes. Odd lot trades usually hold steady through major trends but increase just before the market tops out. Also, odd lot trades increase near the bottom of a market decline.

Odd lot short sales

A composite of odd lot short selling which indicates small investor attitudes. Unusually heavy short selling by odd lotters often will pinpoint a market bottom.

Odd lot theory

A theory that investors who purchase odd lots of securities are not knowledgeable enough to cope with the intricacies and emotional pressures of the stock market and, therefore, will usually make the wrong decision. The theory further holds that timing of stock trading, which is of primary importance, is where the small investor is particularly in error. Therefore, the sophisticated investor is urged to move in the opposite direction from the odd lotter. Statistics do show that the heaviest selling of odd lots occur after a market decline has reached a bottom.

Odd lot trend

An index formed by comparing the daily volume of odd lot buying against odd lot selling. Many analysts and professional investors believe that a significant, continuing difference between such trades indicates that a major change in the market trend is approaching. Since the odd lot theory states that odd lot traders are not knowledgeable traders and, therefore, move opposite to, or may even precipitate major trends, the professional will often buy when odd lot sell off is high, and he will sell when odd lot buying is heavy.

Off board

This term may refer to transactions over-the-counter in unlisted securities or in a special situation to a transaction involving listed shares which was not executed on a national securities exchange. See CROSS and THIRD MARKET for examples of special situations of listed stocks being traded outside the exchange.

Offer

The price at which a person is willing to sell. Opposed to BID which is the price at which one is willing to buy. An offer is the same thing as the asked price. There is a careful distinction in terms for quoting prices. If a dealer quotes the *bid* and *asked* prices at 9½ - 10 it means that the prices are firm. He will buy a round lot from you at 9½ or he will sell a round lot to you at 10.

However, if he says, "The *asking* price is 10," it means that the price is negotiable. Also see QUOTE and INDICATED MARKET for more information.

Offered firm

A valid offer to sell a security at a firm price. The seller will not take less. See QUOTE for additional information.

Offering

A large amount of stocks or bonds which are made available to the public by a corporation, also called an issue or distribution.

A sale of stock is actually a sale of shares of ownership or equity in the corporation while a sale of bonds is actually making private loan arrangements with investors. The bond secures the debt for repayment at a later time. Interest payments provide the income for bond holders. See PUBLIC OFFERING and UNDERWRITER for added information.

Offering circular

A prospectus. A document which describes in great detail all the facts concerning a public stock offer. It will give facts about the company, its products, its officers and directors, its financial reports, its competition, the intended use of the proceeds of the stock sale, and disclosure of the commissions or expenses of the underwriter. It is a required document that, after clearance by the SEC, must be presented to each person solicited as a potential investor in the security during its initial offering to the public. Subsequent trading in the security over-the-counter or on an exchange does not require the offering circular unless the issuer is an open end investment company. Also see PRELIMINARY PROSPECTUS for a special type of offering circular and MUTUAL FUND for an example of an issuer which must always provide a prospectus to any investor.

Offering price
1. In mutual fund shares, this is the price an investor would pay for one share when investing. It amounts to the net asset value with the sales charge added to it.
2. In other securities it is the market price stated separately from commissions.
3. In the case of a new issue of stock the offering price includes a special sales charge, and the regular brokerage commission does not apply.

Offering wanted
It is a notice by a dealer that he has an order for a security and is asking prospective sellers to submit offerings. The notice will appear abbreviated to OW on the pink sheets listing OTC prices and dealers. The pink sheets are published daily by the National Quotation Bureau to list all dealers in all over-the-counter stocks, plus the latest prices on those stocks.

Officer
A member of the management team of a corporation. The team is usually chosen by the board of directors and may even be directors themselves. Usually the officers will include a president, one or more vice-presidents, a secretary, and a treasurer. In some very small companies, one person may fill more than one office.

On balance
An expression which means that the heaviest weight of evidence favors one alternative. For example, if

most indicators and influences are good during a given period, it is said that, "On balance, the outlook for the market is favorable."

Open
The opening sale or the first sale of a trading day for any given stock. This is sometimes viewed as an indication of the trend for the day. If a price opens above the previous day's close, it suggests rising prices for the day for that stock.

Open end fund
A broad term applying to all mutual funds. They are investment companies which offer their shares to the public on a continuous basis, and are obligated to redeem or repurchase those shares at any time at the net asset value. Thus, the number of shareholders may vary from day to day, which gives them the open end designation. Also see CLOSED END FUND.

Open end investment trust
A mutual fund. There are two kinds of investment trusts or investment companies, the open end and the closed end. The open end company is commonly called a mutual fund and is constantly issuing new shares to anyone who wishes to purchase them. The proceeds are then reinvested in other securities according to some stated investment purpose. By regulation, at least 90% of the income and capital gains obtained by the fund must be distributed to shareholders in order to remain non-taxable to the fund. By contrast, the closed end fund issues only a specified number of shares to the public. Those shares then may be traded over-the-counter or even listed on an exchange, but the number of shares outstanding will never increase. The

investment trusts are also called regulated investment companies.

Open market

Open to the public for any one to purchase. This is said of securities, real estate, government surplus, and a myriad other things available to anyone to bid for. Occasionally a market may be limited by a few qualifications, but, if bidding is open, it is still called an open market sale.

Open market operations

The buying or selling of government securities on the open market by the Federal Reserve as a means of expanding or contracting credit. Buying these securities puts extra money into circulation, which has the tendency to expand economic activities, while selling of the securities removes money from circulation to slow the economy. All the decisions pertaining to these open market operations are the responsibility of the Open Market Committee of the Federal Reserve System. These decisions are carefully guarded secrets for 90 days to prevent speculative trading rushes. The buying and selling activities are also carefully guarded so that the public becomes aware of the actions only as they see the effect of the moves.

Open order

An order issued by an investor to his broker to buy or sell a security which remains in effect until it is either fulfilled or cancelled by the customer. Also called a good till cancelled order. See BUY or SELL ORDERS for a list of other kinds of orders used in securities trading.

Operating cost ratio

The ratio between a company's net sales and its operating costs. As an example, if a company has net sales of $10,000,000 and operating costs of $9,000,000, its operating cost ratio would be 90%, and its gross profit would be 10%. These two figures can vary widely between different industries.

Operating deficit

Opposite from operating profit. It consists of any losses that result from normal operations only. It excludes expenses for rent, insurance, interest payments, and property taxes. Also excluded are gains or losses from other investments, liquidated assets, research and development, write-offs from discontinued products, or tax loss carry forward. Those expenses included in operations are raw materials costs, labor, utilities, administrative costs, advertising, and others directly involved in producing a product or service for customers. These operating expenses and resulting profits or losses are totaled up separately, then combined later with other profits or losses. Separating such figures on financial statements makes analysis and planning much more simple.

Operating expenses

The cost of conducting normal business activities. There are several ways of identifying these expenses, depending upon the purposes involved.

1. Speaking in general terms without regard to accurate accounting the term is used to include labor, raw materials, supplies, rent, leasing costs, utilities, advertising, legal costs, or almost any other expense arising from normal operations. In this case the only expenses excluded are losses

from other investments, losses from discontinued operations, write-offs from unsuccessful products, expense of law suits, or other expenses not connected with normal operations.

2. There are other times when it is necessary to report expenses as those directly involved in producing a product or service. In this case fixed expenses are excluded, such as depreciation, mortgage payments, interest, and leasing payments. This may be the most common usage and will appear on many financial statements.

3. At times operating costs will exclude materials and supplies, sales expenses, advertising, insurance, interest, and other items so that the remaining costs pertain only to the expense of converting raw materials into the finished product.

Operating profit
Income in excess of expenses. It consists of the gross profit, or profit from operations before taxes and before adjustments for loss carry forward, losses from discontinued operations, write-downs in investments, income from sale of assets, or income from investments. These other charges against profit are listed separately, so that profitability from operations is easily determined by investors, management, auditors, security analysts, and the regulatory agencies.

Operating statement
Another term for the income statement, profit and loss statement, or P&L sheet. This is one of the three financial reports making up the financial statement published quarterly by public corporations and at varying other periods by privately held companies. The report contains a listing of sales, manufacturing costs,

administrative costs, taxes, depreciation, interest costs, and other income or expenses.

Opposing viewpoint theory

A theory propounded by a few idle economists that if most fundamental security analysts begin to agree with most technical security analysts, it is best for investors to make decisions contrary to the agreeing analysts. The theory is proclaimed in all seriousness, but that does not make it correct. It fits well with another statement that "rules are made to be broken."

Optimal analysis

A technique for analyzing securities and improving the odds for forecasting short term price movements and trends. Optimal analysis is a scientifically developed system based on statistical analysis of over 9,000 days of market movements. It uses fundamental analysis for basic selection of securities according to a profile for investment selections that have good probabilities of trading profits. Then continuous technical monitoring on specially designed proportional charts aids in determining proper timing for trading decisions. Proper use of the system nearly eliminates emotional pressure that can affect good judgment in investing while taking advantage of emotional read-out of the investing public. The system was devised by Investor's Systems, Inc.

Optimatician

A person following the optimal analysis technique in investment management. He makes use of statistical probabilities for analysis and projection of trends, relies heavily upon proportional stock charts, and uses a basic profile which selects the most likely prospects for gain. The optimatician is a short term trader. Note difference from the FUNDAMENTALIST and the TECHNICIAN.

Optimism curve

A graph that indicates a progressive change from optimism to pessimism in the attitudes of investors in relation to time, mental inertia and other market characteristics. One of the tools of the optimal analysis system of security analysis and portfolio management that aids in forecasting and timing of trading decisions. See illustration on page 306.

Option

Any of several types of contracts which give the holder the right to buy or sell specific securities or properties at a specified price within a specified time. One type of option called a right generally expires in a short period of time . . . a few months up to a year. Warrants are another form of these options that usually are good for longer periods of time . . . a year, five years, ten years, and some are good permanently. For more information see RIGHTS, WARRANTS, PUTS, CALLS, STRIPS, STRAPS and STRADDLES.

Optional bond

A bond which may be redeemed prior to the maturity date if the issuer agrees. See BONDS for other types of bonds and comparisons between them.

Orders good until a specified time

A market order or limited price order issued by an investor to his broker which is good for a specified time after which the order or any portion not executed is cancelled. See BUY or SELL ORDERS for other types of orders used in security trading.

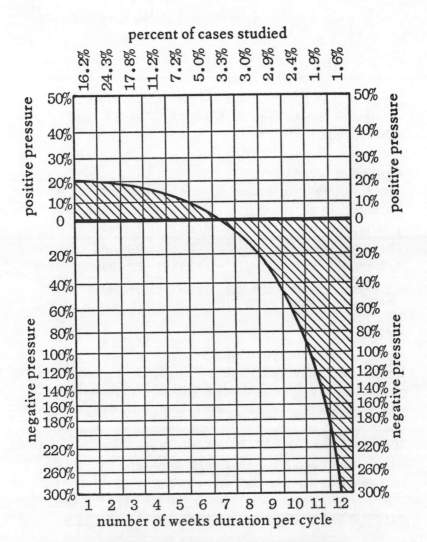

OPTIMISM - PESSIMISM CURVE

Read across bottom for duration of primary wave cycles. Read across top for percentage of cycles which lie in each time span unit. Vertical reading of pressure is the ratio between market price up-turns and down-turns. Evidence yielded: Short down-cycles tend to reverse upward more quickly than the short up-cycles which turn down. Also, longer up-cycles tend to turn down more quickly than the longer down-cycles which turn up. Time is a negative influence. Sampling: 9,200,000 transactions.

Ordinary income

Income received by an individual in his normal course of activities, so designated for tax purposes so that income from the sale of assets may receive special consideration. Ordinary income includes wages, salaries, rents, dividends, alimony, gifts, prizes, some classes of royalties, tips, commissions, gambling winnings, and even illegally obtained money. For tax purposes, ordinary income is differentiated from long term gains or capital gains by allowing lower tax rates on long term gains.

Other assets

Balance sheets and other financial reports frequently list major groupings of assets as plant and equipment, inventory, receivables, and cash. Many other types of assets can be grouped as miscellaneous or other assets. That category can include patents, license agreements, trademarks, deposits by customers, goodwill, credits granted that do not represent adjustments, payments, or trade discounts. Many of the so-called other assets are also called intangible assets.

Other exchange

An infrequently used expression meaning the American Stock Exchange. Much more often called AMEX or ASE. See AMERICAN STOCK EXCHANGE for more information about membership requirements, seats available, etc.

Outside financing

Selling stocks or bonds in order to raise funds for business expansion instead of depending completely upon retained earnings. Outside financing is called equity financing if stock is sold to obtain the money, or debt financing if bonds are sold.

Outstanding stock

The amount of capital stock issued by a company and still in public hands, though not necessarily those of the original buyers. This includes all shares owned by officers of the company or shares owned by any other companies, but it does not include treasury stock or shares bought back by the issuing company.

Over-the-counter market

A negotiated market for securities trading outside of the stock exchanges between dealers acting as principals or as brokers for their customers. The OTC market handles all new issues and is the principal market for bank and insurance stocks, mutual funds, and industrial and utility issues that either cannot or do not wish to meet the listing requirements of national exchanges. Over-the-counter trading volume is far heavier than exchange trading volume, and it is also the most volatile in prices.

Overbought

An opinion as to stock price levels. This may refer to a security that has had a sharp rise, or to the market as a whole after a period of vigorous buying. This, it is said, has raised prices too high, and they are now due for a decline. Opposite to oversold.

Overhead supply

A large block of stock which someone wishes to sell. It will probably be offered in small lots in order to have a minimum effect on the market.

Overlaying bond

A bond which ranks behind another issue by the same company in claims against their assets. See

BONDS for other types of bonds and comparisons between them.

Override

In retail trade it is a payment made to dealers, wholesalers, managers, or other representatives for their efforts in the marketing of a product. This is similar to a commission, except that commissions are usually a percentage of the selling price which may vary somewhat because of negotiations. Overrides are usually flat rates regardless of selling price. Overrides may also be in addition to commission and may become payable only after reaching a specified sales volume.

Oversold

A statement of opinion about stock price levels. It can apply to a single security or to a market that, it is believed, has declined to an unreasonably low level and is due for a turnaround. Opposite to overbought.

Owner's equity

The same as shareholder's equity, net worth, book value or capital of business. It is the difference between all assets and all liabilities as they are carried on the books. See NET WORTH for expanded definition.

P

P. E. multiple

The same as P.E. ratio, which is a shortening of price-earnings ratio. Also called earnings ratio, earnings multiple, or simply multiple. See PRICE EARNINGS RATIO for expanded information.

P-E ratio

A shortening of price-earnings ratio, the ratio between the market price of a stock and its issuer's earnings per share. Also called times earnings, earnings multiple, multiple, or earnings ratio. See PRICE-EARNINGS RATIO for additional information.

P & L statement

The profit and loss statement issued by a corporation to its shareholders or to financial institutions. It will list expenses from operations, payroll, various administrative expenses and other expenses, and finally, the bottom line figure: the resulting profit or loss for the period. Sometimes also called the P&L sheet, operating statement, or income statement. Often included with the statement of assets and liabilities (balance sheet) and a statement of capital in a combined report called the financial statement. Quarterly or annual reports to shareholders usually contain the financial statement, along with a brief review of operations for that period, and a general forecast for the next few periods, by the chief officer of the company.

P R

Short for public relations. It can refer to the existing public image of an organization or individual, or it can refer to the determined effort to improve and expand upon that public image. PR is the foundation of all advertising and political campaigns, and often a company will employ special public relations personnel to arrange news releases and press conferences, cultivate community awareness and friendly associations with banks, newspapers, local business and political officials.

Paid in surplus

An accounting term for the difference between the par value, or stated value, of a company's stock and the amount received when it was first sold. After a period of operation, some original capital is consumed and replaced by retaining earnings. It then becomes necessary to compute the paid in surplus by other means. This, then, is the difference between assets and liabilities plus the par or stated value of the stock less the earned surplus or retained earnings. Also called capital surplus.

Paint the tape

An expression describing the effect of a stock which is undergoing heavy trading in small lots. The frequent trades cover the ticker tape with trading reports.

Paper

Also called commercial paper, it refers to short term notes or instruments of indebtedness sold by large corporations, banks, and other agencies. They can take the form of a negotiable promissory note. Typically, such paper matures in 90 to 180 days but can be as short as two days or a weekend. A trend is beginning to take form which causes banks to base the prime interest rates on commercial paper rather than the federal discount rate; the thought being that paper is much closer to the supply and demand for funds, and, therefore, can be more representative for the need of changes in rates.

Paper gold

A term applied to created assets in the international monetary fund. Properly called special drawing rights or SDR's, they are credits assigned to certain nations, equivalent in value to gold, for settling international accounts.

Paper losses

An unrealized loss in the market value of a security which has declined below the price at which it was purchased. It would become a real or realized loss only if sold at that low price. Unrealized profits are also referred to as paper profits.

Paper profits

Sometimes called unrealized profits, they are the

gain in market value of a security held by an investor since the original purchase. This is also called appreciation and growth. When the security is sold, the gain becomes realized profits. For tax purposes the gain will then be called short term gains if sold less than 6 months after purchase or long term gains if held more than 6 months before being sold.

Par

In the case of common stock, par is the dollar value per share assigned by the company's charter for bookkeeping purposes. It is primarily used to compute the dollar amount of outstanding common shares on the balance sheet. It has little relationship to the market value of a stock, but once reflected the book value at the time of issue. Now that usage has passed, but if a shareholder demands that the company buys back his shares, the company must pay at least the par value, even if the market value has declined below par. For that reason, common stock is now often issued with no par value. All equity is then shown on the balance sheet as paid-in surplus. Bonds and preferred stock are often sold at the stated par value, since interest and preferred dividends are calculated on the par value. Even if the market prices change on these senior securities, the par value is still the basis for calculating interest and dividend payments.

Parent corporation

A company which owns all or a major portion of another company called a subsidiary. The parent company may start the subsidiary or it may acquire it in one of many ways: by buying the stock on the open market, exchange of stock for financial assistance, exchange of stock for licensing agreements, joint ventures, etc. Often a parent company will place certain operating officers or directors, on the board of the subsidiary to aid management or to help assure that the parent's purposes are met.

Parity

A condition of equality or rate of conversion for equality. It can be used for comparing standards of living between dissimilar areas as a basis for government subsidies. Also, it is a basis for international exchange for currency.

Participating bond

One type of industrial bond which provides that the holder may share in the profits of the company, just as a shareholder, in addition to the regular guaranteed bond interest. See BONDS for other types of bonds and comparisons between them.

Participating brokers and dealers

Brokers and dealers who have agreed to assist in the selling of a new issue of stock or a bond. They are not part of the underwriting syndicate and do not take part in the preparation of the issue for the public. They only assist in selling the issue on a commission basis so that a broader market may be obtained for the stock. They are also called selling group or selling concession.

Participating preferred

A special class of preferred stock which has an added benefit. Along with the customary position as a senior security (prior claim to assets in liquidation) and the usually specified dividend, it also is entitled to additional dividends based upon payment of dividends on common shares. See PREFERRED STOCK for other kinds of preferred and STOCK for a list of other types of stock.

Partnership
An unincorporated business formed by two or more individuals which gives the strength of combined assets while retaining the simplicity of operation and tax considerations of an individual. See GENERAL PARTNERSHIP and LIMITED PARTNERSHIP for added information.

Passed dividend
Omission of a regular or scheduled dividend. In some cases a passed dividend will be paid at a later date, as in the case of cumulative preferred.

Patent
An official recognition by a government that a person or company has originated a device, process, or design. It does not prevent others from copying, but does give the originator the legal right to prosecute if infringed upon. The major value is its use as a marketable asset. Corporations carry the value of patents on the books as goodwill or other assets.

Patterns
Shapes which appear in the charts used in stock charting. Different methods of charting attribute special significance to different patterns. Some are widely accepted and others are merely smiled upon. Some patterns are:

Base	Cone
Bottom	Consolidation

Correction	Rally
Cycle	Recovery
Cylinder	Reversal
Double bottom	Saucer
Double top	Secondary wave
Flag	Sell off
Fundamental wave	Shelf
Head and shoulders	Spike
Line	Top or peak
Plunge	Trend
Primary wave	Wave

Some of the above patterns are shown on sample charts under the heading STOCK CHARTS.

Payable date

The official date on which dividends or other distributions to shareholders become payable. Also called record date because the payments are made to stockholders of record on that date. This is the official acquisition date to establish proper ownership of the security for payment of dividends, although the actual payment is usually made at a later time. Notice the difference from payment date and settlement date. The payment date is the date for issuing checks for dividends or interest payments, while the settlement date refers to payment for securities purchased by an investor or delivery of certificates for securities sold by an investor. See separate headings for more information.

Payment date

The actual date on which dividend or interest checks are mailed to owners of securities. This date is later than the payable date. See separate listing. Also note difference from settlement date, which refers to payments for securities that are purchased by an investor.

Payout

The annual amount of dividends paid by a company on each share of stock stated as a percentage of the market price of the stock. Notice that payout is only a *portion* of the company's earnings. Retained earnings are plowed back into the business for growth. Also referred to as the payout ratio. The same figure if referring to bonds is called yield. From the standpoint of the investor who receives the payments, dividends or bond interest are both called yield and are stated as a percentage of the market price of the stock or purchase price of the bond. See YIELD and COUPON RATE for differences.

Peak

Also called top. In stock charting, these terms are used to describe the highest point reached for a given period of time on a stock chart. It can only be used in retrospect and must be followed by a break. If a following break is brief, it is termed a correction or a technical correction. If the reversal following the break continues a week or more it is called a sell off. If it continues for several months, it becomes a downside trend which verifies that the peak was truly a peak. If a peak is followed by a break and then recovers to another peak in the same price range, it is termed a double top, which is considered a resistance line that probably cannot be exceeded. A double top is considered as a selling signal. See STOCK CHARTS for illustrated chart patterns.

Penalty plan

A name for prepaid charge plans offered by mutual funds. They are used with plans which call for periodic payments for the purchase of new shares in a mutual fund where all of the sales charges are paid in the first year or two of the plan. See PERIODIC PAYMENT PLANS or other special features under the heading INVESTMENT COMPANIES for more information and comparison of these plans.

Penny stock

Extremely low priced stocks, generally of a speculative nature, if not totally worthless. Prices have ranged up to several dollars, but most have been under one dollar. They blossomed some years ago as a fad when everyone was on a stock buying binge, and numerous promoters took advantage of it. Regulations have since reduced such operations considerably. Some prices may fall into the penny category, while the reason may be vastly different from the fast buck activities of the past. See STOCK for more information and a list of other types of stock.

Per share net

Earnings after taxes divided by total common shares outstanding. Usually called earnings and stated in dollars per share. Not to be confused with payout or yield, which are the per share amounts of dividends paid to shareholders. The retained earnings portion of profits not paid to shareholders is used for operation of the business and expansion.

Percentage order

A market order or limited price order issued by an investor to his broker to buy or sell a stated amount of a specified stock after a fixed number of shares of that stock have been traded. See BUY or SELL ORDERS for a list of other kinds of orders used in securities trading.

Performance

1. In referring to a corporation, performance is the earnings or increase in earnings per share for any period compared to a similar period in a prior year.
2. In referring to the market price of a security it is either its volatility or its ability to maintain overall increases in prices.
3. In referring to a security itself and not just its market price, it is its ability to show steadily increasing earnings, which in turn will affect market price. In this case a person speaks of the security, but actually means the issuing company.
4. In referring to top management of industrial firms, it is the ability to maintain or increase earnings for the company. Unfortunately, the ability to maintain sound financial conditions, quality personnel, and soundness of corporate planning are not considered until they affect earnings per share.
5. In referring to lower levels of management in industry, it means the ability to maintain or improve productivity, control costs, and reach corporate goals.
6. In referring to management of investment companies, it is the ability to maintain or increase net asset value per share.

Performance bond

One of several types of bonds that are not investment securities. This bond is a cash deposit by one party of a contract to the other party to guarantee that he will perform his part of the agreement. Construction contractors frequently must post performance bonds with cities to insure satisfactory completion of public works programs. An entertainer or other public figure may post such bonds when renting an auditorium. The bond money is returned upon completion of the contract terms. The bond may take the form of an advance deposit toward the full payment of the rental fee.

Performance fund

An aggressively managed mutual fund which buys stocks that are expected to show near term growth. These funds trade frequently in glamour stocks and may use short sales, puts, calls, and other speculative measures to increase return. Managers of such funds are judged by the gain they can produce. Some funds which may use short sales, puts, calls, and other speculative activities, for increased gain, and to protect other potentially weak investments, are called hedge funds. These are not really mutual funds, but closed end investment companies. See INVESTMENT COMPANIES for other types of funds and descriptions of each. Also see INVESTMENT COMPANY ACT OF 1940 for definitions, purposes, and limitations.

Performance stock

A stock issue that exhibits a spectacular growth in value. It may also be called growth stock or glamour stock. See STOCK for listing of other types of stock.

Periodic payment plan

In mutual funds it is a general term referring to a

program for purchasing additional fund shares at regular intervals, also called an accumulation plan. Several types of plans are available in both voluntary or contractual varieties. *Voluntary* plans do not require any specific amount for each purchase, nor do they have set time schedules for each purchase. Among the *contractual* plans several names are used to describe the plan, such as prepaid charge plan, contractual plan, and penalty plan. Under these plans an agreement is made to purchase a fixed dollar amount of shares at fixed time intervals. The sales charges are generally paid off more heavily during the first year or two of the plans, hence the penalty name. These are definitely long term investment programs for the unsophisticated investor. See *special features* under the heading of INVESTMENT COMPANIES for more information on these plans.

Perk
A shortening of the term PERQUISITE listed below.

Perpetual bond
Another name for annuity bond, one that bears no maturity date. It will continue drawing interest indefinitely. See BONDS for other types of bonds and comparisons between them.

Perquisite
An additional benefit or prerogative given to someone by virtue of his status or position. Frequently officers and management of large corporations will be given automobiles, club memberships, plush office furnishings, personal investment counselors, or other side benefits in addition to salaries as inducement for lower management to strive for the top, or as an in-

ducement to the top management to remain loyal in the face of offers from other companies. Often the term is shortened to perk.

Phantom stock

Imaginary stock being listed to the account of a corporate executive as compensation in addition to his salary. It does not have voting rights, nor can it be traded, but it does earn dividends for him, and it is treated as regular stock for purposes of stock splits. One of many perquisites used to attract top management. See STOCK for listings of other types of stock.

Pink sheets

A list of over-the-counter stocks and dealers who make a market in those stocks, along with the latest bid and asked prices for the stocks. The list is published daily by the National Quotation Bureau. Since different colors of paper are used for different types of securities, the term is often shortened to sheets, although the predominant pink color is loosely applied to describe the entire publication. Many over-the-counter stocks are now reported on electronic quotation machines along with listed stocks. These OTC listings are called NASDAQ listings.

Pit

An area on a commodity exchange floor that corresponds to a trading post on the New York Stock Exchange. The pits are arranged as broad circular steps where traders in the various commodities can stand to see and hear one another more easily. Also called trading pits.

Plain bond

Another name for a debenture bond which is a bond with no specific collateral pledged, basically an IOU. Many government bonds are of this type. See BONDS for other types of bonds and comparisons between them.

Play the market

A term not meant to be flattering, used in reference to speculative activities in securities. The term usually identifies the speaker as one who knows very little or nothing at all about investments or securities trading. It suggests gambling, or buying and selling in hopes of getting profit while having no knowledge of the market or skill in interpreting market influences. It is trusting chance. Contrary to the meaning inferred by those who use the term "to play the market," speculators who are trading frequently are very knowledgeable and very studious in their efforts. See INVESTMENT for comparison of terms investor, trader, and speculator.

Plum

An especially profitable stock that was purchased at the right time to give unusually strong growth while being held, or to realize an unusually high profit when sold.

Plunge

1. In charting: a sudden and sharp drop in the price of a stock. The drop may amount to 20% or more of the price of the stock in a single day.
2. In investing: the term is also used to describe a heavy investment made in an almost reckless manner. An excessively speculative move.

See STOCK CHARTS for illustrated chart patterns.

Plunger

A person who is inclined to plunge or invest heavily in a speculative manner. Buying with little investigation into the quality of the investment.

Plus-tick

The report on a stock ticker of a securities transaction made at a price higher than the preceding transaction for any given stock. It is also called an up-tick. You may sell short only on an up-tick. The zero-plus tick is a transaction which took place at the same price as the preceding transaction but still higher than the next preceding different price. Also see DOWN-TICK or ZERO-MINUS TICK.

Point

The unit of measure in reporting security prices. In the case of prices on shares of stock, a point means $1; on bonds it represents $10; in foreign exchanges it is 1/100 of one cent; and in commodities, it can be almost anything (1 cent, 1/5 cent, 1/10 cent, 1/100 cent or any fraction suitable for convenient trading in a given commodity). The units of trade can be pounds, gallons, dozens, bales, ounces, bags, tons, etc.

Point and figure chart

A stock chart using a linear or arithmetical type graph paper which does not record exact prices but small increments of movement. The movements are recorded as x's and o's. The marks are made in vertical columns with each successive move representing a basic unit of change of as little as 1/8 point, or as much as 5 points. Usually a 1 point basis is used. The price may not be recorded for days until it has changed the complete basic unit (1 point, 3 points, etc.). A change in direction of price trends will advance the chartist to the next column. This type chart gives no indication of time or short term emotional influences, and is strictly one dimensional. It is used by many long term investors. The sample below shows a typical point and figure chart. See STOCK CHARTS for samples of other types of charts.

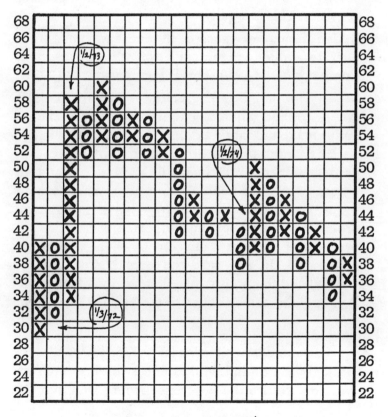

(two points per unit)

POINT AND FIGURE CHART

Pool

The combined assets of several investors. Depending on the circumstances, it can be legal, illegal, or circumstantial.

1. It is illegal for several large investors to pool assets and efforts in an attempt to influence stock prices for their profit.
2. Some forms of corporate mergers are called pooling of assets. This is legal.
3. Hedge funds are pooled investment funds that operate under regulations of the Investment Company Act of 1940. This is legal, also.
4. In the commodity trading market there are pools of orders formed when a given commodity makes a limit move, and market demand continues to build. As long as the price on that commodity moves the predetermined limit, the trading is blocked and all orders go into the pool. When traders begin taking profit, the prices can weaken. This absorbs some orders from the pool, and others are cancelled to practically eliminate any pool when trading is moderated. In this case the pool is just circumstantial and not an organized effort by anyone, but is simply the name applied to the backlog of orders.

Pooling of funds

A project undertaken where the principals contribute only the capital, and talent is hired to manage the venture. Notice the difference from POOLING OF INTERESTS below.

Pooling of interests

Combining of effort and assets for a common goal. It may be a formal merger, partnership, syndicate, consolidation, a new corporation, or an informal working agreement. Usually each party has special skills to contribute along with capital. Notice the difference from POOLING OF FUNDS on page 326.

Portfolio

The total list of securities owned by an investor or investment company. The true meaning is a briefcase or carrying case, but the term, as used in the field of securities has gradually come to be used in most cases for the total number of securities owned by an individual that he might carry in his briefcase.

Position

The extent of your commitment in an investment account. If you own stock, bonds, or commodities, you are said to have a long position of that many shares or contracts. If you have sold short any shares or contracts, you have a short position. At times a person may buy long and sell short at the same time, as happens frequently in commodity trading. The long and short positions cancel out some of the risks, as well as some of the growth potential, and the trader is said to be in a spread position. If he has a greater commitment to the long side than the short side, it is said that he has a net position on the long side or a net long position. In commodities trading and option trading a net position one way or the other can be called a strip or a strap.

Positioner

One who buys a security for his own account. It may be said of a dealer who, while handling trades for his customers, will buy some of the securities being offered by customers for his own account. When he does so, he takes a position in those securities.

Post 30

A trading post on the floor of the New York Stock Exchange where inactive stocks are traded. These inactive stocks are traded in units of 10 shares, 25 shares, or 50 shares, instead of the normal trading unit of 100 shares. This trading post consists of a group of filing cabinets which is quite different from the usual horseshoe-shaped counter around which exchange members conduct their business. Also called the inactive post.

Power of attorney

A document that, when signed by a person, gives full legal authority to another party to act for the signatory person.

Pre-emptive right

The right of all shareholders to maintain their proportional share of ownership by buying that same portion of any subsequent issues. Most stock offerings have pre-emptive rights clauses, but some may specifically eliminate the right. A shareholder may forfeit his right by simply not purchasing additional shares. He may also sell the right to others in some cases.

These rights are evidenced by documents called subscription rights and can be traded on the open market. The market value of a right is the difference between the market price of the stock and execution price stated on the right. Also see RIGHTS, WARRANTS, and OPTIONS.

Pre-tax profit margin

The percentage of gross revenues that a corporation realizes as profit before federal corporation taxes, but after all expenses of operations and any special charges or tax loss carry forward.

Preference stock

Another name for preferred stock. It has preference over common stock in the event of liquidation and distribution of proceeds. It does not have voting rights, however, as the common stock has. There may be several additional classifications and positions of rank for stock issues. Sometimes a prior preferred is issued which ranks ahead of other preferred. Classified stocks are any of those which are issued after the original issue and have slightly different conditions of ownership, voting rights, claim of assets, transferability, dividend payments, or other terms of preference or rank. These stocks are often labeled class A common, class B common, class C common, class A preferred, class B preferred, etc., and together are all called classified stocks. The purpose of preference stocks or classified stocks is to meet requirements of existing stockholders while raising additional capital. Shareholders may be willing to surrender claim on assets in order to obtain more working capital. In return, potential new shareholders may demand certain dividend advantages to give up voting rights on new shares. See STOCK for listings of other types of stock.

Preferred dividend coverage

The ratio of a company's net income, *after* taxes and interest payments have been deducted, to its annual dividends payable to preferred stockholders. Notice the difference from bond interest coverage, which is calculated on gross profits *before* taxes. This difference is due to the fact that interest payments are considered an expense of doing business, while stock dividends are a distribution of the profits of business being paid to the owners of the business. For comparisons between bond coverage and preferred stock coverage, assume a hypothetical company: Company XYZ has 3000 bonds out at $1,000 par, paying 7%. It also has 20,000 shares of preferred at $100 par, paying 5%. Then there are 1,000,000 shares of common, no par, earning dividends as voted by the board of directors. This year 10 cents a share is voted. If the company earns $1,000,000 *before taxes*, the payout will be as follows:

Gross income before taxes	$1,000,000
Bond interest (3000 x $1,000 x 7%)	-210,000
Pre-tax net	790,000
Federal taxes (approximate)	-380,000
After tax earnings	410,000
Pref. stock div. (20,000 x $100 x 5½%)	-110,000
Balance	300,000
Common dividends (1,000,000 x $.10)	-100,000
Retained earnings	200,000

The retained earnings, also called earned surplus, are plowed back into the business for expansion.

Preferred stock

A senior equity security which ranks above common stock in claims on the assets of a corporation. It is a limited form of ownership and lies midway between common stock, which is equity with voting rights, and bonds, which represent debt only, and not equity. Dividends on preferred stock are usually fixed for the life of the security unlike the dividends on common stock. There are several kinds of preferred stock in common use:

1. Convertible preferred: one which may be exchanged at some time for a voting common stock.
2. Cumulative preferred: one which has a clause providing that if any dividend payments are ever missed, they will be accumulated to be paid before any common shares may receive dividends.
3. Participating preferred: one which may participate with common shares if profits permit any extra dividends. This would provide the normal dividend plus an extra dividend for the preferred. If profits decline so that common shares get no dividends, the preferred will still get its normal dividend.

Also see STOCK for other kinds of equity securities in use.

Preferred stock funds

Mutual funds which have a policy of investment only in preferred stocks for income and safety of capital. These are planned as very conservative funds for certain types of investors. Also see INVESTMENT COMPANIES for other types of funds and INVESTMENT COMPANY ACT OF 1940 for definitions, purposes, and limitations.

Preliminary prospectus

Also called a red herring prospectus. It is an information circular which gives information on a forthcoming issue before the final approval of the registration statement by the SEC. This prospectus may not reveal the offering price and cannot be used as an offer to sell. It must be submitted to the SEC for approval before distribution, just as the formal offering prospectus which follows. At the time the formal prospectus is distributed, the preliminary prospectus must be returned. See PROSPECTUS for more information.

Premium

An extra charge or an increase in the selling price of some asset such as, for example:

1. The amount a bond or preferred stock may be selling for above its par value.

2. In some cases when a new issue is offered to the public the demand is so high that the market price immediately rises above its original offering price. This increase is called a premium.

3. There are times, too, when the term applies to a charge made when a customer borrows stock to make delivery on a short sale.

Premium bonds

Any bonds selling at a market price above the face value. This is determined only by market demand and economic conditions, rather than by the issuer. Solid financial strength of the issuer may enhance the market price. Bonds that are issued during periods when interest rates are high may command high market prices during later periods when newer issues are being offered at lower coupon rates. If the market price rises above the par value or face value, the extra cost is called a premium. Premiums have gone more than 20% above par on some issues.

Prepaid charge plan

One name for a contractural periodic investment plan in a mutual fund. See PERIODIC PAYMENT PLANS, one of several *special features* listed under the heading of INVESTMENT COMPANIES.

Prepaid expenses .

An accounting term used in financial reports which refers to payment for materials for services not yet received. Examples would be rent and lease payments, some insurance costs, advance payments for materials, advanced consulting fees, and performance bonds. These prepaid expenses are similar to deferred expenses, except that prepaid is usually understood to mean that it applies to goods and services that will be received within a year, while deferred is usually understood to mean that it applies to goods and services that will not be received within a year. Both prepaid and deferred expenses are carried on the balance sheet as assets.

Price earnings ratio

The market price divided by earnings per share for the previous 12 months. Stock selling at $24 and earning $2 per share has a price earnings ratio of 12 to 1, or simply 12, and is said to be selling at 12 times earnings. The lower the ratio, according to some analysts, the better the bargain. According to others, the higher the ratio, the better the market and growth prospects are for the security. The interpretation may be debatable, but, at least, the higher ratios do indicate that investors expect great things from the issuer, and, therefore, the demand for the stock is high.

The average PE ratio for the Dow Jones Industrials or for all stocks listed on the New York Stock Exchange will change from time to time according to overall public moods. In bearish markets PE ratios may average 6 or 8, but in bullish times they may average 16 to 20. In mid-1973 the PE average for the Dow Jones Industrials stood at 12. By mid-1974 it had dropped to

6.7. Some good stocks in bear markets can go as low as 2 simply because of association. Those same companies in better times can demand a ratio of 10 with no change in earnings. Glamour stocks, in contrast, can have ratios over 100. Also called PE, PE ratio, PE multiple, earnings multiple, or times earnings.

Price earnings ratio line

A calculated index which shows where market prices for a given stock *would be* if traded at an arbitrarily selected, but theoretically acceptable PE ratio. Acceptable ratios are calculated by plotting moving averages of earnings over several years. It is intended as an index of desirability for investment.

Price spread

The difference between a bid and asked price. This spread can narrow for widely traded stocks or widen on little known stocks with narrow markets.

Price support

Federal subsidies. A government program designed to hold prices up for producers of certain products, chiefly agricultural, while supply and demand on international markets is yielding lower prices. The government merely pays the producer a high price for the product and then resells it at a lower price. Generally there are also limits placed upon production volume so that shorter supply will help to raise prices. In the case of agricultural products, the government will pay the farmer for not planting a certain portion of his land, thus making up for his losses in meeting the artificial shortage scheme.

Primary distribution

The original sale of any issue of stock or bonds. Also

called primary offering. Also see SECONDARY
DISTRIBUTION or AFTER MARKET for opposing
terms.

Primary market
1. In the securities industry this is the total of all the
   investors who buy a given security at the time of the
   original issue to the public. Contrast to the AFTER
   MARKET or SECONDARY MARKET.
2. In other areas of business the primary market for a
   product is the major category of consumer the
   product is directed toward. In this sense a secondary market for a consumer product would not
   concern a resale of the product, but a group of
   consumers of lesser importance to the manufacturer. Also an after market for consumer products
   would concern the sale of other products that add on
   to the major product or are used in conjunction with
   it.

Primary offering
The original sale of any issue of stock or bonds to the
public. The same as primary distribution above.

Primary wave
In the wave theory of the optimal analysis method of
securities analysis, there are three basic wave patterns
or cyclical patterns on a stock chart. The primary wave
is the most important to this theory, because it reflects
investors' emotional changes and the inertial
movements in the market. It most often lasts two to
five weeks and is of considerable value in short term
investments. See CYCLIC PATTERNS for other chart
patterns that are useful in technical analysis of
securities. Samples of various waves and patterns are

shown under heading STOCK CHARTS.

Prime rate

The interest rate charged by major banks to their top rated corporate clients. This is usually a guide for establishing other interest rates and is an indicator of economic conditions. Higher prime rates tend to suppress business expansion, and, thus, they have a negative effect on the stock market. Traditionally the prime rate is based on the federal discount rate, which is the amount the banks themselves must pay to borrow money from the Federal Reserve System. There is now the beginning of a trend to use the rate charged for commercial paper as a basis for the prime rate. See COMMERCIAL PAPER and FEDERAL RESERVE SYSTEM.

Principal

1. The person for whom a broker executes an order.
2. A dealer buying or selling for his own account.
3. A person's capital.
4. The face amount of a loan.
5. The face amount of a bond.
6. In corporate structure it refers to top ranking officers or major stockholders if actively involved in corporate activities.

Note that the spelling is different from principle, which means a natural law or fundamental truth. Notice the contrast to the term AGENT. Also see DEALER for more information.

Prior lien bond

A bond which ranks ahead of another issue by the same issuer in claims against the company's assets.

See BONDS for other types of bonds and comparisons between them.

Prior preferred

A preferred stock that usually takes precedence over other preferreds and common stocks issued by the same company. See STOCK for more information and listings of other types of stock.

Private offerings

New issues of stock which are offered directly to a limited number of institutions or other investors not exceeding 25. The private offering is also usually limited to less than $300,000 for the total value of securities being sold. They need not comply with registration requirements of the SEC, but they cannot be resold to the public until the proper registration procedure is completed. Also see PUBLIC OF-FERINGS and PRIVATELY OWNED and PUBLICLY OWNED corporations and REGULATION A offerings for issues less than $300,000.

Private placement

A transaction in which a corporation borrows money from another company or individual. This operates much like a bond issue except that it is much less complicated. Occasionally the term is applied to mean the same as a private offering, which is a sale of securities to a limited number of investors.

Privately owned corporation

A corporation which is owned by one or only a few stockholders. According to certain regulations, an issue of stock sold to more than 25 shareholders is a public offering; however, the company itself may still be called privately owned if the shares cannot be purchased later on the open market. This will often be the case, since the original shareholders keep their stock as a long term investment. Also notice difference from PUBLICLY OWNED CORPORATION, listed separately, and compare PRIVATE OFFERINGS and PUBLIC OFFERINGS for additional information.

Probability

The calculated or estimated odds for something to happen or for certain conditions to exist. Calculated odds can be mathematical probabilities or statistical probabilities. *Mathematical probabilities* depend upon a mathematical formula which is based on the laws of chance. The formula considers variables combined in all possible arrangements. Each variable is a constant for any single computation.

Statistical probabilities are odds based upon analysis of a mass of historical records which were compiled in graphic form to indicate the numerical distribution of various possibilities. Statistical probabilities are the basis of the wave theory that is followed in optimal analysis. Optimal analysis is a technique for analyzing securities and portfolio management. In theory, statistical probabilities should coincide with mathmatical probabilities, but the unknown variable of human emotion escapes mathematics. The statistical record, to the contrary, shows every reaction to every stimulus. This makes statistical probabilities much more useful to an investor or security analyst.

Optimal analysis was originated by Investor's Systems, Inc., using original statistical research and developing original probability curves. Publication of the book *Optimal Analysis* culminated a 20-year statistical research program. See OPTIMISM CURVE for illustrated sample of chart showing probabilities for stock trading activities.

Productivity
The amount of goods produced by an industry divided by the man hours required to produce it. Increases in productivity are the result of new processes and equipment and can also be affected over a short term period by management efficiency and worker motivation. Decreased productivity is abnormal and can be traced to inefficiencies due to aging equipment and worker motivation, both of which follow poor management. Some inefficiencies are also traceable to restrictive labor contracts. An index of productivity is used as an indicator of economic progress. Lowering productivity coincides with and follows a peak in economic growth. Increased productivity precedes an upturn in economic growth.

Profile
A basic tool of the optimal analysis system of security analysis and portfolio management which is used to select securities with the highest probability of providing trading profits. It consists of a list of characteristics that have been observed in some of the most profitable investments. It is presumed that the greater the number of these characteristics present in a new candidate for investment, the better the odds for profitable trading.

Profit
An imprecise term related to the gain from business operations. Accountants use terms like income, earnings, net, surplus, etc. and specify whether before or after certain charges, deductions, allowances and

reserves. It is the basis of all business of any type at any time in history and the objective of any investor. It is the basis of backyard bartering of marbles for slingshots, or of international negotiations for shiploads of oil or bananas. It is a most beautiful word to anyone making it, and a most heinous, immoral insult when anyone *else* makes it.

Profit and loss statement

A quarterly or annual financial report which lists total revenues or sales, costs, expenses, taxes, and profits for a corporation. Along with the breakdown of general expenses and income, it will separately identify extraordinary expenses or income such as disaster losses, write-offs for discontinued products, legal judgments, sales of properties and securities, and interest income and expenses. Often stated as P&L statement or income statement. The profit and loss statement, along with the balance sheet and statement of capital, make up the financial statement of a corporation.

Profit margin

The difference between the cost and the selling price. A business must provide for all its operating expenses out of this margin. Rent, utilities, insurance, advertising, warranty service, maintenance, administrative expenses, commissions, salaries, and taxes are all paid out of the profit margin before the net profit or operating profit is realized. Sometimes profit margin is stated as a percentage of the retail price. The same profit margin stated as a percentage of mark up will appear as a larger figure. For example, an article costing a dealer 75 cents and selling for $1 would be stated as a 33% markup (markup $25 \div 75$ cost $= 33\%$)

but only 25% profit margin (.25 ÷ 1.00 selling price =
25%). Note the difference from the term margin as
used in investments. See NET PROFIT and EARN-
INGS.

Profit taking

Selling to take a profit that has accrued after a
security price has risen sufficiently above the purchase
price. The process of converting paper profits into real
profits. A person receiving such a profit is said to
realize a profit.

Sometimes after a brisk rise in the market, there will
be a flurry of *sales* by sophisticated investors which
causes a brief dip in market prices. This period of
decline is referred to as a profit taking sell off. See
STOCK CHARTS for illustrated chart patterns.

Projection

A forecast for some condition based upon an extension of known statistics.

Proportional chart

Stock charts which use specially designed logarithmic charts so that the user, when using Investor's
Systems' techniques of security analysis, may reduce
all stocks to easily compared basic dimensions. The
user can read directly in proportional percentages of
change regardless of price range. Ordinary logarithmic
charts or the more common linear charts and point and
figure charts will not work with Investor's Systems'
special materials. See sample proportional chart on
page 342 and other types of charts under STOCK
CHARTS.

Proprietorship

An unincorporated business owned by one person

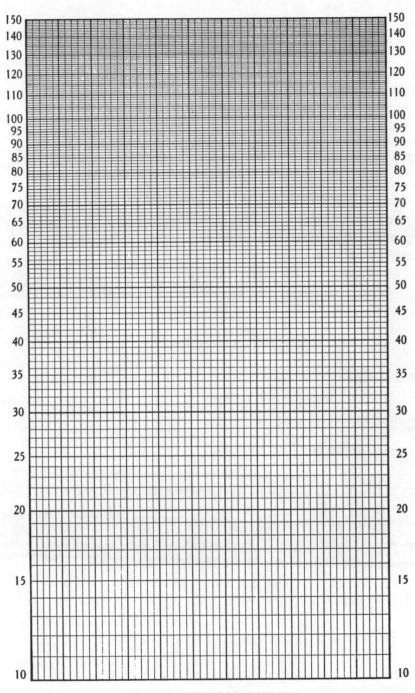

PROPORTIONAL CHART

and, perhaps, operated by the same person. He receives all the profits and is liable for all expenses and losses. It does not have stockholders, and when the proprietor dies, the proprietorship ceases to exist. Also see GENERAL PARTNERSHIP, LIMITED PARTNERSHIP, PUBLIC CORPORATION, and PRIVATE CORPORATION.

Prospectus

A circular that describes securities being offered for public sale. It is required by the Securities Act of 1933 and must be presented to each prospective buyer of any new issue being offered to the public. Its purpose is to make complete disclosure of pertinent facts concerning the company, its financial status (with financial reports), its products, its officers, any special conditions or restrictions to investors, any possible negative factors such as competition, market condition, and law suits. It also reports the intended use of the proceeds of the offering and disclosure of commissions or expenses of the underwriter. The circular is quite detailed and can consist of more than 200 pages of information, although most run 20 to 40 pages.

After the initial offering the prospectus is no longer used when the shares are traded. Mutual funds are different, since their shares are not traded but sold back to the issuer; therefore, a prospectus is always used for every sale or sales presentation. A prospectus is also called the offering circular. Often a preliminary prospectus is distributed prior to the formal offering of securities is made. See separate heading for a description of the PRELIMINARY PROSPECTUS, which is also called a red herring prospectus.

Proxy

Authorization given by a stockholder to another party to vote in his place. Frequently these proxies are solicited by management. Most holders of very small portions of the stock of a company will assign their votes to management to vote in any manner desired by management. The shareholder may designate how the vote should be cast if he wishes.

Proxy fight

A struggle between stockholders to win voting control through gaining proxy support of other shareholders. The winner of such voting control generally elects himself as the chief executive officer and installs a majority of the Board of Directors who will support his policies. To conduct such a proxy fight, opposing factions present their views in a proxy statement to shareholders and request proxies from shareholders. At a duly called shareholder's meeting, views are again expressed and a vote taken. Often the proxy votes assigned by absentees carry the deciding weight of votes, and the winner realigns management, the board of directors, and company policy to suit his own point of view.

Proxy statement

An information statement supplied by a corporation to its shareholders as a requirement by the Securities Exchange Commission before solicitation of proxies. It explains the proposals that will be voted upon at a shareholder's meeting.

Prudent man rule

An investment standard to guide persons who control investments for others. In some states, the law provides that a fiduciary, such as a trustee, may invest the fund's money only in a list of securities designated by the state, the so-called "legal list." Other states require that the trustee may invest in a security if it is one that a prudent man of discretion and intelligence, who is seeking a reasonable income and preservation of capital, would buy. In some states the prudent man rule is imposed in addition to any other standards.

Public corporation
The same as PUBLICLY OWNED CORPORATION listed on page 346.

Public offerings
New issues of stocks which are offered to the public through investment bankers, only after they have complied with the registration requirements of the Securities Act of 1933. Those requirements are concerned mostly with complete and thorough disclosure of facts about the company, its products, its officers, its market, its financial status, the intended use of the proceeds of stock sale, and any special conditions of ownership of the stock. See PRIVATE OFFERINGS, PRIVATELY OWNED and PUBLICLY OWNED CORPORATIONS, and REGULATION A OFFERINGS.

Public relations
It can refer to the existing public image of an organization or individual, or it can refer to the determined effort to improve and expand upon that public image. It is the foundation of all advertising and political campaigns. Often a company seeking to improve its image or expand its influence will employ special public relations personnel to arrange news releases and press conferences, cultivate community

awareness and friendly associations with banks, newspapers, local business, and political officials. Often referred to as PR.

Public utility

A company which supplies some necessary service to the general public, such as telephones, electricity, water, gas and sewers. Most utilities operate as monopolies and are under government regulations. Since these services have a continuing demand as the population grows and living standards rise, they are usually considered very safe and stable investments. During the economic slump of 1973-74, utilities and banks both tested our traditional belief in the unquestioned safety of these securities. Now more investors feel the need to investigate *any* kind of investment candidate before buying.

Publicly owned corporation

A company owned by a number of people who have bought shares of its capital stock. It is unclear how many shareholders are required to constitute public. The number can vary from two on up, depending upon what regulation you are complying with. Some regulations refer to a corporation as private if there are less than 15 investors. In other places, private means up to 25 investors. Disregarding regulations, a commonly applied definition calls a corporation public if its shares are traded on the open market, however limited the market may be. All listed stocks and over-the-counter stocks represent publicly owned corporations. See REGULATION A and PUBLIC OFFERINGS for more information. Also see PRIVATELY OWNED CORPORATIONS and PRIVATE OFFERINGS for contrast.

Purchase and sale memorandum

A form mailed to commodity traders after a transaction listing financial information about the trade. It is the commodities exchange equivalent of a stock market transaction slip.

Put

An option to sell a stock at a given price within a given time. If the price of the stock goes down, the holder of the put may exercise his option for a profit. A put obligates the seller of the contract to take delivery of the stock and pay the holder of the option the specified price. The amount of profit to the holder of the put option is the difference between the market price and the contract price minus the fee paid for the option. If the market price rises and the option holder chooses not to exercise his option, he then forfeits the price he paid for the option.

Often puts and calls are mentioned simultaneously, since they both refer to the purchase of an option for a future transaction. The call is opposite to a put. See separate listings for CALL, STRIP, STRAP, and STRADDLE for other forms of option contracts that are traded.

Pyramid

1. In investments the term applies to reinvesting profits and using the maximum buying power in margin accounts. Sometimes it describes the practice of buying additional shares of a security you already own if that stock is rising in market value. This is an aggressive and perfectly legal investment practice.

2. There is, however, another illegal practice that uses the same term. In this case an overly aggressive

person establishes a business which is usually a direct sales type operation and sells franchises and licenses to other individuals, who in turn recruit other investors to take sub-franchises and sub-licenses. The program is always based on a product or service which may be very good, but all efforts are spent in recruiting in order to earn overrides and commissions from those lower in the structure. Each new salesman is cultivated as a sub-franchisee who will recruit more like himself. The only profits usually come from sales of franchises or inventory to sales persons, and the only winners are the founders of the scheme.

$\mathcal{Q}$

Quick assets

Current assets minus inventory. Generally it amounts to cash on hand plus government securities held, plus accounts receivable. Quick assets, as the name implies, are part of a quick method of judging a company's liquidity or financial resistance to sudden economic disturbances. See QUICK RATIO for more information.

Quick ratio

A ratio of financial data that is considered a fast way to measure the liquidity, and, therefore, the financial strength of a company. It is formed by deducting the inventory from current assets, then comparing to current liabilities. Another term for quick ratio is acid test. In 1974, the quick ratio of all manufacturers was .91. In more normal times it is considered alarming if the ratio falls below 1. In 1955, the average of all manufacturers was 1.36.

Quotation

The same as a quote. The highest bid to buy and the lowest offer to sell a given security in a given market at a given time. The difference between the two is the spread. A quote is a firm price for buying or selling. If the prices are stated "The market is . . .," it means that the prices are approximately as stated, but the prices are not firm. Further checking would be required to get a quote. Also see INDICATED MARKET, SUBJECT MARKET, and ESTIMATED MARKET for contrast.

Quotation board

A large display board in a brokerage office where daily prices are posted in selected securities. It can be electronically operated and show successive trades as they occur, or they can use clip-on numbers changed manually. Some offices will even use a chalk board. Prices shown are often the open, high, low, and close of the previous day.

Quote

Also called a quotation. A firm price for both buying and selling a security. A dealer quoting a given stock at 21½ to 22 is saying that he will buy that security from anyone at 21½ or will sell from his own account to anyone at 22. When a dealer gives a quote he is obligated to buy or sell at least 100 shares from anyone requesting the quote. Usually the dealer will be able to handle much larger quantities if requested. Bid and asked prices are also called a quote. If a dealer does not want to be obligated to trade at the prices he gives, he will say "The market is 21½ to 22," or he may call it the indicated market, estimated market, or subject market.

Quoting machines

Any of several machines used to secure information about stocks. They are desk top devices that can give electronic readout of open, high, low, closing prices, latest trade, volume, earnings, and other information on thousands of stocks traded on national exchanges and over-the-counter. Some of the machines used are Video Master, Quotron, Telequote, and Ultronic Stockmaster. Other devices are designed to give a continuous display of ticker tape transactions or updated information on selected stocks. Some of these are Lectrascan, Teleregister, and Translux. See separate listings for each device.

Quotron

An electronic stock quotation device which supplies market data to brokers and dealers. It looks like a calculator with many buttons, and, with the right combination of buttons pressed, it will print out information on a narrow tape concerning stock prices, earnings, dividend rate, yield, price earnings ratios, and trading volume on all listed stocks for the New York Stock Exchange, and American Exchange, plus 1500 over-the-counter stocks. Also see VIDEO-MASTER, TELEQUOTE, and ULTRONIC STOCK-MASTER. Other automatic devices which give a continuous display are LECTRASCAN, TELE-REGISTER, and TRANSLUX. See separate listings for each.

R

ROI

Return on investment. The amount of annual pre-tax profit from any investment stated as a percentage of the original purchase price. The term is most often used to describe earnings for investors who own a majority of the equity of a particular enterprise. If the investor owns only a small portion of the equity, he may refer to the "yield" on the securities he owns, rather than return on investment.

R & D

Research and development. The efforts of a company to find and develop new materials, processes, products, and even new uses for some known products. It is a behind-the-scenes portion of most businesses which is sometimes looked upon as a frill. R & D is, in reality, the father of practically every product, service, and nugget of knowledge we enjoy in a modern world.

Raider
An enterprising person or organization which buys control of a company in order to milk it of assets, profits and perhaps personnel which are then legally or illegally channeled into other ventures controlled by the raider. They have little concern for the successful operation of the acquired company. The term is not used to describe acquisitions which produce mutual benefit.

Railroads or rails
The market quotations of the Dow Jones Index for a selected group of railroad stocks. Now called transportation averages. Originally based on stock averages for 20 railroads. Half of these have since been dropped and replaced by trucking companies and shipping lines, hence the new designation transportation stocks. There are other indexes using a composite of the entire transportation industry. See TRANSPORTATION, UTILITIES, and INDUSTRIALS for additional information.

Rally
A brisk rise following a decline or inactive period in the general price level of the stock market as a whole, or in an individual stock. The sequence of conditions is as described: the decline is stopped by an up reversal, then a rally is the brief rising period following the up reversal. If the rally continues a few weeks it is called a market turnaround (compared to the prior decline). If it continues for several months, it is called an up market or an uptrend. If it continues many months it is called a recovery. If a recovery moves strongly above previous highs, it becomes a bull market. See STOCK CHARTS for illustrated chart patterns.

Random walk theory

A theory which states that, since the stock market is an auction, the prices are based on what people know at the time. Prices and events of previous days are said to have no effect on today's prices. It is a fatalistic resignation to forget all that had preceded and take the same chance that everyone else is assumed to take. The theory is an extremely inefficient and lazy way to handle investments, yet it has been named the efficient market theory, which only proves that, if men are left alone long enough, they can rationalize anything. It is a theory that offers intellectual exercise in conversation or written commentary, but is ignored by all serious investors.

Rating of securities

1. The activity of assigning relative ranking to securities based on their history and risk. The terms rating, grading and ranking are used interchangeably, but at times certain words are preferred. For example, people speak of high *grade* bonds, but at other times they may say that *Moody's* has lowered their *rating* on a certain bond.

2. Various advisory firms have their own systems for grading or ranking stocks and bonds. *Standard and Poor's Corporation* provides a rating system with very wide acceptance. They stress that such grading does not evaluate a security for the purpose of recommendation for buying or selling the security, but rather the gradings represent financial strength or stability. Their grading of common stock is based on earnings, dividends, rate of growth and consistency in dividend payout over a period of eight years or more. These gradings by *Standard and Poor's* for common stock are as follows:

A + highest	B + average
A high	B below average
A- above average	B- low
	C lowest

Standard and Poor's ratings for preferred stock are intended to imply a stability in yield and safety of investment. These ratings are:

AAA prime	BBB medium grade
AA high grade	BB lower grade
A sound	B speculative
	C sub-marginal

3. *Standard and Poor's* bond ratings are similar and are based on management performance, reflecting financial resources, earnings of company, debt ratios and the like. These ratings in declining rank are:

AAA	BB
AA	B
A	CCC
BBB	CC
	C

Moody's provides bond ratings, also, but base them on maturity, yield, and other factors to indicate risk. These ratings in declining rank are:

Aaa	Ba
Aa	B
A	Caa
Baa	Ca
	C

There are times when a low grade stock is so under-priced that it becomes a good investment for growth without regard for income. Also a high grade stock which may be very stable in income may be comparatively over-priced, so that a loss on market price could cancel out earnings yield. Careful analysis is always wise before investment.

Ratio analysis

A method of analyzing the performance of a company or the market in general through ratios of data found on balance sheets and income statements. Some ratios used are sales to earnings, sales to inventory, sales to capitalization, sales to payroll, sales to administrative costs, sales to material costs, earnings to capitalization, earnings to debt.

Ratio chart

A logarithmic chart that can show proportional changes. See STOCK CHARTS for comparisons and explanations of their use. Samples are also shown for various types of charts.

Ratios

A method for rapid evaluation of a company. Various bits of statistical data are compared by dividing one by another to produce the ratio. The ratios are then measured against other companies or against an industry average to indicate the strength of any particular company. Some of the ratios that are the most commonly used are:

Collection period
Current assets less inventory to liabilities
   (Quick ratio)
Current assets to current liabilities (Current ratio)
Funded debts to net working capital
Market price to annual earnings per share
   (P E ratio)

Net profits on net sales
Net profits on net working capital
Net sales to net working capital

Other ratios that are not quite as common but have value are:

Bond coverage
Current debt to inventory
Current debt to tangible net worth
Fixed assets to tangible net worth
Inventory to net working capital
Inventory turnover
Net profits on tangible net worth
Net sales to inventory
Net sales to tangible net worth
Total debt to tangible net worth
Turnover of net working capital
Turnover of tangible net worth

See each ratio listed elsewhere in the dictionary with expanded definition and average figures for each ratio.

Reaction

Any movement of a stock price that is contrary to a previous sharp or prolonged move. The theory behind the term is that the strong previous move up or down carried a bit too far simply from inertia so a rebound is easing the pressure which was building up. It is a stock market term for the tendency for all forces to seek a normal stability. A pronounced departure from normal must in time return toward normal.

Realizing

Another term for receiving something that is due. A gain in the value of a security is a paper profit or unrealized profit until the security is sold; then it becomes a real profit or realized profit which is taxable. The same term applies to losses when converting a paper loss to a real loss. Also see PROFIT TAKING.

Recapitalizations

Changing the financial structure of a company, usually by adding more capital. It is often accomplished by selling additional stock or bonds but sometimes by capital donations by existing shareholders. See NEW ISSUE, CLASSIFIED STOCK, DILUTION, and PREFERENCE STOCK for more information. Notice the sharp distinction between the terms RECAPITALIZATION and REORGANIZATION, which is a form of bankruptcy.

Receding market

Falling prices for stocks in general. Usually indicated by falling Dow Jones Industrial averages. Also called a bear market, a down market, falling market or a slump. The declining prices reflect a lack of interest by investors which can result from declining profits, higher materials costs, higher interest rates, higher taxes, declining demand for products, national political uncertainty, international unrest, or even mere rumors.

Receivables

The amount of money due from any outside sources for goods shipped or services performed. A manufacturing company may ship goods to retail outlets and not receive payment for the goods for 30 days or more. The retail outlet may receive installment payments for goods sold, or it may sell its accounts to a finance company. It is a receivable until complete payment is received from some source.

Receiver's certificate

Certificates of deposit which represent stock or bonds of a company in receivership. They are traded on the open market at prices which represent the receiver's evaluation of the securities they represent.

Receivership

A form of bankruptcy. It is the operation of a business during reorganization, by a trustee appointed by a court. The trustee, called a receiver, attempts to solve the financial difficulties of a company while under court protection from creditors. If difficulties are too severe, the receiver may liquidate the firm, which usually results in creditors getting only a small portion of the money due them. Also see BANKRUPTCY.

Recession

A wide spread economic downturn accompanied by lay offs, high interest rates, lowering stock prices, reduced corporate profits. Recession is a period of hardship for many and belt tightening for all, but not a calamity like a full depression. Some economists have established a standard of measurement which classifies an economic recession as a period during which the gross national product index declines two quarters in succession.

Record date

Date on which you must be registered as a shareholder in order to receive a declared dividend. If shares have changed hands, the dividend is paid to the owner of record, or the person whose name was on record on that specified date. Notice the difference from payment date which is the date on which dividend checks are mailed to shareholders. This date will be sometime after the record date.

Recovery

An extended period following a long market decline during which the general trend of market prices is upward. By contrast, a short period of rising market prices would be called a reversal or up reversal. If the up reversal continues several weeks, it is then known as a rally. After a rally continues for several months, it becomes a recovery. If the recovery reaches a level that is considered normal but continues to climb, it is then a bull market, or even a boom.

Red herring

A preliminary prospectus. It gives information concerning a forthcoming issue of stock before the final approval by the SEC. This prospectus may not reveal the offering price or cannot even be used as an offer to sell. When the final prospectus is distributed, the red herring prospectus must be returned.

The red herring prospectus must be submitted to the SEC for clearance before distribution, just the same as the final offering prospectus. See PROSPECTUS for more information.

Redeem

It means literally to buy back. Bond holders turn in their bonds at maturity to be redeemed by the company. The company then pays the face value amount to the bond holder. Some bonds can be called in early for early redemption.

Redeemable bond

Another name for callable bond, one that may be called in before maturity for repayment. Early redemption is possible only on issues that were so arranged at the time of issue. An exception to this is the event of reorganization, during which the issuing company may offer to exchange some combination of new securities for the original issue. Such a move must be approved by the bond holders themselves. See BONDS for other types of bonds and comparisons between them.

Redemption

Paying off corporate bonds or retiring stock which is called in for repurchase. Each issue will have indentures or contract terms, which state the conditions of time and price at which the issue may be recalled for redemption or conversion if that privilege has been planned.

Redemption price

1. The price at which a bond may be redeemed before maturity at the option of the issuer.
2. The payment that a shareholder of mutual fund shares receives when he sells his shares back to the fund. The net asset value. Also called liquidating price or repurchase price.

Rediscount rate

Usually called federal discount rate or simply discount rate. It is the rate of interest paid by member banks when they borrow from the Federal Reserve System. The rediscount term is used because there may be a two stage transaction between the Federal Reserve and the commercial customer. A corporation may borrow $100,000 from the bank agreeing to pay 8½% which may be in the form of a discount, yielding the customer only $91,500. The bank then takes the $100,000 note to the Federal Reserve to borrow against it. The bank must pay the rediscount rate of perhaps 7%, so they receive only $93,000. The bank thus receives an immediate profit of $1,500 and then repays its loan as payments are received from its corporate customer.

Refinancing

In corporate finance it is using the proceeds of a new issue of bonds or stock to pay off existing debts or to extend the maturity of outstanding loans. In effect, it is only delaying the final payoff. Notice the sharp distinction from the term reorganization which is a form of bankruptcy.

Refunding

Also called refinancing. In corporate activities it has nothing to do with paying back money, rather, it is the renewing of pledges to investors. When refunding, a company will issue new debt securities (bonds) to replace an issue that is falling due for redemption. It is regular practice by the Federal government, which almost continuously offers new securities. See TREASURY BILLS, BONDS, NOTES, and CERTIFICATES.

Regional exchanges

Security exchanges which deal in the newer, unseasoned issues, or local issues. The regional exchanges are important, but handle a very small portion of the security trading conducted in the U.S. All the regional exchanges combined do less volume than the

American Exchange, which in itself does less than 15% of the volume of the New York Stock Exchange. Some of the regional exchanges are as follows:
Boston Stock Exchange
Chicago Board of Trade
Cincinnati Stock Exchange
Detroit Stock Exchange
Midwest Stock Exchange (In Chicago)
National Stock Exchange (In New York)
Pacific Coast Exchange (Los Angeles and San Francisco)
Philadelphia - Baltimore - Washington Stock Exchange
Pittsburgh Stock Exchange
San Francisco Mining Exchange
Spokane Stock Exchange

All exchanges require membership from any broker or dealer who desires to trade on the exchange floor. See exchange SEATS for explanation of memberships. Also see NEW YORK STOCK EXCHANGE for description of typical exchange and TRADING FLOOR for explanation of the operation of an exchange.

Regional funds

Mutual funds that have a policy of investment in securities of a specific geographical area such as the West Coast, Florida, and the Midwest. See INVESTMENT COMPANIES for other types of funds and descriptions of each. Also see INVESTMENT COMPANY ACT OF 1940 for definitions, purposes, and limitations.

Register

1. To submit a new issue of a security to the SEC or state agencies in preparation for offering it to the

public. See REGISTRATION for more information.

2. To record the names of shareholders on the books of a corporation. Usually done by the registrar or transfer agent, which may be a bank or other party acting for the corporation.

Registered bond

A bond which is registered like stock on the corporate books in the name of the holder. It can be transferred only by the endorsement of its registered owner. Some other bonds are negotiable, which means that they belong to any person who holds them. See BONDS for other types of bonds and comparisons between them.

Registered investment company

Another term for regulated investment company, mutual fund, or investment trust. See INVESTMENT COMPANIES for other types of funds and descriptions of each. Also see INVESTMENT COMPANY ACT OF 1940 for definitions, purposes, and limitations.

Registered representative

A representative of a broker or dealer who handles security trading orders for the investor. He is trained and licensed by the NASD and state agencies to sell securities. He is also referred to as an account executive, a customer's broker, or a customer's man. Although technically not correct, most people refer to him as "my broker."

Registered stock

Stock which has been properly submitted to the state agencies or Securities Exchange Commission (SEC) with all pertinent information for evaluation and approval before being sold to the public. Some small or restricted stock offerings do not have to be registered but they have limitations as to where they may be sold and how one may purchase them. See PRIVATE OFFERINGS, PUBLIC OFFERINGS and REGULATION A offerings for differences. Also see STOCK for listings of different types of stock.

Registered trader

A member of a stock exchange who trades in stocks on the floor of the exchange for an account in which he has an interest. A floor trader.

Registrar

Usually a trust company or bank charged with the responsibility of the issuance of the proper amount of stock authorized and sold to investors by a corporation. Any time shares are traded after the original issue, the registrar cancels the old stock certificates and issues new ones to the new owners.

Registration

In general, registration means to comply with all the requirements of the Securities Act of 1933 when preparing any public offering of securities. Before a public offering of any security may be made, the security must be registered with the Securities Exchange Commission (SEC). It must disclose all pertinent information related to the company, its management, and the purposes of the offering. Registration is the process of submitting for and receiving approval of the request for offering the security to the public. Certain small offerings, involving only a limited number of purchasers and limited to residents of the state in which the corporation operates, are exempt from SEC registration. Generally these are subject to Blue Sky Laws of that state. See PUBLIC OFFERINGS, PRIVATE OF-FERINGS, and REGULATION A offerings.

Regular way delivery

Unless otherwise specified, securities (other than government) sold on the New York Stock Exchange are to be delivered to the buyer and payment made to the seller by the fifth business day after the transaction. Most securities are sold regular way. In some cases, however, for tax purposes or other reasons a trade may be made under seller's option, which gives the seller the right to make delivery any time within a specified period ranging from 5 to 60 days.

Regulated investment companies

Companies organized for the purpose of investing money for other people. The funds are obtained by selling shares of the investment company to the public. The proceeds of the sale of stock may then be invested in any manner desired, consistent with the company's charter and subject to regulations of the Investment Company Act of 1940. At least 90% of the profits of the investment company must be distributed to its shareholders. Most investment companies are called mutual funds and investment trusts. Hedge funds are one type that are not a mutual fund. They may be open end or closed end investment companies and may be front end load or no-load companies. See INVEST-MENT COMPANIES for a list of other types of funds and descriptions of each. Also see INVESTMENT COMPANY ACT OF 1940 for definitions, purposes, and limitations.

Regulation A
A federal regulation applying to the registration of securities offerings totaling more than $50,000, but less than $300,000. The regulation requires the use of a prospectus to describe the security and the company, but it is much less complicated than the registration requirements for a *public* offering of more than $300,000. This type issue is commonly called a Regulation A offering. For those issues less than $50,000 in total value, the company will file a simple Form 6 or some other state-oriented document, and no prospectus is required.

Regulation Q
A regulation of the Federal Reserve Board which sets the maximum interest rates that member banks may pay on savings accounts.

Regulation T
A federal regulation which governs the amount of credit which may be advanced by a broker or dealer to his customers for the purchase of securities. This credit regulation is referred to as the margin requirements and may be adjusted from time to time, depending upon the need to relax or tighten investment credit, as determined by the Federal Reserve Board. For example, if margin requirements are 50%, investors would have to put up at least half the cost of any securities purchased on margin. Then, if the Federal Reserve Board determines that investment attitudes are becoming relaxed and too speculative, they may raise margin requirements as required by regulation T, so that investors may have to put up 70% of the purchase price.

Regulation U
A federal regulation which governs the amount of credit which may be advanced by a bank to its customers for the purchase of listed stocks. See MARGIN for credit buying of securities.

Reinvestment
An arrangement under which a mutual fund will apply dividends or capital gains distributions for its shareholders toward the purchase of additional shares for growth in the shareholder's investment if it is left in the fund for a number of years. Such arrangements are also called dividend reinvestment plans, cumulative agreements, or systematic investment plans. A fund offering such plans is called a full service fund. Note the difference from a fully managed fund. See *special features* under the heading INVESTMENT COMPANIES for more information.

Reorganization
It is a form of bankruptcy, a change in the financial structure and operation of a corporation which is having financial difficulties. Management is replaced and trustees are appointed by the court to reorganize operations and attempt to recover business profitability. This is known as Chapter 10 bankruptcy. There are several other forms of bankruptcy which can be used if court directed reorganization is not required. See BANKRUPTCY for variations. Also notice the sharp distinction from REFINANCING and RECAPITALIZATION, which are plans for issuance of new securities for expansion or extension of debt.

Repurchase
Redeeming, redemption, or buying back of shares

from an investor by an issuer. This is the only way a shareholder of mutual fund shares may liquidate his fund shares.

Research

1. In industry and science, research means a systematic study and investigation of some field of knowledge in order to learn or establish new facts and develop new products or services from the facts.

2. In the securities market, research is the study of printed data and news about specific companies or market influences. It is assumed that accuracy in predicting market moves is related to the quantity, accuracy, appropriateness, and timeliness of the information gathered.

Industrial research can be carried as a budgeted expense item on accounting records, or, in some cases, it is amortized off over a period of years if the costs can be identified with specific products.

Reserve requirements

The amount of money member banks of the Federal Reserve System must have in cash or on deposit with the Federal Reserve based on the amount of the bank's demand deposits. This requirement, stated as a percentage of total deposits, may vary from time to time as the Reserve Board determines the need. Note the difference from the meaning of the single word RESERVES used by other businesses.

Reserves

An accounting term used on a corporation's balance sheet to define an amount of cash set aside to meet unforeseen needs such as uncollectable accounts, additional taxes, pending law suits, damage, or loss in foreign countries due to political instabilities. The funds are drawn from earned surplus or retained earnings and on the financial records will be shown as a transfer from the asset column to the liability column. Note the difference from the term reserve requirements, which refers to a bank's reserves.

Resistance line

Some technical analysts or chartists draw a dotted line across their charts connecting previous highs. If a price rise is strong enough to break through that line of resistance the chartists believe it is strong enough to establish a new trend upward . . . hence, a signal to buy. Also see SUPPORT LINE and TREND LINE for similar interpretive devices and STOCK CHARTS for sample charts showing many different chart patterns, signals, and interpretations.

Retained earnings

The amount of money retained by a company out of its net earnings for expansion of the business after having paid all taxes, bond interest, and all dividends to shareholders. This is the portion of profits that is plowed back into the business for growth. Retained earnings are also called earnings surplus or simply surplus. Note the difference from capital surplus or paid-in surplus, which is part of the original investment which produced the earnings.

Retired stock

Stock that has been repurchased by a company and formally removed from the list of authorized shares by action of the board of directors. Retiring stock has the effect of reducing the breadth of the market for a security and increasing the book value per share. It can no longer be sold or distributed by the company, unlike treasury stock, which is often used for acquisitions and stock option plans. See STOCK for a list of different types of stock.

Retirement
In the investment field this refers to withdrawing a security from circulation so that it will never be sold again. When a bond is redeemed, it is paid off and retired. Preference stock may sometimes be called and retired, which means the issuer repurchases it. Occasionally a company will repurchase some of its common stock on the open market. It may then hold it as treasury stock for use later in acquisitions or executive bonus plans, or it may retire those shares permanently in order to increase the book value per share of outstanding stock and probably cause a market price increase as well.

Return
Dividends or interest earned by holders of securities. It is also called yield and is stated as a *percentage of the market price* of the security. Notice the difference from coupon rate or stated rate, which is the income earned on the security stated as a *percentage of the par value* or face value of the security. Since the market value can fluctuate, the yield rate can be quite different from the rate of return on investment, although some people reserve the term return on investment for application only where the investor, either corporate or individual, owns a major portion of the enterprise.

Return of capital
A payment of cash to shareholders which is specified

as a return of a portion of the original investment and not a dividend from earnings. It will show on the books as a reduction in capital surplus. It is non-taxable as a dividend but must be applied to reduce the original cost of the security, which will result in an increase of the capital gain when the security is sold. It is also called a tax-free or non-taxable dividend and is sometimes used to satisfy dividend-seeking shareholders when earnings do not justify payment.

Along with the psychological advantage in paying tax-free dividends, there is also a real advantage. It substitutes a long term gain (from increase in *effective* growth in market value) for a short term gain (the regular dividend it replaces).

Return on investment
The amount of annual pre-tax profit from any investment stated as a percentage of the original purchase price. The term is most often used to describe earnings for investors who own a majority of the equity of a particular enterprise. If the investor owns only a small portion of the equity, he may refer to the "yield" on the securities he owns, rather than return on investment.

Revaluation
Adjusting the value of a currency upward, the opposite of devaluation. Such a readjustment in values would occur in an effort to offset international trade imbalance by increasing incentives for exporting and decreasing imports. The move would have little effect on business within the nation, but international currency exchange rates would be adjusted.

Revenue bond
Bonds issued for special projects like toll roads,

bridges, transit systems, and sewers, where the income generated by the facility is used to pay the interest. Revenue bonds are usually some type of municipal bond. Also see BONDS for other types of bonds and comparisons between them.

Revenues
The term applied to the total amount of money received from all sources by a service type industry, such as a utility or airline company. It is comparable to the term gross sales used by a manufacturing company. There are times when the terms are used interchangeably without regard to the type of company. There are times when the term cash flow has been used to mean revenue, but usually cash flow suggests an accounting of money from all sources and its use for various operations.

Reversal
Any change in the *near term* trend of market prices. Day to day changes are called fluctuation of prices, but a steady rise or decline for several days or several weeks becomes a near term trend. It is common for charts to show market price cycles of alternate up reversals and down reversals with the cycles extending from a few weeks to a few months. Reversals usually apply to the early portion of a cycle. For instance, a secondary wave may last only a week, so the reversal which started the cycle may be applied to two or three days of the move. A primary wave may continue six weeks, so the reversal which started it may apply to several weeks on the chart. Some changes that last longer are described as turnaround, bottoming out, topping out, rally, and recovery. See PATTERNS for a list of chart patterns that give meaning to analysts and

STOCK CHARTS for samples of charts with typical patterns and conditions shown.

Reverse split
The process of calling in unattractively low priced shares to be replaced by a smaller number of higher priced shares. All shareholders continue to hold their correct proportion of equity but have fewer shares. As an example, a company whose shares are trading at $4 may feel that $20 shares would be more marketable, so they carry out a 1 for 5 reverse split. An investor who previously had 1,000 shares for a $4,000 total market value will now have only 200 shares with a $4,000 total market value.

Rigging
An illegal practice of manipulation of stock prices by wash sales, matched orders, or publicizing false information.

Rights
Privileges given to shareholders of a corporation at a time when a new offering is being made to the public to purchase a specified number of the new securities in order to keep their equity position unchanged. Usually they are offered at a price under the existing market prices. These rights have value, so that if a person holding rights is unable or unwilling to exercise those rights, he may sell them to another party. Also called subscription rights. Rights usually expire in a month or so. Warrants are similar to rights, except that the life of a warrant may run a number of months or years, even perpetually. Also notice differences from OPTIONS.

Rights offering

A new stock offering made only to *existing* shareholders. The new issue offers shareholders additional shares in proportion to their existing stock as of a specified date, called the record date. Anyone becoming a shareholder after that record date is not elegible for the rights being offered. Any unsubscribed shares are then re-offered to the remaining shareholders.

Risk

Uncertainty of future events, values, income, markets, or influences, or the chance of loss. Often calculated in percentage of probability. Investment and financial risks arise from several areas of uncertainty, some of which are as follows:

1. Financial uncertainty: Also called business risk. Possibility of changes occurring in the company issuing the security.

2. Interest rate uncertainty: Rates may change company earnings, and payout or market prices may change due to changing interest rates.

3. Market uncertainty: Price changes due to investor attitudes.

4. Political uncertainties: Revolution, devaluation, nationalization of industry, or other national policy may limit, reduce or eliminate possessions or resources.

5. Purchasing power uncertainties: Changing market prices and exchange rates make values of investments or reserves uncertain.

6. Social uncertainties: Shifting public attitudes strongly influence markets and market values.

Risks and uncertainties abound in every activity and

ambition of man. The manner in which a person handles the risks indicates the character of the person and ultimately determines the results achieved. There are three ways to handle risk:

1. Blindly offering one's resources to the whim of chance with the hope of receiving gain, which is called *gambling*.
2. Studying the alternatives and selecting a course of increased probability of success, which is taking a *calculated risk*.
3. Calculating the risks and applying diligence to direct a course through areas of uncertainty, which is called *enterprise*.

Risk capital

Money invested in stock, also called equity capital. It is called risk because in the event of failure in the business, the investor may lose part or all of his investment. Bond money is not called risk capital, but debt financing, although a failure could wipe out that investment as well. There is no investment or device for preservation of our money that is completely free of risk, not even savings deposits, government bonds, or a coffee can buried in the ground. See VENTURE CAPITAL, a specific kind of risk capital and DEBT CAPITAL, which is more secure. Compare with EQUITY CAPITAL.

Roll over

Concerning bond investments, it is the practice of reinvesting the proceeds of bond redemption in a new issue of identical type. For example, an investor may have a given amount of money in government bonds maturing in 10 years. At the maturity of these bonds he may purchase an identical quantity of new government bonds. These have the same effect of perpetual bonds or annuity bonds, except that the interest rates may vary on the different issues purchased at different times.

Round lot

A unit of trading which usually consists of 100 shares. The round lot is contrasted to the odd-lot, or normally any number less than 100 shares, and the block, or units of 10,000 shares or more. There are a few inactively traded stocks which are traded in units of 10, 25, or 50 shares. These are handled on the exchange floor at the inactive post or post 30.

The typical broker or dealer will handle only round lot orders through his own firm. If he receives an odd-lot order, he will take it to an odd-lot dealer to be traded. That will add a small additional fee (typically 1/8 to 1/4 point) which is based on the price of the stock, and, more importantly, on the market for the stock. If a broker receives an order for 375 shares, it would be handled as 3 round lots and 1 odd lot of 75 shares.

Round trip

In the stock market a round trip is a complete cycle in a securities trade, or buying a security and later selling out the same shares. The term also applies to short selling and then covering those same shares. The round trip term has no consideration of time between purchase and sale. Also called in-and-out trading or two-way trading.

Round turn

Two cancelling transactions which involve both the purchase and sale of a commodity futures contract. The purchase may occur on the same day as the sale, or it may be separated by months. The round turn in commodities is the equivalent of a round trip in stock trading.

Round turn commission

A single commission on the commodities exchange which covers both the purchase and sale of a commodities contract. All commodities contracts expire on given dates that never extend more than 18 months beyond issue date. Many may call for delivery within a few weeks after the purchase date. Since the resale of a contract is certain, and the average contract may be traded within days after the original purchase, the commodities commissions are applied only at the time of the sale (close out of a position).

Royalty

Payment to an investor, designer, author, or prominent person for the use of his product or his public image. Compensation may be a one time payment, or it can be in terms of percentages of sales, frequency of usage, or a combination acceptable to all parties involved.

Rule of 78

A system of calculating interest refunds so that the amount of refund is less than the amount of interest paid for the same period. The method is also called sum-of-the-digits because of the method of calculation. The months are numbered 1, 2, 3, 4, 5, and so on up to 12 for the twelve months in a year. These digits are then totaled to yield 78 points for a year. Usually, on consumer loans, the interest is charged on an add-on basis, which charges the full rate of interest for the full principal for the full life of the loan. If an early pay-off is made, the last month is given credit for 1 point, the 11th month is 2 points, the 10th month is 3, and so on. A 3 month refund then gets a total of 6 points out of 78 or 6/78 of the total amount paid in. See INTEREST for other methods of charging interest and for comparative examples showing the actual cost on a sample loan subject to the different types of interest.

S

S D R's

Special drawing rights, commonly called paper gold. They consist of created assets or credits in the International Monetary Fund which member nations may draw upon as if they were actual gold deposits. These credits are used to facilitate exchanges in international trade.

S E C

The Securities Exchange Commission, an independent federal agency, established to protect investors by supervision of investment trading activities. Among the acts of Congress interpreted and administered by the SEC are The Securities Act of 1933, the Securities Exchange Act of 1934, the Trust Indenture Act, the Investment Company Act of 1940, the Investment Advisors Act, and Public Utility Holding Company Act. Corporations wishing to sell stock to the public must register the security with the SEC. The process is quite involved and requires a great deal of information to be published about the company, its officers, and the plans for the proceeds of the sale. The "non-approval" that the SEC gives in no way guarantees that the company is sound, successful or even ethical. It merely says that apparently all pertinent facts have been disclosed.

SOP

Statement of policy. A formal set of standards issued by the Securities Exchange Commission to which all investment companies must comply. The statement of policy, often referred to as the SOP, requires a very careful, conservative approach to the sales of mutual fund shares. It has eighteen sections which, in general, require the following:

1. Sales presentation must make a complete explanation of the risks involved.

2. Implication of future performance based on past performance or in comparison to any other industry is forbidden.

3. Unqualified reference to regulations, or comparison to other securities or industries to imply that there is any safety or growth in mutual funds is forbidden.

4. Full disclosure of costs and possible loss at the time of redemption or from switching accounts into another type of fund is required.

5. Rigid standards must be followed for preparation of any performance charts, and presentation of them must not imply anything other than what has actually happened in the past. Charts must be complete for the most recent 10 years, or for the

entire life of the fund if less than 10 years old.

6. No material, either printed or oral, may be used for sales presentation which has not been cleared by the Securities Exchange Commission for sales use.

7. An overall, careful, conservative approach must be followed in sales efforts for all mutual funds.

See INVESTMENT COMPANY ACT OF 1940 for more information on the limitations, purposes, and definitions of mutual funds. See INVESTMENT COMPANIES for more information and comparisons between a number of investment companies.

Safety of income

The measure of likelihood that the issuing company will be able to continue interest payments or dividend payments on a given security.

Safety of principal

The measure of likelihood that the initial investment in a stock will remain safe or free from adverse price movements, or that a bond will be redeemed at maturity.

Sales

1. On financial reports this usually refers to net sales or the gross receipts for all goods or services sold *less* any allowances, guarantee costs, shortages, or uncollectable accounts. At times there is a distinction of terms, so that the term *sales* is used to describe the receipts from merchandise, and the word *revenues* is used to describe the receipts from services. The two different terms never appear on a single financial statement, but a company involved in manufacturing may use the word *sales*, and a

company involved in services like insurance will use the word *revenues*.

2. Another distinction occurs in the defining of operations. Sales and marketing are often used interchangeably, but marketing experts usually insist upon a delineation of responsibilities. These differences apply the word *sales* to activities oriented toward the *product*; demonstrating it, extolling its advantages, writing orders for it, etc. *Marketing*, then, is applied to activities directed toward the *customer*. It is a study of people; their needs, wants, reactions to various product differences, their income, employment, family size, distribution, habits, age brackets, etc. The marketing expert tries to find the best ways to reach the customer, and the salesman tries to convince the customer that he has just the right product for him.

Sally Mae
A popular nickname given to the Student Loan Marketing Association. This is a federally sponsored, private corporation formed to provide liquidity in a secondary market for student loans. In operation it loans money to universities and financial institutions, who re-loan the money to students. The government guarantees the repayment so that the lending institutions have incentive for making such loans. Also see FANNIE MAE, GINNIE MAE, and FREDDIE MAC. These are other government sponsored programs intended to provide liquidity and assistance in other financial areas.

Salvage value
The value expected or actually received for used

capital equipment after its useful life has expired, and all depreciation deductions have been claimed. In calculating depreciation, the expected salvage value is deducted from original cost, then the remaining depreciable cost is charged off against earnings each year by some approved method. If the equipment is still useful after all allowable depreciation is claimed, no further deductions are claimed. It is then called fully depreciated. When equipment is replaced, there may be a difference between the allowed salvage value and the actual price received for it. The adjustment is accounted for on the books and may result in a loss to charge off on income that is subject to taxes. See DEPRECIATION for various methods of charging off the amortized cost of equipment. Straight line depreciation and four methods for accelerated depreciation are shown.

Saucer
A pattern appearing on certain stock charts that has significance to some chart readers. The shape shows as a long, shallow, inactive period that eventually turns up. The longer the inactive period, the stronger the recovery is expected to be when it comes. If it climbs higher than the lip of the saucer, it is persumed to indicate a sure winner. See STOCK CHARTS for illustrated chart patterns.

Savings and loan company
A financial institution which sells savings shares for savings accounts and pays dividends in place of interest on these savings accounts. It reinvests its deposits in real estate loans, as do mutual savings banks.

Savings bonds

Bonds sold by the U. S. Treasury to individuals, usually in small amounts. Series E savings bonds are sold at discounts in minimum denominations of $25 and mature in seven to ten years. Series H bonds are sold in minimum denominations of $500 and mature in ten years with interest payments semi-annually. See GOVERNMENT BONDS for other types of government securities and BONDS for comparison to industrial bonds.

Scale order

An order issued by an investor to his broker to buy or sell a certain number of shares of a given security at different price levels.

Scrip

A certificate exchangeable for stock or cash before a specified date after which it may have no value. Usually issued for fractions of shares in connection with a stock dividend or split or in reorganization of a company. Scrip has also been used by some retail businesses as a substitute for small change. The military forces have used it as a substitute for money for trade within the limits of a military base that is in a remote location. Normally, the use of scrip in lieu of money is illegal.

Seat

1. A traditional figure of speech for a membership on a security or commodity exchange. Price for a seat and admission requirements vary with demand and potential gain from having such a membership. They are sold on the open market and are negotiated between buyer and seller. Currently the

New York Exchange has 1366 seats, the American Exchange has 650 seats, and the Chicago Merchantile Exchange (commodity trading) has 500 seats. See EXCHANGE SEAT and MEMBER FIRM for more information.

2. The term is also used to refer to the membership of a Board of Directors of a corporation. It means the number of positions open to be filled. Board seats are filled by shareholder voting. See CUMULATIVE VOTING, NON-CUMULATIVE VOTING, and BOARD OF DIRECTORS for more information.

Secondary distribution

The re-distribution of a large block of stock sometime after its initial offer. This may result from the settling of an estate or a large corporation divesting itself of major holdings in another corporation. This is registered with the SEC, just as if it were a new issue and is offered at a fixed price somewhat near the current market price. It is sometimes referred to as a secondary offering, or simply as a secondary. Notice the difference from secondary market, which is an after market. See EXCHANGE DISTRIBUTION for handling of slightly smaller blocks of stock. Also see SPECIALIST BLOCK PURCHASE OR SALE and SPECIAL OFFERING OR BID.

Secondary market

1. The market of supply and demand for trading of a security on the open market after its initial offering is terminated. The term applied whether it is traded over-the-counter or on an exchange. Notice the difference from secondary distribution, which is re-registration.

2. The term has been used to describe a two step loan arrangement where the secondary level is the consumer, and the primary level is the lender who has borrowed the funds from another source.

Secondary reaction

A term describing a movement in stock prices opposite to the major trend. It is interpreted as a self-stabilizing force that tends to return market prices to realistic levels after they have departed strongly, due to some major disturbance.

Secondary wave

In the wave theory involved in the Optimal Analysis method of security analysis, the secondary wave is the smallest pattern shown on the chart. It represents the small changes in price that occur daily or over several days. Secondary waves on a stock chart represent the volatile emotional reactions of investors and do not indicate trends. See PRIMARY WAVE, FUNDAMENTAL WAVE, and OPTIMAL ANALYSIS for more information. Also see STOCK CHARTS for illustrated chart patterns.

Securities

Documents representing shares of ownership in a corporation (stock), or representing debt of the corporation to the owner of the security (bonds). The term security comes from the word secure, which means to guarantee or make safe. These documents then represent a legal claim to guarantee payment of debt or proof of a shared ownership. See STOCK or BONDS for more information on different forms of each type of security. Also compare JUNIOR SECURITIES, SENIOR SECURITIES, EQUITY SECURITIES, and DEBT SECURITIES.

Securities Act of 1933

An Act of Congress, which was enacted after the careless and speculative stock buying binge of the late 1920's, to protect investors. It primarily spells out the requirements for full disclosure during registration of a stock offering prior to public sale in its primary market (original issue). Some major points of the act are to require complete disclosure of all pertinent information about the company, its products, market, competition, financial structure, condition, obligations, management, major stockholders, any law suits, major contracts, new products, associations, and use of the proceeds of the offering. The Act defines private and public corporations, with varying limitations on each.

Securities Exchange Act of 1934

An Act of Congress intended to assist the Act of 1933 to protect investors. The main purpose is to regulate the trading of securities after they reach the secondary market (open market trading).

Securities Exchange Commission

Also called the SEC. An independent federal agency established to protect investors by supervision of investment trading activities. Among the acts of Congress interpreted and administered by the SEC are the Securities Act of 1933, the Securities Exchange Act of 1934, the Trust Indenture Act, the Investment Company Act of 1940, the Investment Advisors Act, and Public Utility Holding Company Act. Corporations wishing to sell stock to the public must register the security with the SEC. The process is quite involved and requires a great deal of information about the company, its officers, principal stockholders, its product and market, its financial status, the use of the proceeds of the offering, and special conditions of ownership of the stock. The SEC issues a "non-approval", which in no way guarantees that the company is sound, successful, or even ethical. It merely affirms that apparently all pertinent facts have been disclosed. The liability for complete disclosure still rests upon the registrant.

Security

1. In investments, a security is a document giving evidence of ownership rights such as stocks, bonds, mortgages, notes, etc. Notice that the term security includes bonds with stock, while equity includes only stock, both preferred and common. Stocks represent ownership *by* an investor, while bonds represent debt *to* an investor.

2. Property pledged as collateral for loans. It is possible to pledge any asset, such as real estate, equipment, stocks, bonds, cash, receivables, contract rights, or other intangibles, and even goodwill, such as the name or reputation of a well known and wealthy person.

3. The term is also used to suggest the prospect of financial safety in future years, as when discussing the security of a good job.

Seigniorage

The profit made by the government in marking coins at a higher value than the actual cost of their metal content. Sometimes used as a synonym for brassage. One of the reasons for holding the actual metal value below the face value is to discourage hoarding that would then cause shortages. Notice GRESHAM'S LAW which discusses the principle of hoarding.

Sell, sell order

The authorization by a shareholder for a broker to sell some specific number of shares of his stock. Very often the transaction is conducted in a telephone conversation with the broker. There are a number of different kinds of orders that have special significance to investors and brokers. Each of the following is listed under separate headings with definitions.

All or none	Hit the bid
Alternative order	Immediate or cancel
At market	Limit order
At the close only	Market order
At the opening only	Not held
Buy order	Open order
Contingent order	Percentage order
Cancel order	Stop limit
Day order	Stop loss
Discretionary order	Stop order
Do not reduce	Switch order
Either/or order	Time order
Fill or kill	Today order
Firm order	When, as and if
Good till cancelled	

Sell off

A period when the stock market undergoes falling prices due to heavy pressures to sell. For every seller there is a buyer, but since prices are on a "bid-asked" basis, selling pressure makes the seller more willing to accept what he can get, thus, the downward move. It is an important fact, too, that during declining markets many stocks that are offered for sale are not purchased by other investors, but by dealers who hold them in their own accounts until the market returns to a buying atmosphere.

Seller's market

Circumstances which by short supply or popular demand tend to cause buyers to be willing to pay whatever price is being asked for a product or service. Since the seller is likely to get prices in his favor, it is a seller's market. During periods known as seller's markets, the market prices tend to rise. The opposite is true in a buyer's market, where demand is slack. In this case the buyer may be able to negotiate lower prices for himself.

Seller's option

A special transaction on a stock exchange which gives the seller the right to deliver the stock or bond at any time within a specified period, usually ranging from five business days to not more than 60 days. Seller's option is a special arrangement devised to meet a specific need of the seller, such as tax considerations at the year's end. The delay may permit a delay in reporting taxable income. On the other hand, the selling price for a seller's option transaction may also afford the buyer a special price that is below the current market. Seller's option is not often used. Most securities are traded "regular way", which requires payment and delivery within five business days.

Selling against the box

A method of protecting a paper profit. Assume that you own 100 shares of XYZ which have advanced in price, and you think the price may decline. You may sell 100 shares short, borrowing the 100 shares to make delivery. You retain in your security account the 100 shares which you own. If XYZ advances, the loss on your short sale is exactly offset by the profit in the market value of the stock you have retained. You can close out your short sale by buying 100 shares to return to the person from whom you borrowed, or you can send them the 100 shares which you own. Your only cost is the commission on the transaction. This seems to be a pointless exercise, but it is a way of protecting one position for long term gains by offsetting a similar dollar amount of short term loss.

Selling concession

A group of brokers and dealers who assist the underwriters in the distribution of a new issue of stock. They work on a commission basis and do not share the liability of underwriting. Also called the selling group and participating brokers and dealers. Notice the difference from SYNDICATE, INVESTMENT BANKERS and UNDERWRITERS, who actually purchase the entire issue and then resell it to the public. See separate listings for each.

Selling group

A group of brokerage firms which join together in selling a new issue of some security. Also called participating brokers and dealers or selling concession as above. The purpose of the selling group is to assist the underwriters by trying to broaden the market for the security.

Selling on balance

A time when either an individual investor or the market in general is selling more securities than buying. This does not suggest selling out completely, but, rather, reducing the number of shares held. It does suggest a bearish attitude or doubts about the market. Since there must be a purchase for every sale, it seems contradictory that sales would outnumber purchases for a bearish trend. It is explained in two ways: many of the surplus shares accumulate in the accounts of specialists and dealers, also, the auction nature of the market will show heavier selling pressure than buying pressure, so prices will be declining in search of buyers.

Selling signal

A progression of prices as charted on a stock chart that exceeds what could be considered normal. It is read as an indication that self-stabilizing forces will soon take effect to cause a reversal in trend. Trading on such signals is "moving with the odds."

Several of such conditions are as follows:

1. A sharp climb in prices that continues several days, following a longer period of slowly rising prices.
2. A leveling of prices following a period of unusually strong price gains.
3. Any spike, which is a sharp jump of 20% or more in a single day.
4. A high point on a wave pattern that appears to duplicate the duration and intensity of several preceding waves. These signals should be interpreted in the light of fundamental conditions which may reveal reasons for some departure from normal chart patterns.

Also see BUYING SIGNALS, CHART PATTERNS, TREND LINES, TECHNICAL ANALYSIS, and OPTIMAL ANALYSIS for more discussion of stock chart interpretation, and see STOCK CHARTS for sample charts that illustrate many patterns.

Senior capital

The same as senior security. It will include preferred

stock and bonds. Notice the difference between related terms as follows:

Senior security: The same as senior capital, includes both bonds and preferred stock.

Senior equity: Preferred stock only. It represents equity, but ranks above common stock.

Junior equity: Common stock only

Equity: All forms of stock, both common and preferred, but excludes bonds which are debt.

Security: All stock and all bonds. The certificates issued for these securities represent invested capital and offer guarantees of various forms and degrees for the investor.

Capital: Invested money in all forms: stock, bonds, cash deposits, receivables, equipment, and facilities.

Senior equity

Preferred stock, contrasted to junior equity, which is common stock. The preferred position relates to its rank in the event of liquidation and distribution of assets of the issuing company. In spite of this preferred rank, it is only the common stock that has voting privileges. Notice that *equity* includes only stock and represents ownership of a company, but *security* includes bonds and stock with other obligations, since they all give evidence of responsibility of the issuer to investors.

Senior security

Any security that ranks above common stock in claims against the assets of an issuing corporation. This includes bonds with preferred stock. Notice that *security* includes both bonds and stock while *equity* refers only to stock, which is evidence of ownership.

Serial bonds

Bonds of a single issue which mature on successive dates rather than all at once. Notice the difference from series bonds which are issued on successive dates. See BONDS for other types of bonds and comparisons between them.

Series bonds

A single issue of bonds which are programmed for issuance at successive dates rather than all at once. Notice the difference from serial bonds, which are issued all at the same time, but mature on successive dates. See BONDS for other types of bonds and comparisons between them.

Series E bonds

U. S. Government savings bonds sold at discounts in denominations of $25 and larger maturing in 7 to 10 years depending on the date of issuance. Compare with SERIES H BONDS, and see GOVERNMENT BONDS for other types of federal securities.

Series H bonds

U. S. Government savings bonds sold in denominations of $500 or larger, sold at face value, paying interest semiannually. They mature in 10 years. Compare with SERIES E BONDS, and see GOVERNMENT BONDS for other types of federal securities.

Settlement date

The date on which an investor must pay his broker for securities he purchases, or the day on which a seller must make delivery of negotiable certificates for securities he has sold. There are two methods for delivery, they are as follows:

Regular way delivery: The designation that calls for settlement on the fifth day after the transaction takes place. Extensions are possible, and some brokers will try to avoid harsh measures; however, the rules permit the broker to close the account of the tardy customer, sell out securities bought for him, and even sue to collect the due amount.

Delayed delivery or *seller's option:* A special arrangement whereby delivery is made from five to sixty days after the transaction. The buyer must pay for the transaction, but the transfer does not take place until the agreed date as a special concession to the seller, who may be seeking tax benefits from delaying a profit. In return, buyer may get a lower price on his purchase.

The settlement date is sometimes called the due date. Notice the difference from payment date and payable date, which refer to payments for bond interest and stock dividends. Also see GOOD DELIVERY for explanation of proper form for transferring securities.

Shake out

A period when an industry undergoes strong competitive forces and financial strain following a turndown from a highly profitable period of expansion. During a growth period many weaker companies grow and prosper with little real ability. Market demand is high and profit is easy to make even with inefficiencies. Those weaker and less experienced companies are often forced to drop out when demand slackens and profits vanish, leaving only the more solid and established ones to serve the market. The shakeout term is roughly parallel to the case of a fruit tree being shaken by the wind to dislodge the less healthy fruit.

Shareholder

Also called a stockholder, a person who shares ownership of a corporation. Ownership is evidenced by stock certificates or shares which state the exact number of shares owned. Since the company may issue more shares of different classes of stock at a later time, the shares cannot state the percentage of ownership. Market prices may vary considerably with market demand, so the purchase price is not shown on the certificate.

A shareholder's rights are the same regardless of the number of shares owned. Shareholders elect a board of directors who in turn elect the operating officers and set the major policy of the corporation. The stock purchased by the shareholder represents equity in the company and entitles the investor to his portion of the assets in the event of liquidation. As part owner he is also entitled to his share of the profits which are paid out as dividends. Part or all of the profit may be retained for business expansion or acquisitions, as determined by the board of directors. See SENIOR SECURITY for preferential treatment of some shareholders. Also see STOCK for a listing of different types of stock, and see BONDS for many types of non-equity securities.

Shareholder's equity

Another term for net worth, owner's equity, book value or capital of business. It is the difference between all assets and all liabilities as they are carried on the books. See NET WORTH for expanded definitions.

Shares

Certificates representing a portion of ownership of a corporation. One certificate may represent one share or many thousands of shares. This is referred to as stock, either common or preferred. Common stock is called junior equity and is the only type with voting privileges. Preferred stock is senior equity and has a higher standing in claims against assets in the event of liquidation. The term *shares* suggests proportional ownership and often specifies the number of shares, whereas the term *stock* suggests more of the concept of public ownership or investment without quantitative reference. See STOCK, EQUITY CAPITAL, and SECURITY for methods of classifying corporate capital, and see STOCK for a list of special classifications and characteristics of equity capital.

Sheets

A daily publication listing of current trading prices and the dealers who make markets in the thousands of securities traded over-the-counter. It is published by the National Quotation Bureau. The sheets consist of many long sheets of listings using different colored paper for different kinds of securities. Most brokers use the term pink sheets because of the predominant color of paper used.

Shelf registration

A registration of stock for sale at some undetermined time in the future.

Short, short selling

To sell stock which has been borrowed for that purpose. It is legal when following certain procedures and requires that the seller put up cash to cover the value of the borrowed stock. Borrowing stock sounds like a difficult and questionable task; however, for the investor it involves no more than saying the word to the broker. The customer must have an active margin account and must have sufficient buying power to cover the transaction. He will tell his broker, "Sell short 100 shares XYZ at market." The broker then handles the rest. The transactions are recorded as bookkeeping entries for the customer, and the borrowed shares are held in the broker's name for all street name accounts.

The seller in such a transaction is expecting the price of that stock to fall, so that he might buy other shares at a lower price to replace the ones borrowed, thereby making a profit on the transaction. If he guesses wrong and the price goes higher; he must pay more to replace the borrowed stock. It is a very speculative practice that can be quite expensive to anyone who does not have a great deal of experience and information.

Short covering
Buying stock to replace stock that was previously borrowed for delivery on a short sale.

Short interest
The number of shares of stock borrowed and sold by short sellers and not covered by a given date. A high short interest can indicate fears of trouble. However, because the short interest builds up with some inertia, many consider it a good time to buy, since those short will soon have to cover and, therefore, push the price up.

Short interest ratio
An index comparing uncovered short positions to average volume over a 30 day period. A ratio above 1.5 is considered bullish, and a ratio below 1.0 is considered bearish in investor attitudes.

Short position

The condition of the account of a trader who has stocks sold short and not covered as of a particular date. See SHORT SELLING and POSITION listed separately for more expanded definitions.

Short term

Something that is planned for or expected to involve a relatively short period of time. A short term profit is a profit realized from the sale of an asset held less than six months (a designation determined by tax laws), but a short term market rally may be one which terminates less than a month after it begins. Short term market forecasts concern expected market movements over a few weeks or months, contrasted to long term, which refers to market moves which follow a trend over many months or even years. Also notice a difference from near term market moves, which are essentially the same thing as short term, except that near term market moves may concern only the next half of a market cycle or the next reversal. The short term market moves may cover several cycles but still be limited to a relatively short period of time. When applied to trading, a short term position in commodities may last for less than one day. In securities trading, short term positions may be held for several days or several months. None are planned to be held longer than six months. Note the difference from SHORT POSITION and SHORT SELLING listed separately.

Short term capital gains

Profits on assets held less than six months. This is taxable as ordinary income.

Short term debt

Corporate obligation due in less than five years. This

may include bank notes due in 6 to 12 months, money borrowed on inventory, or other current liabilities.

Short term investment

A security or property purchased for the intention of reselling in less than six months at a profit. A person who makes a purchase of a security with the intention of selling within six months is actually not *investing* in the fullest sense of the word, but is *trading* with the hope of making profit on each trade. Investing, by contrast, is the purchase of a security or other asset with the intent of holding it for income or security in future years.

Short term trading

Buying and selling securities with the intention of holding them only long enough to take advantage of market price fluctuations. Positions may be held only a few days or weeks, and no thought is given to dividends or future stability. Profits gained in short term trading are nearly always taxed as ordinary income. This is opposed to long term investing, which seeks stability and dividend income in the future. The dividends on both short term and long term investments would be taxed as ordinary income, but profits from selling long term investments are taxed at lower rates.

Sidewise market

Indecisive chart movements that swing slowly in both directions but show no trend up or down. See STOCK CHARTS for illustrated chart patterns.

Signal

Any charting pattern, index movement, or significant

occurrence in timing or numerical systems which indicates to a searching investor that something important is about to happen. There are hundreds of different signals and systems with varying qualifications and reliability. See BUY SIGNALS and SELL SIGNALS for some specific examples. See PATTERNS for a list of chart formations that have significance to technical analysts, and STOCK CHARTS for samples of charts that illustrate some signals.

Signal pattern

Any of a large group of patterns that can appear on a stock chart and carry significance to a technical analyst. Contrasting to cyclic patterns which tend to recur with a loose but recognizable frequency, the signal pattern may occur at any time or any place on a chart. This represents an important event when a number of influencing conditions coincide to exert strong pressure on a security price . . . either upward or downward. These combined pressures force a market price outside of normal ranges, signaling very high odds for a self-stabilizing adjustment back toward the normal condition. An investor interpreting stock chart patterns will make quick decisions when certain signals occur. Also see CYCLIC PATTERNS, which are more regular chart formations and indicate investor's mental inertia, news distribution and assimilation lag, and sympathetic emotional diffusion among investors. A number of signal patterns are described under BUY SIGNALS, SELL SIGNALS, and PATTERNS. Some samples of signal patterns and cyclic patterns are shown on charts under the heading STOCK CHARTS.

Sinking fund

An amount of cash, or its equivalent, set aside at

regular intervals to provide for the redemption of bonds at or before maturity.

Sinking fund bonds

Bonds which make it mandatory that the issuer set up a sinking fund to provide for their redemption. See BONDS for a comparison of many types of bonds.

Six and ten

A common expiration term for an option. The expression means the option will expire in six months and ten days. Also common is a 95 day term. If the parties negotiating the option wish to, they may set any date for expiration that is agreeable to both.

Sleeper

A security which is potentially strong but is underpriced and out of the public interest.

Slow market

A period when the stock market shows relatively few trades and only minor price changes. A slow market is a dull, inactive market. It may also be called a flat market or sidewise market, which would mean that there is little definitive direction of trends.

Slump

A temporary downturn in the stock market, characterized by generally falling market prices, but not severe enough to rate as a bear market. Sometimes called a period of consolidation, profit taking, or regrouping.

Small investor

Often called the little man or average investor, the largest of four classes of investors. The distinctions are: institutions, corporations, large investors, and small investors. The small investors comprise 80% of the market, but they hold only 20% of the securities. They may buy a few shares at a time or a few hundred of low cost shares. Almost all odd-lot transactions represent the small investors. Their presence in the market is vital to market liquidity, and their trends in trading are valuable indications for the professionals who analyze and forecast market conditions. By contrast, the institutions are banks, mutual funds, pension plans, and various foundations and trusts.

Corporate investors are companies who buy large blocks of stock to participate in the operation of other companies. Some also buy for investment. Large investors are individuals who buy for investment in very large amounts. They are wealthy, knowledgeable, and experienced in investments.

Smart money

A term that refers to investment moves of sophisticated investors, generally accepted to mean large investors and institutions. The term suggests that the greater knowledge and experience of these sophisticates will cause their investment money to move toward the lower risk situations or the more profitable situations.

Soft goods

A term found most often in retail trade which refers to textile products or other products that are consumed relatively quickly. Opposed terms would be hard goods or durable goods.

Soft market

A period of market weakness with some prices falling and others drifting aimlessly. Market volume is small.

Soft prices

Prices that are lower than ususal. It may also mean that although one price is announced, there is good opportunity to bargain for lower prices. It may also apply to a period of dropping prices.

Soft sell

Sales practices which are difficult to recognize as sales techniques. The salesman's knowledge, sincereity, thoroughness, and professional manners are the qualities which sell the customer rather than showmanship, slogans, and relentless verbal cornering of the prospect. Quite different from the hard sell where the customer is overwhelmed with sales pressure, enticed by promises, entertained, flattered, motivated, and otherwise pushed into a purchase.

Software

A shortening of the term computer software. This is the term applied to the supporting supplies and services used to operate computers. It contrasts to computer hardware, which refers to the basic electronic and mechanical equipment itself.

Sold-out bull

A person who has a favorable opinion of market trends, but has sold out most of his holdings to realize his profits and is currently having difficulties finding more good buy opportunities for reinvesting. While he expects the market to continue rising, he prefers to buy securities during a time when prices drop. In a strong market these price dips may not occur, so the optimistic investor is unable to buy in. Those securities he sold during the climb yielded profits, but, in retrospect, he sold too soon.

Solvent

The condition of a company which has at least enough assets to meet all its liabilities. It is also said to be a liquid company.

Sophisticated investors

The educated, experienced investors who are also usually wealthy. This group is usually more successful than the institutions because of size and restrictive regulations that slow the institutions. They are vastly more successful than the small investors because they have years of experience, devote a great deal of time to studying investment opportunities, and can afford good reference materials and investment advisory services.

Special bid

A method of filling an order to buy a large block of stock on the floor of the NYSE. In a special bid, the bidder for the block of stock . . . a pension fund, for instance, will pay a special commission to the broker who represents him in making the purchase. The seller does not pay a commission. The special bid is made on the exchange floor at a fixed price which must be at or above the last sale of the security or the current bid in the regular market, whichever is higher. The transaction is the reverse of a special offering.

Special drawing rights

A credit or created asset in the International Monetary Fund that member countries may draw against. Member countries voted to create these credits to replace the need to transfer gold or silver for international transactions. Special drawing rights are commonly called paper gold or SDR's.

Special offering

Occasionally a large block of stock becomes available for sale which, due to its size and the market in that particular issue, calls for special handling. A notice is printed on the ticker tape announcing that the stock will be offered for sale on the floor of the exchange at a fixed price. Member firms may buy this stock for customers directly from the seller's broker during trading hours. The price is usually based on the last transaction in the regular auction market. If there are more buyers than stock, allotments are made. Only the seller pays a commission on a special offering. The transaction is the reverse of a special bid.

Special purchase

An often-used expression by retailers to satisfy federal controls when advertising special sales. The advertising usually accents the low prices available, and the customer usually makes mental comparisons with prices on the retailer's regular line of merchandise. The term "special purchase" indicates that it is not his regular line, but is usually a lower cost, lower quality line of goods being sold at its regular price. It also suggests that repair parts and service will be difficult or impossible to obtain, since it is not regularly handled by the retailer.

Special situation

A situation in the securities market in which some particular development is counted upon to yield a satisfactory profit, regardless of what the general market does. An example would be a pending merger between a small company and a larger, well known company with solid financial structure. It would make the stock of the smaller company rise prior to the merger.

Special subscription account

A special kind of investor account set up with a broker specifically to purchase shares of a new issue of an already listed security through subscription rights. It is similar to a margin account in some respects, in that the account may be opened with part payment, but there are many differences. It operates as follows: The existing shareholders of the issuing company are given rights to purchase a specific number of the new shares at a reduced price. That price differential is the open market value of the right. The investor who wishes to exercise those rights may open the account by paying 25 % of the total value of the rights he has received, plus the underwriter's cost as stated on the prospectus, which may run from 10 to 15 % of the selling price. This payment will reserve the shares for the investor. The rights themselves serve as part of this down payment. Later, when the investor wishes to take possession of the shares, he must pay off the debit balance, and the account is closed. If a person receives rights from the company but either cannot or does not wish to exercise his rights, he may sell them to other investors on the open market. The buyer may establish the same kind of special subscription account.

Specialist

A member of a stock exchange who presides over a trading post. He carries an inventory of each stock assigned to him which he has to purchase with his own capital. It is from this inventory that floor brokers purchase for your account when you place an order with a local broker. The specialist is charged with the responsiblity of attempting to maintain an orderly market, which means that if there is a heavy flow of sell orders causing the prices to drop, he must buy anyway to try to maintain a normal condition. Only if it becomes evident that his support will not help is he permitted to decline to buy additional shares. There are about 350 specialists registered with the New York Stock Exchange.

Most of the trading is conducted by hand signals, and all orders are considered binding contracts. It is one of the few places left in modern life where a person's word is accepted at face value.

Specialist block purchase

Purchase by the specialist for his own account of a large block of stock outside the regular market on the exchange. Such purchases may be made only when the sale of the block could not be made in the regular market within a reasonable time and at reasonable prices, and when the purchase would aid the specialist in maintaining a fair and orderly market. If the specialist has other orders on his book that are closer to the going market price, he is not required to fill those orders at the same specially negotiated price obtained for the block purchase. This transaction is opposite to the SPECIALIST BLOCK SALE below.

Specialist block sale

Opposite of the specialist block purchase. Under exceptional circumstances, the specialist may sell a block of stock outside the regular exchange market out of his own account at a price above the prevailing market. The price is negotiated between the specialist and the broker for the buyer. If the specialist has other orders closer to the going market price, he is not required to fill those orders at the same specially negotiated price for the block purchase.

Speculation

Investing with little concern for the risks involved and more concern for capital appreciation in a short time. Usually investing in any new company is considered speculation. The more knowledgeable analysts tend to consider any security speculative that has depressed prices or possible favorable changes underlying its present market acceptance. Some observers consider any security speculative if it possesses more risk than they care to accept. Ironically, they will buy gold or silver when fever pitch buying has pushed it to record highs in an effort to avoid the risk of depressed stock prices.

Speculative security

One which is of uncertain strength. It may have very great potential, but must fight strong odds to succeed. Most new issues are considered speculative. Some conservative analysts consider almost any stock which has a depressed price to be speculative. Other, more aggressive, and, perhaps, realistic analysts consider a stock speculative when it is pushed up to new highs. Risks should properly be determined by financial strength, management strength, product acceptance, market penetration, and consistency in performance.

Speculator

A person who buys and sells securities for his own account with the hope of making a profit as market prices fluctuate. He is an aggressive trader who uses leverage to its greatest extent and frequently uses margin trading, short selling, option buying, commodity trading, special situations, and any other device which can increase his return. He accepts high risk for the promise of high profits. He is usually a very knowledgeable, professional trader who understands what he is doing and is not "playing the market" or gambling on chance. Note the difference between investing, trading, and speculating as listed under the heading INVESTMENT.

Spike

A sudden and sharp increase in a stock price. A jump from 20 to 30% or even more in a single day, which has a special significance to chartists using Investor's Systems method of account management. See STOCK CHARTS for illustrated chart patterns.

Spin-off

In business activities the term refers to the action taken by a corporation to divest itself of a subsidiary by distributing the stock of the subsidiary to its own shareholders. It is sometimes done under federal pressure to satisfy anti-trust charges. The term is also used to refer to a by-product of some other activity. For instance, much of our consumer goods in the electronics industry originated in our space research, so those consumer products are said to be a spin-off from the space program.

Split investment company

Another term for a leverage fund which may borrow money for investment in order to increase return for its shareholders. See INVESTMENT COMPANY for other types of funds and descriptions of each. Also see INVESTMENT COMPANY ACT OF 1940 for definitions, purposes, and limitations.

Splits

The division of higher priced shares into a larger

411

number of lower priced shares. Splits may be as little as 5 new shares for 4 existing shares, or more than 1,000 new shares for 1 existing share. The decision is determined by the Board of Directors as they understand the need. The purpose may be to pay a dividend in stock (not really a split), or to reduce the market price which may widen the marketability of the stock, and it also has the psychological effect of keeping the shareholders happy through the feeling of owning more shares. Typically, the rate of growth in a stock price is slightly greater after a split.

Sponsor
In an unincorporated mutual fund a sponsor is the group who performs the normal duties of a Board of Directors. Although incorrect, the term is sometimes applied to the underwritter, since he may dominate management policy. Also called a trustee.

Spot prices
Prices for commodities that are currently in effect for the merchandise on hand for immediate delivery. This contrasts with futures prices, which are the prices available now for commodities which will be delivered at a later time.

Spread
1. Most often the term spread is used to mean the difference between bid and asked prices for a stock. It may also be called quotation spread.
2. The term is also used to mean a straddle. It is the practice of purchasing a put and a call (options to sell and to buy) for the same stock at the same price on the same day. It is done with the thought that if a loss is sustained on one, it would be offset by a

profit on the other. See STRADDLE for more information.

3. A trader buying a spread in commodities may buy a contract for delivery in one month and sell a contract for delivery in another month. If conditions are such that the prices for the different months widen or narrow, the trader will profit or lose from the shift.

Stabilization

The legal manipulation by the underwriters of a new issue designed to prevent the market price of a security from dropping below the public offering price until the entire issue is sold.

Staff management

A middle strata of management above line management, which is responsible for production and operations, and below top management, which sets policy and long range plans. Staff may include vice presidents and division managers and is responsible for interpreting policy and implementing long range plans of top management.

Standard and Poor's

A highly respected investment advisory service serving brokers, institutions, and sophisticated investors. Their research materials are available in any library, and their stock guide can be obtained from nearly any broker. They publish data on over 5,000 corporations and compile indexes and indicators used by most professionals.

Standard and Poor's 100 industry indexes

Separate indexes of 100 different industry groups

computed weekly by Standard and Poor's Corporation. They show areas of strength and weakness within the general market. See indexes, averages, and composites for listings of some indexes.

Standard and Poor's composite index

A composite index of 500 common stocks listed on the New York Stock Exchange. The index includes market prices for 425 industrial stocks, 20 railroad stocks, and 55 utility stocks. It is computed every half hour during trading days by Standard and Poor's Corporation. The method of computation for this index is known as base-weighted aggregative, which means that each stock used is compared to a base period (1941-1943) and given a weighted value or a multiplier which is based on the market value of the aggregate of all its outstanding stock. This index is considered to give a reasonably accurate view of general market conditions, more indicative than the popular Dow Jones Industrial average, since it represents approximately 90% of the market value of all common stock listed on the New York Exchange.

Standard and Poor's stock and bond ratings

A system for comparing relative quality of numerous securities. Various issues are assigned letter grades to indicate financial strength, safety, returns, or stability. The system is explained more fully under RATINGS OF SECURITIES and compared with *Moody's* rating systems. Letter grades are listed.

Stated value

A per share, arbitrary value listed on a company's

accounting records for their stock. This is an accounting procedure for carrying a fixed figure on the books while the market value of the stock may fluctuate widely. The difference between the stated value and true book value is then shown as retained earnings. There is no relationship to market value of the stock.

Statement

1. A monthly billing sent out by companies to their regular customers, listing all purchases and credits. Most companies issue individual invoices for each separate purchase but do not ask for payment until the monthly statement is sent.

2. A monthly summary of purchases and credits intended to state the condition of the account. Payment is due when invoices are sent for each individual purchase. This practice is less frequent than the method in #1 and is usually more common with smaller companies. Either method is accepted, and there is no standard procedure.

3. An announcement or release of information, usually stating an official position.

Also see INCOME STATEMENT and FINANCIAL STATEMENT.

Statement of capital

Another way of saying capital statement. It is a brief report included in a company's financial statement, along with the balance sheet and the income statement. The statement of capital shows the capital at the beginning of the reporting period, any additions or subtractions, and, finally, the capital as of the end of the reporting period. The capital of a company is the same as the net worth.

Statement of condition

A formal term used for a company's balance sheet. The balance sheet may also have an attached income statement and capital statement.

Statement of Policy

A formal set of standards issued by the Securities Exchange Commission to which all investment companies must comply. The Statement of Policy, often referred to as the SOP, requires a very careful, conservative approach to the sales of mutual fund shares. It has eighteen sections which in general require the following:

1. Sales presentation must make a complete explanation of the risks involved.
2. Implication of future performance based on past performance or in comparison to any other industry is forbidden.
3. Unqualified reference to regulations or comparison to other securities or industries to imply that there is any safety or growth in mutual funds is forbidden.
4. Full disclosure of costs and possible loss at the time of redemption or from switching accounts into another type of fund is required.
5. Rigid standards must be followed for preparation of any performance charts, and presentation of them must not imply anything other than what has actually happened in the past. Charts must be complete for the most recent 10 years, or for the entire life of the fund if less than 10 years old.
6. No material, either printed or oral, may be used for sales presentation which has not been cleared by the Securities Exchange Commission for sales use.

7. An overall, careful, conservative approach must be followed in sales efforts for all mutual funds.

See INVESTMENT COMPANY ACT OF 1940 for more information on the limitations, purposes, and definitions of mutual funds. See INVESTMENT COMPANIES for more information and comparisons between a number of investment companies.

Statistical probabilities

Market forecast probabilities derived from statistics rather than from mathematical computation. Using a very large quantity of test cases, statistical probabilities should theoretically coincide with mathematical probabilities. However, if human influences are introduced, the statistical results may depart from mathematical forecasts. These anomalies are accounted for in the optimal analysis method of investment analysis to greatly improve probabilities of correct forecasting and resulting growth in investment.

Statutory subsidiary

As defined by the Public Utility Holding Company Act, this is any company in which there is 10% or more ownership of the outstanding voting shares held by another company.

Sterling

In financial circles the term refers to British currency or other documents based upon British currency.

Stock

A general term also called capital stock and equity that refers to certificates representing partial ownership in a corporation. Such ownership is divided into a suitable number of equal shares for sale to the public. A single stock certificate may serve to indicate any number of shares owned by a single investor. There is also a move which is gathering support to record ownership by bookkeeping entries only. This would speed and simplify the back office work in the securities industry. Street name accounts are already handled in a similar manner.

Stock represents equity, or shared ownership, as opposed to bonds, which represent a debt of the corporation to an investor. Equity is also called capital. Stock can be issued to give preference to a particular category of investor, or it can be converted from one class to another if it is so stipulated at the time of issue. It can have restrictions placed upon it to limit its original sale or its resale. It can carry special tax concessions to its owner. (See PHANTOM STOCK and 1244 STOCK). Some of the different terms used to identify or classify stock are listed below and also under separate headings. The individual headings carry definitions for the terms with comparisons to other terms.

Barometer stock: A single stock which fluctuates in price approximately the same as economic conditions in general. This type of stock is watched as an index to the whole market by verifying any reversal that the market makes. If a reversal takes place in the market averages but not in the barometer stock, it is considered not to have significance to chartists.

Blue chip stocks: Those stocks which are issued by leading corporations which have outstanding records of earnings, financial strength, and stable stock prices.

Capital stock: All stock of any class or type that is

issued by a corporation. It represents ownership and is called equity. The proceeds received by the company for the sale of the stock are called equity capital. Bonds are not included, but are called debt securities and represent obligations to be repaid.

Classified stock: Any of the many categories of stock which can be issued by a corporation beyond common stock. It will include various classes of common that are usually labeled Class A common, Class B common, etc. There may also be Class A preferred, Class B preferred, Prior Preferred, Convertible Preferred, Second Class Preferred, Debenture Stock, Restricted Common, and even a Phantom Stock. The term *classified* has no specific qualifications, but means that there are several types of stock outstanding for the company. The reason for having several different types of stock is to suit the needs of the company as well as to please various groups of stockholders. If a company needs to expand, it may raise additional capital by issuing more stock. Existing stockholders may want to retain control, but are willing to sacrifice some claim on assets to induce others to invest. A later issue offered for another expansion move may take a subordinate position in claims on assets and may offer a lower dividend payout, but may have a conversion privilege giving those shareholders a substantial advantage for gain in future years. The conditions and benefits for each issue are worked out to the satisfaction of shareholders before the issue is made available to the public.

Common stock: The first issue of stock offered by any corporation. Normally, common stock is the only class of stock that has voting rights. It represents an undivided interest in the ownership of the assets of the corporation and has no set rate of return. Dividends are determined by vote of the board of directors.

Convertible preferred: A preferred stock which earns specified dividends and has a superior rating compared to common stock in the event of liquidation. Its special feature is the privilege of being exchanged for common stock at some time in the future. This type stock is often issued during a growth period for a small company. Buyers of the convertible issue want the preferential position in claims on assets to justify their non-voting position, and they want the opportunity to gain voting privileges in the future if their capital has produced the growth that is anticipated.

Corporate stock: This is actually a misnomer as far as equity securities are concerned. This name is applied in some states to bonds that are issued to finance local public works projects. Most states call them municipal bonds. They can be issued by any taxing agency except the federal government and very often carry tax-exemptions on interest payments to the stockholder. These tax benefits are offered by the government to induce investors to assist in the financing of otherwise unattractive public projects.

Cumulative preferred: A preferred stock which has the provision that if any dividends are omitted for any reason, such as severe profit declines, that all dividends will accrue and be paid at a later time before any dividends may be paid to holders of common stock.

Gilt-edged stock: The same thing as a blue chip stock. The term gilt-edged is usually applied to bonds of high quality, while stocks of high quality are called blue chips.

Glamour stock: A stock that has captured the public's collective fancy because of some real or imagined potential for fast growth or high earnings. Glamour stocks are usually in an industry with recently developed technology, and the issuing companies show histories of regular growth and high earnings. Such stocks tend to have high price-earnings ratios because of the demand for the stock. P-E ratios of over 100 are not impossible for glamour stocks, compared to ratios for average stocks of 10 to 20 in normal times and 5 to 10 in bear markets. Market prices on the glamour stocks can be 10 to 20 times the book value in bull markets, when other stocks may be only two times book value. In bear markets the glamours decline disastrously, so that market prices may be less than half the book value and P-E ratios may be from 0 to 5.

Growth stock: A common stock representing a company that has a record of steadily increasing earnings and sales. The growth can be achieved by internal expansion resulting from product success and management efficiency, or it can come from external expansion resulting from acquisitions and mergers. Growth stocks are characterized by heavy trading volume, steadily increasing market prices, perhaps with volatile price swings and high price-earnings ratios. The difference from a glamour stock is both degree and public interest. Part of the interest in a glamour stock results from publicity. The growth stock has earned its reputation by actual performance, but also has some public interest as a result of publicity. Growth stocks usually do not pay dividends early in their growth periods because the income is plowed back into the business for expansion. Investment in growth stocks is appropriate for individuals who have many years before retirement and do not need the extra income. Growth in the portfolio may be many times the income received on income type investments.

Inactive stock: An issue traded on an exchange or in the over-the-counter market in which there is a relatively low volume of trading. Volume may be less than a few hundred shares a week. A stock listed on the New York Stock Exchange which is inactive may be traded in units of 10 shares, 25 shares or 50 shares instead of the traditional 100 share round lots.

Income stock: A stock which has a record of high yield or dividend income for stockholders. This type stock is considered a conservative type investment suitable for retired people and those others who need to supplement other earnings. Income stocks are also some of the most secure for protecting the principal invested. Growth is not considered by investors seeking income investments. Typical income stocks are public utilities, railroads, large food chains, and some other large, well established corporations that have a history of stable market prices and good dividend history.

Letter stock: A common stock sold privately by a corporation to certain individuals without the normal SEC registration. The purchaser must submit a letter stating that his intention in buying the stock is for investment and not for resale. The stock cannot be resold on the open market, so it gives the owner some liquidity problems. This is also called a restricted stock or unregistered stock.

Listed stock: A stock accepted by a stock exchange for trading on that exchange. Each exchange has its own requirements for listing, and they will include market breadth, financial strength, and earnings. In addition, a fee is charged, and the issuing company must agree to publish accurate financial statements at regualr intervals. At the New York Stock Exchange a listing company must meet the following requirements for initial listing:

1. Have at least 1,000,000 shares outstanding in public hands.

2. Have at least 2,000 shareholders, each of whom own 100 shares or more.

3. Have a current market value for publicly held shares of $16,000,000 or more.

4. Have at least $2,500,000 in pre-tax earnings in its latest year before listing and $2,000,000 in each of the two preceding years.

5. Pay a listing fee of $50,000.

6. Agree to publish promptly all financial reports and maintain a transfer agent and a registrar to insure knowledge of stock transfers.

The company may decline from these standards after listing due to changing market conditions, but there are minimums below which the exchange may delist the stock. The requirements may change from time to time as the exchange considers appropriate.

Non-cumulative preferred: A preferred stock which stipulates that its dividends, if not paid, do not accrue for later payment. This is normal for common stock, but more preferred stocks accrue any dividends that are missed.

Participating preferred: A special class of preferred stock which has an added benefit of earning extra dividends based upon the dividends paid to holders of common stock. The preferred still maintains its preferential standing in claims on assets and the guaranteed dividend based on its par value. The additional dividends are paid only if common shares receive payment and in some fixed proportion to the amount paid on common.

Penny stock: Extremely low priced stocks, generally of

a speculative nature, if not totally worthless. They blossomed some years ago as a fad when everyone was on a stock buying binge, and numerous promoters took advantage of it. Regulations now have reduced such plans to memories. Prices have ranged up to several dollars, but most were under one dollar, even less than 10 cents a share. Some prices today fall to the penny category in price, but the reason is vastly different from the fast buck activities of the past.

Phantom stock: Imaginary stock being credited to the account of a corporate executive as compensation in addition to his salary. It does not have voting rights and is not registered in any way with the SEC, nor can it be traded, but it does earn dividends. It is also treated as regular stock in the event of stock splits or stock dividends. This type stock is used as one of the many perquisites used to attract and hold top caliber management personnel.

Preferred stock: A senior equity security which ranks above common stock in claims on the assets of a corporation. Preferred is a limited form of ownership and lies midway between common stock, which is equity with voting rights, and bonds, which represent debt only and do not have voting rights. Dividends on preferred are usually fixed for the life of the security, unlike the variable dividends on common that can increase, decrease, or be cut off entirely. There are several kinds of preferred stock in use. They are identified by any special features and sometimes by classifications as Class A, Class B, etc. Some common forms used are as follows:

1. Convertible preferred: A preferred stock which can be exchanged at some time in the future for common stock with voting privileges.

2. Cumulative preferred: A preferred stock which has

a clause providing that, if any dividends are ever missed for any reason, they will be accrued and paid before any dividends may be paid on common stock.

3. Participating preferred: A preferred stock which may earn additional dividends if common stock earns any increase in dividends. If profits decline so that the common shares receive no dividends, the preferred will still be paid the guaranteed dividend based on par value.

Prior preferred: A preferred stock that takes precedence over other classes of preferred or common stock issued by that same company.

Registered stock: A stock which has been properly submitted to the Securities Exchange Commission (SEC) and state regulatory agencies together with all pertinent information for evaluation and approval before being sold to the public. Registration is required for all securities that are sold to the public. Some small or restricted offerings do not have to be registered, but they have limitations as to where they may be sold and who may purchase them. Registration pertains to the process rather than to the fact that clearance must be obtained before offering the securities. Unregistered issues still must be filed with state authorities and are subject to state blue sky laws.

Restricted stock: A common stock sold privately by a corporation to certain individuals without the normal SEC registration. The purchaser must submit a letter to the SEC stating that his intention in buying the stock is for investment and not for resale. The stock cannot be sold on the open market without registration. It is the same thing as letter stock or an unregistered stock.

Retired stock: Stock that has been repurchased by a company and formally removed from the list of authorized shares by action of the board of directors. Retiring stock has the effect of reducing the breadth of the market for a security and increasing the book value per share. The stock can no longer be sold or distributed by the company, unlike treasury stock, which is often used for acquisitions and stock option plans.

Treasury stock: Stock that has been issued to the public and repurchased by the company. It receives no dividends and has no voting rights. The purpose of the re-acquisition may be to increase the book value of outstanding shares, or it may be to hold the shares in anticipation of use in acquisitions of other companies, bonuses to employees, or stock dividends.

Unlisted stock: Any security that is not listed on a stock exchange. The term does not refer to quality of the security, but many unlisted stocks do represent new companies and small businesses. Many utilities, banks, and insurance companies are unlisted by choice, even though they may rank very highly in investment circles. Unlisted securities are also called over-the-counter stocks, meaning that they are traded in brokerage offices any place in the country.

Unregistered stocks: Certain stocks issued on a limited basis, for special purposes or by small companies for sale to a limited number of people within one state. They are perfectly proper under the designated conditions but are not permitted to be sold outside the state of issue or to larger numbers of investors without being registered with the Securities Exchange Commission. These stocks are also called restricted stocks and letter stocks.

Voting stock: Generally, this is common stock. There may be some classifications of common that do not have voting rights, and there may be certain times that voting rights are subordinated. Voting rights are suspended on all stock held by the treasury, but if those shares are resold or issued in any way, the voting rights resume.

Watered stock: Stock that has been issued without adding a corresponding value to the issuing company. A watered stock is said to be diluted. The condition occurs frequently when a company, particularly a new one, will issue shares to an individual in return for patents or production rights. Other investors supply the capital to operate, while the inventor supplies the product and knowledge. The new product and knowledge are most important to the future of the company, so the dilution is not at all unfair. In fact, it is quite a bargain for investors. They do not have to pay out any cash to obtain the new product. In some cases organizers of new companies have issued themselves an unfair portion of stock compared to the contribution made. This leaves a stock far overpriced in relation to the book value of assets, and it may be a long time before investors have an equitable value. This is dilution, or watered stock, in an unfair sense.

1244 stock: Any stock issued under a special regulation of the Internal Revenue Service and registered on a special form, so that in the event of liquidation the shareholder gets special tax treatment for the loss. Instead of a long term loss on such cases, the holder may claim an ordinary income loss, even though the stock was held for several years. This will apply only to the original purchaser of the stock. The 1244 designation arises from the identifying number on the IRS form used to register the owners of such stock.

Following the original issue or offering, stock is sold on the open market on a bid and asked (auction) basis.

Prices may then be unrelated to asset value. Prices are quoted in points and eighths of a point, one point equaling $1. A few very low-priced stocks traded over-the-counter are quoted in sixteenths of a point. See RISK CAPITAL, VENTURE CAPITAL, EQUITY, SECURITY, and CAPITALIZATION for more information.

Stock, 1244

1244 stock is the designation of stock that is sold under a special regulation which gives the holder special priviliges in the event of liquidation. His loss may be deducted from regular income rather than treated as a long term loss. The 1244 designation refers to the number on the government form used to register the stock. See STOCK for listing of other types of stock in use.

Stock ahead

An expression that is used to explain a condition where an investor places an order with his broker, and that order is not executed at the designated price or time, even though the record shows other trades being executed at that price and time. The reason is that the specialist had other orders at the same price which were received ahead of his, and they must be executed first.

Stock certificate

The actual piece of paper evidencing ownership of stock in a corporation. A single certificate may be issued for one share, 100 shares, 25,000 shares, or any other number. The certificate will bear the name of the issuing company, signed by at least one officer of the company or transfer agent, and the name of the shareowner. The serial number of the share is recorded on the corporation records. At the time a shareholder sells his stock, he must sign the certificate in the appropriate place on the reverse side. This will show the ownership transferred *from* that owner, but the certificate then becomes negotiable, or ownership is determined by the possession of the certificate until that certificate is voided by the transfer agent, and a new certificate is made out to the person buying the stock from the original owner.

Stock charts

A method of recording stock prices and other data which might influence the prices so that analysis of an investment is made more mechanical and scientific. The charts usually record the closing prices for the day for any given security, or perhaps average prices for a particular industry, or even the whole market. There are several types of charts in use, each with some distinct advantages, and each with strong support from different investors or analysts. Three basic types are line charts, bar charts, and point and figure charts. Descriptions of each are as follows:

Line charts: A single line connecting the closing prices for consecutive days. See sample on page 430.

Bar charts: A short vertical line is used for each day.. The line continues from the lowest price for the day to the highest price for the day. The closing price for the day is shown by a little flag at the appropriate point on the vertical line. See chart for MEI Corporation on page 431.

Point and figure charts: A one dimensional chart that records only price changes in units of 1 point, 3 points, 5 points, or some other selected value. The chart cannot show time periods other than by a written note

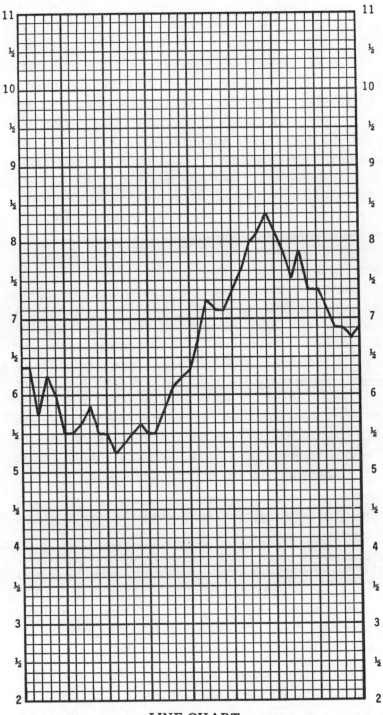

LINE CHART

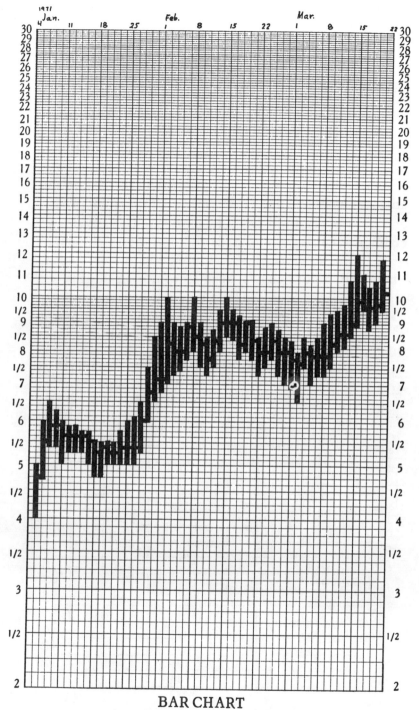

BAR CHART
Company: MEI Corporation

431

entered at some point. It does not even show exact prices. As changes occur in the selected increments, small x's and o's are marked in an appropriate column of boxes. All changes are marked in a vertical direction in a single column until a reversal in trend takes place. The new direction of movement is then recorded in the adjacent column. The x's are used for rising prices, and the o's are used for falling prices. The advantage claimed for this type chart is that is ignores the small price fluctuations and shows only the major trends. The chart below shows MEI Corporation during an eight week period of 1971. Compare with pages 431, 434, and 435 showing the same period on different charts.

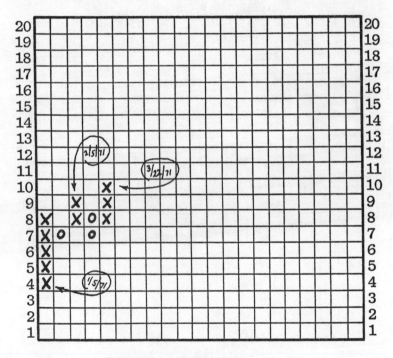

POINT AND FIGURE CHART
Company: MEI Corporation

There are two basic kinds of graph paper used for stock charts. They are:

1. Arithmetical: The grid lines are all equally spaced with equal values for any price changes. The advantage is low cost for the supplies and easy availability. Again MEI Corporation is shown on page 434 on a more typical chart.

2. Logarithmic: The price changes in the vertical direction are recorded on lines that are progressively closer together. The advantage is that all prices for all stocks are shown in exact proportional changes. You can, with a glance, compare a 2 3/4 point change in a $12 stock with a 12 point change in an $87 stock and know immediately that the $12 stock made a larger percentage of gain on investment. Logarithmic charts, which are also called ratio charts or proportional charts, are more difficult to obtain, but they serve very effectively for the elite of the professionals. Charts of any type are the primary tool for techanical analysis. Notice on the sample logarithmic chart on page 435 how the higher prices seem to be subdued in comparison to the straight arithmetical chart.

In use, stock charts do far more than just record prices. Skilled investors and analysts can interpret various formations that appear on the charts to indicate changes in investor emotion and reactions to economic or market conditions. These chart patterns tend to recur reliably enough that the chartist is able to recognize a pattern as it takes shape and with experience is able to greatly improve his odds on investment decisions. The patterns defined on the next 30 pages are accompanied by charts that illustrate each pattern.

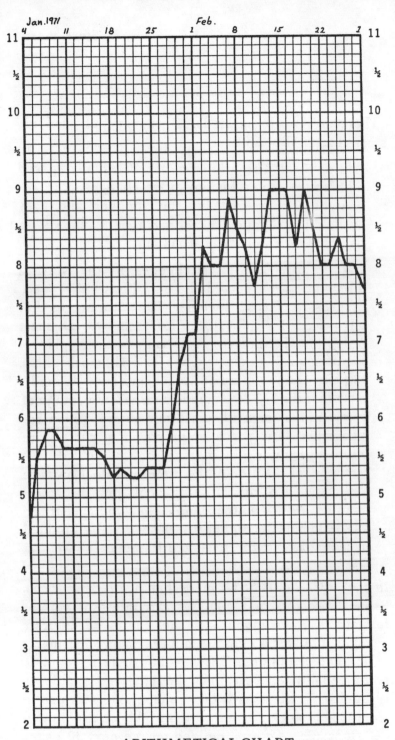

ARITHMETICAL CHART

Company: MEI Corporation

434

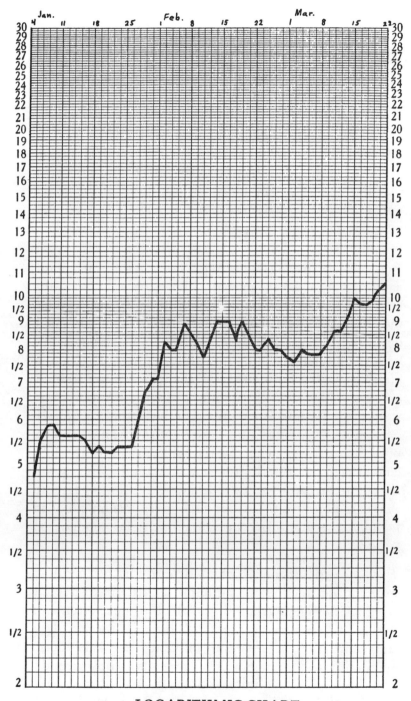

LOGARITHMIC CHART
Company: MEI Corporation

Base: An area on a stock chart which shows a narrow range of trading prices over an extended time span. The period is called a consolidation period if it follows a period of general decline. Technical analysts expect this type pattern to lead into an upward trend. If a rally does not materialize from a base, and a decline takes place, the analyst will adjust his appraisal of the chart and say that the flattened area was a shelf instead of a base. Refer to chart on page 437.

Bottom: The lowest point that a stock price reaches on a chart for a given period. It can only be said in retrospect, and it must be followed by a recovery on the chart. If a chart shows a price pattern that has been declining but seems to be slowing, and the chartist believes a recovery is approaching, he may say that it appears to be bottoming. If the price does indeed recover only to decline again to the same level in a few weeks, the pattern is called a double bottom. A double bottom is interpreted as a sure sign that the price can not fall any lower. The chartist will draw a dotted line connecting the two bottoms and extend it for some time into the future and declare that it is a support line that is impervious to further decline. A bottom can also be a base, a line, or a consolidation. Refer to chart on page 437.

Break: A point on a chart where prices begin a pronounced decline. It can show as a definite decline from a sidewise market or a shelf, but most often it is applied when a rising market reverses direction. It is different from a reversal in that reversals occur frequently and may lie within uptrends or downtrends. The break is a definite change from uptrend to a decline of a few weeks or longer. Refer to chart on page 439.

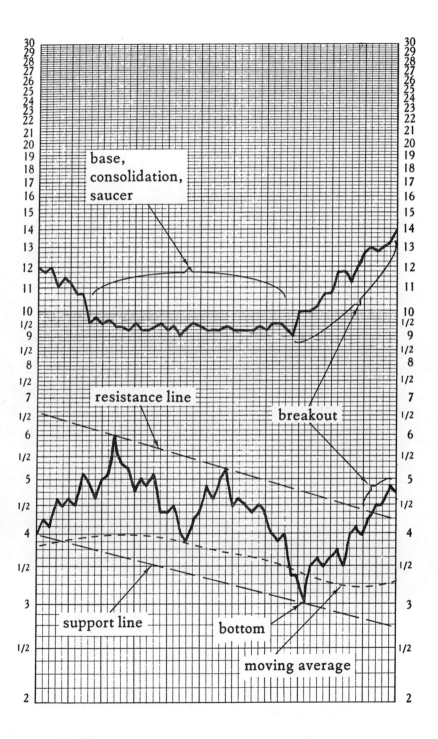

Breakout: A term used in technical analysis to describe a decisive move upward with heavy volume following a consolidation period on a chart. It is also applied to the point at which a price crosses a resistance line or support line. In this case the term is applied to either an upward or a downward direction. When a price breaks out of the confinement area between a resistance line and a support line, it is interpreted to mean that a trend has been established, and the price will continue in that direction for some time. Refer to chart on page 437.

Buying signal: A progression on a chart that exceeds what could be considered normal and that because of self-stabilizing forces will soon lead to an up-reversal. Statistical analysis shows a correlation between certain price progressions and economic developments of a given nature. When these conditions repeat and chart patterns appear to be developing the familiar forms, an investor will feel confident that the odds are on his side in assuming the pattern will develop as usual. Several of the signals are as follows:

1. A sharp decline that continues for several days, following a longer period of slowly declining prices.

2. A leveling of prices following a period of unusually strong declining prices.

3. *Any* plunge, which is a sharp decline of 20% or more in a single day.

4. A low point on a wave pattern that appears to duplicate a previous wave pattern for duration and intensity.

These signals should be interpreted in the light of *fundamental* conditions, since these conditions could alter current market values. Refer to chart on page 439.

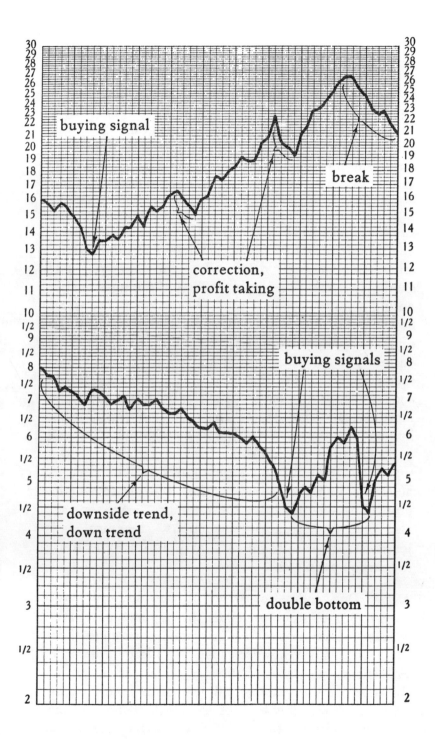

buying signal

break

correction,
profit taking

buying signals

downside trend,
down trend

double bottom

Consolidation: A period on a chart where the charted market prices show as a horizontal trend following a declining period. This is especially significant if the trading volume is heavy but the prices change very little. The pattern will look like a base or saucer and, like these other terms, is expected to lead up to an uptrend. Refer to chart on page 437.

Correction: A break in the trend whether up or down. The term is used to explain a change when there is no other fundamental reason for the change. For example, if the price of a stock is climbing strongly during healthy economic conditions, a sudden reversal downward is unexplained other than to credit it to the market adjusting itself. This means that traders have earned good profits during the climb and are now ready to sell to take that profit. The economic forces concerning profits cause prices to stabilize toward a more average line on the chart. It also verifies that human emotion is a very strong influence that will outweigh fundamental values. Investors holding stock that has made unusually strong gains become nervous about holding the gains, so they sell off to fix the profit. The sell off causes the set back. Corrections are also called technical corrections, technical adjustments, reversals, sell offs, and profit taking. Refer to chart on page 439.

Cycle: One complete round of the up and down movements of stock prices as they appear on charts. Market prices are continuously moving through these cycles, but, since they are caused by a large number of influences, the cyles may vary widely in intensity, duration, configuration, and the price levels at the beginning and the end of the cycle. The Optimal Analysis system for investment management has

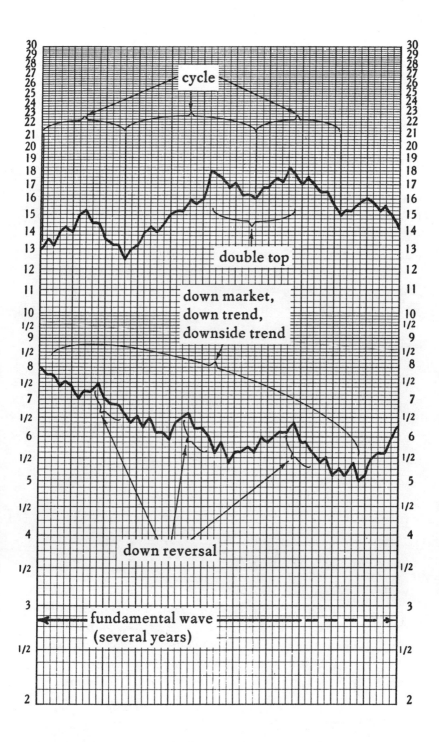

cycle

double top

down market,
down trend,
downside trend

down reversal

fundamental wave
(several years)

441

identified three basic cycles called primary waves, secondary waves, and fundamental waves. A special condition exists when several market influences coincide to cause an unusually strong price change. This is called a spike if the price jumps upward, or a plunge if it drops sharply. Spikes will fit into the secondary wave designation for duration. Refer to chart on page 443.

Double bottom: A "W" shaped pattern that may appear when a long downtrend begins its turnaround for an uptrend. Some chartists believe that the first bottom establishes the support line and the second bottom verifies that the price could not penetrate that support. It is interpreted to mean that a strong uptrend should follow and is considered as a buy signal. Refer to chart on page 439.

Double top: An "M" shape that may appear on a chart after a long period of rising prices. It is interpreted to mean that the market has reached a peak and is certain to decline for some time afterward. Many chartists believe that the first reversal from the top establishes the resistance line, and the second reversal from that area verifies that the price can go no higher. It is considered a sell signal. Refer to chart on page 443.

Down market: A period when market averages are declining in trend. Refer to chart on page 443.

Down reversal: A sudden decline in market price following a rising trend. This term is applied only during the early stage of the decline or to a short term period of decline. It is also called a technical adjustment, a technical correction, or profit taking. If the price continues to decline for several weeks or more, it is called a sell off, soft market or downside trend. Refer to chart on page 443.

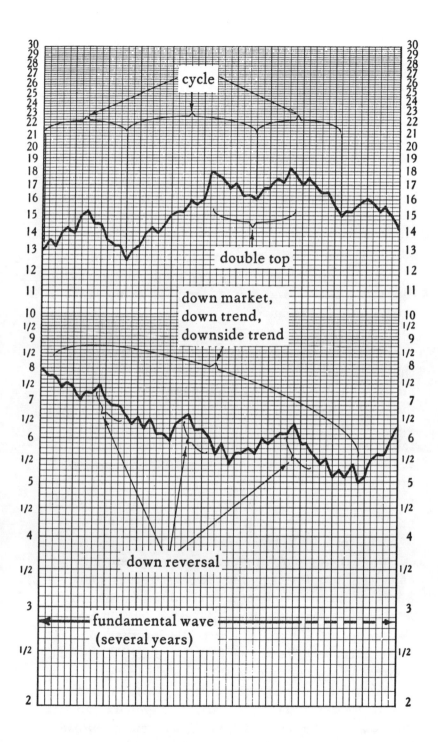

cycle

double top

down market,
down trend,
downside trend

down reversal

fundamental wave
(several years)

Downside trend: The portion of a fundamental wave that shows declining prices. It may continue for several months while permitting several smaller up-reversals to occur during the general decline. The term is often shortened to downtrend if the downward movement continues longer than just the back side of a cycle. Refer to chart on page 443.

Fundamental wave: A long term cycle that contains a major trend upward and a major trend downward. The cycle may extend from two years to as long as ten years or more. It represents general economic conditions for the entire nation and will encompass many smaller cycles and disturbances to market prices. Refer to chart on page 443.

Head and shoulders: A pattern which appears on a chart as a series of three waves, with the central peak higher than the other two high points. It is similar to the double top in its interpretation. The pattern was more frequent several generations ago and also more reliable in use. The appearance of institutional investors and more rapid access to information by all investors has altered the forces that led to the formation of this pattern. When used, the pattern signals a probable end to a rising trend and the beginning of a down market. Refer to chart on page 445.

Moving average: Average prices for a stock when calculated progressively for the most recent specified period of time. Such averages are often calculated for 10 days, 30 days, 90 days, 180 days, or 200 trading days, depending upon who is preparing them and for what purpose. The average is calculated daily and plotted on a graph along with the closing prices for each day. Each day as a new current price is added, the oldest price is deleted from the average. Its value is considered to be that it will more accurately represent

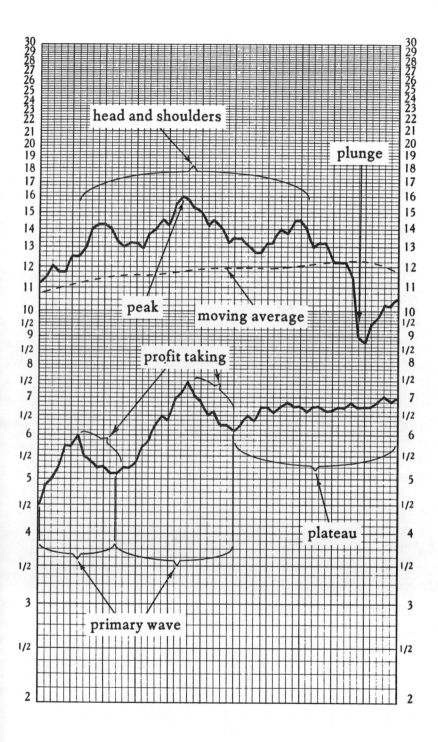

head and shoulders

plunge

peak

moving average

profit taking

primary wave

plateau

true value than the current market prices will. Therefore, when the price falls below the moving average, this is considered a buying situation, or, similarly, when it rises above the moving average, a sell is in order. It is a method of keeping on the right side of the odds. Different time periods are used for different objectives. A long term investor may be interested in values in relation to long periods of time, so he will follow 200 day moving averages. By contrast, a short term trader may prefer a 10 day average which will not show value in terms of economic conditions but will measure an average of investor attitudes and emotions for a recent time period. On a chart this will appear as a dotted line following a gentle contour between the peaks and valleys of the current market price. Refer to chart on page 447.

Peak: The highest point of a market price for any given period on a chart, also called a top. The term can only be used in retrospect after the prices have declined from that point. If the time period is well defined, such as a year or a month, the peak will usually be called the high for that period. The period immediately following the peak is called a down reversal. If the reversal is brief, a few days to two weeks, it is called a technical correction, a sell off, or a period of profit taking. If it continues many weeks or months, it becomes a downside trend and verifies that it truly was a peak or top. Refer to chart on page 447.

Plateau: A period covered by a chart when market prices hold relatively steady following a period of rising prices. It represents a time of uncertainty for a short term trader and probably is a sell signal. He considers the stock to be demonstrating strength in holding its previous gains, but he thinks further gains to be unlikely for some time. He will sell to put his

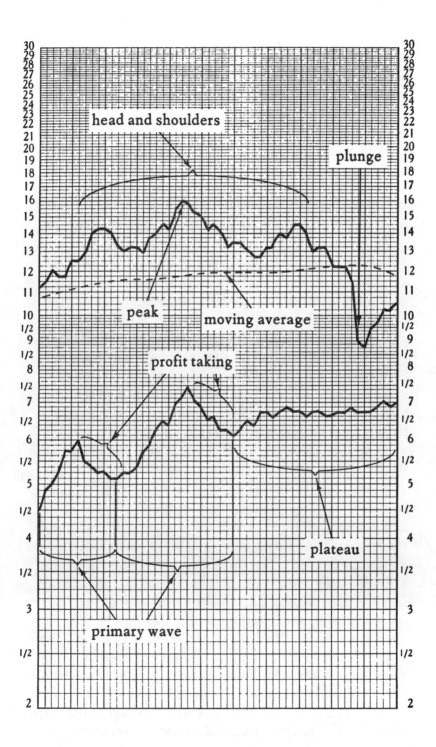

head and shoulders

plunge

peak

moving average

profit taking

plateau

primary wave

money to work in other securities. Refer to chart on page 449.

Plunge: A sudden and sharp drop in the price of a stock. The decline may amount to 20% or more of the market price in a single day and is considered as an immediate buy signal. Refer to chart on page 449.

Primary wave: A wave cycle on a chart which extends from a week to as long as four months, but which averages three to four weeks in length. This is one of the three types of wave cycles identified by the Optimal Analysis method of portfolio management, along with the secondary wave and fundamental wave. The primary wave is so named because it is the most important to short term traders. It ignores the rapid reactionary fluctuations of the secondary wave and de-emphasizes the long term trends that show economic values to give an investor an advantage in predicting cyclic mental attitudes of other investors. The primary patterns are the most common cycles on charts and the most predictable. They offer a distinct advantage in timing of investment decisions. Refer to chart page 449.

Profit taking: Aside from the obvious reference to investors cashing in on securities, a sell off will show as a definite dip in market prices during a period when market interest is running high. The charts will show an abrupt decline a few days after the start of a strong rally. If a rally continues for several months, there may be several periods of profit taking during the rise. This indicates that short term traders have earned some good paper profits and are nervous about how long the rally will continue, so they sell to take the gains while they have them. The longer a strong rally continues, the more likely it is that a profit taking dip will set in. These dips are called technical adjustments or technical corrections, since fundamental conditions are

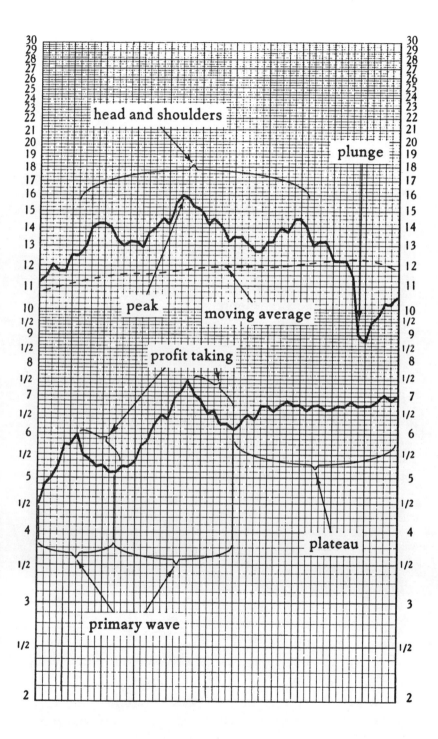

still strong, and declines can only be attributed to self-stabilizing conditions within the market. Refer to chart on page 449.

Rally: A brisk rise in market prices following a longer period of decline or following a long, dull, inactive period. An up-reversal becomes a rally after a week or so of strong gains. If the rally continues longer, it may later be called a market turnaround and then a recovery. After a recovery extends for many months, it will be called an up trend or even a bull market. Refer to chart on page 451.

Recovery: A period of rising market prices that may extend from the first month to the time when prices begin to approach normal. The initial stage of the price rise is called a rally as it turns up from the low point. When the rise has become established, the term recovery is applied. Later, as prices approach normal, the term recovery is dropped, and it becomes simply an up market or up trend. Refer to chart on page 451.

Resistance line: An arbitrary line drawn on a chart connecting any two or three high points and extending for several weeks into the future on the chart as an indication of the highest price range that is expected. The high points to be selected are up to the chartist, so the price levels dictated by the resistance line are variable. The basic premise in using this type of trend line is that once a trend is started, the tendency is for that direction to continue. This is one of the most widely used techniques in stock charting, and it is popular with many professional people, but it has the fault of ignoring the self-stabilizing forces of the laws of averages. Resistance lines and support lines are called trend lines. Refer to chart on page 451.

Reversal: Any change in the *near term* trend of market prices. Day to day changes are called fluctuations. If a

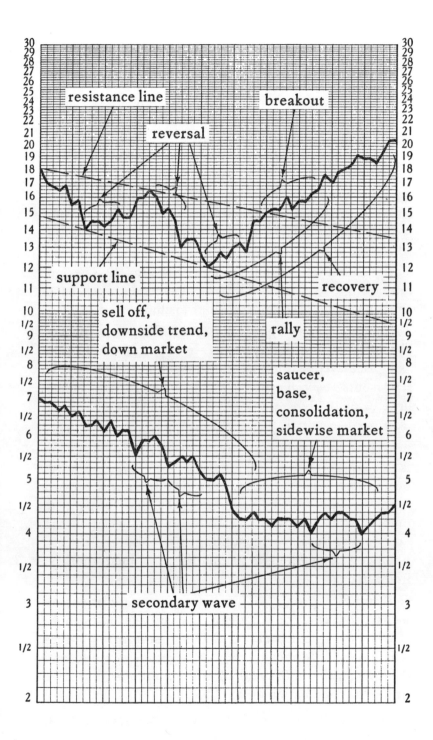

resistance line

breakout

reversal

support line

recovery

sell off,
downside trend,
down market

rally

saucer,
base,
consolidation,
sidewise market

secondary wave

trend continues for several days, it becomes a reversal. If a price changes from a declining trend to a rising trend, it is an up-reversal, and a change from rising prices to declining prices is a down-reversal. The term reversal is not applied after a trend has continued more than a few weeks. Refer to chart on page 451.

Saucer: A pattern that shows as a long, shallow, inactive period on a chart following a declining period. It is also called a base or a consolidation period during which the stock is thought to be gathering strength for a rally. It is thought that the longer the inactive period the stronger the rally will be. A saucer is taken as a time to be prepared to buy. Refer to chart on page 451.

Secondary wave: The shortest of the wave cycles identified by Optimal Analysis. It will show on a chart as a price cycle extending not more than two weeks. It represents reactionary moves by investors, and it has little value to investors. Refer to chart on page 451.

Sell off: A period covered on a chart when market prices are falling due to heavy pressure of selling. This is not the short profit taking dips that occur in a rally, but a more serious decline resulting from widespread fears and gloom. Selling is stronger than buying so many shares end up in dealer's inventories or in the accounts of floor specialists. It is a wide spread action, but not strong enough to qualify as a bear market. Refer to chart on page 451.

Sell signal: A progression of upward moving prices on a chart that exceeds what could be considered normal. It is read as an indication that self-stabilizing forces will soon take effect to cause a reversal in trend and declining prices. Several of the conditions that give this selling indication are:

1. A *sharp* climb in prices that continues several days,

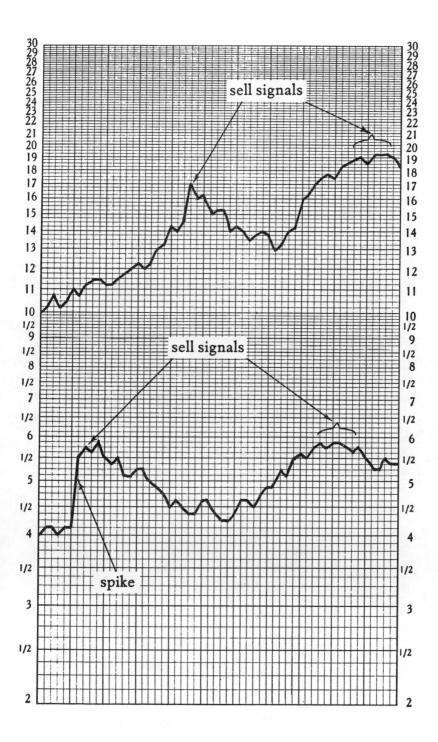

following a longer period of *slowly* rising prices.

2. A leveling of prices following a period of unusually strong price gains.

3. *Any* spike, which is a sharp jump of 20% or more in a single day.

4. A high point on a wave pattern that appears to duplicate the duration and intensity of several preceding waves.

These condiditions are considered signals to sell because the weight of statistics show that the odds are very strong that a decline will follow. Moving with the odds is the whole purpose of traders, but they will also research fundamental conditions that may give clues as to why current cycles could depart from normal values. Refer to chart on page 455.

Sidewise market: A period of time on a chart when prices show little change up or down. It traces a horizontal path with minor fluctuations. If it occurs after a period of decline, it is said to be a period of consolidation when the stock is forming a base from which to make a rally. Traders do not buy during this period but are in readiness for the rally to begin. Refer to chart on page 451.

Slump: A temporary downturn in market prices. Declines are widespread, but not severe; and investor moods are depressed, but not in panic or despair. Refer to chart on page 457.

Spike: A sudden and sharp increase in a stock price. It will show as a jump of 20% or more in a single day. It is a very obvious departure from normal and is considered as a signal for an immediate sell. Unless facts are known about the cause of the jump, a trader will sell to take his profit while it is there. The odds are that a decline will soon follow. Refer to chart on page 455.

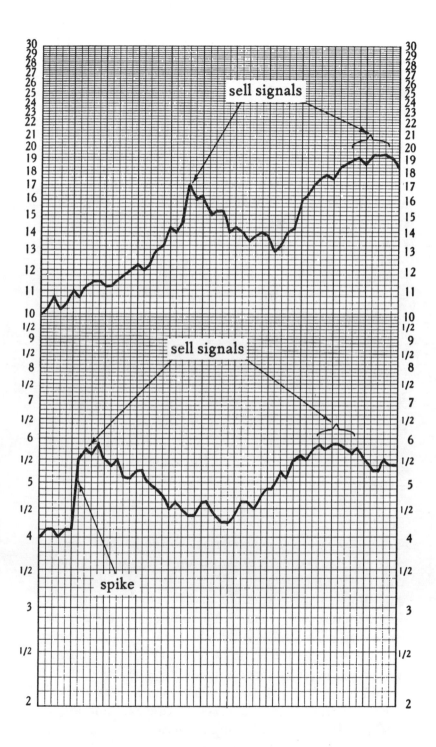

Support line: A line drawn on a chart as a technique of technical analysis to determine likely limits for price declines. The chartist will draw a dotted line across his chart connecting two or three recent low points and then extend that line for a few weeks into the future. He then declares that any decline is not likely to penetrate that line. Many analysts will hedge that statement by selecting two other low points that could generate another support line falling below that first line. When using these lines, the chartist will recommend buying when the price approaches the first support line. If the price does turn up, it is a strong buy signal. However, if the price penetrates the support line, it is a sell signal, and he will then declare that the lower support line is the area where a turnaround is expected. These lines are used to guide investment decisions on the premise that once a trend is begun, the tendency is to continue that direction. This ignores the law of averages which says that the longer a trend continues, the greater the probability for a reversal. Support lines and resistance lines together are called trend lines. Refer to chart on page 457.

Technical adjustment: The same as technical correction below. Refer to chart on page 457.

Technical correction: Any brief change in the direction of trend of market prices that is opposite to the general trend, whether up or down. The term is applied to the early portion of a reversal if that reversal is contrary to fundamental conditions. For example, if the trend has been upward and suddenly reverses downward following the announcement of a large bank failure, it would *not* be considered a technical correction. But it would be technical if fundamental conditions are very favorable when a brief setback occurs that can only be explained as a self-adjusting move in the market. Self-

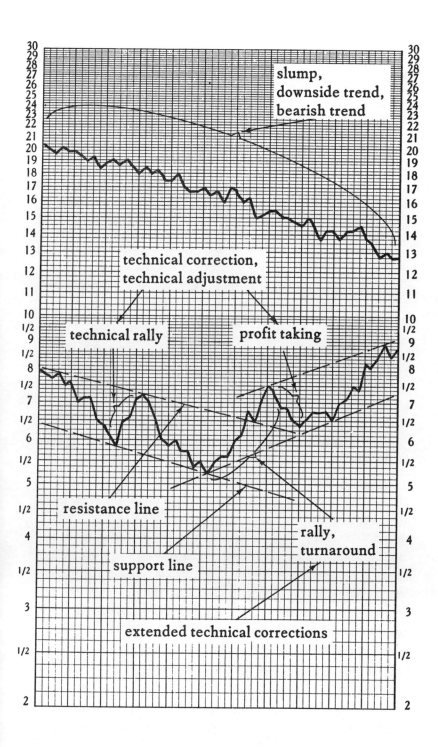

slump,
downside trend,
bearish trend

technical correction,
technical adjustment

technical rally

profit taking

resistance line

rally,
turnaround

support line

extended technical corrections

adjustment amounts to profit taking in a period of rising markets and bargain hunting in times of declining markets. Several other terms also carry the same definition but apply to special cases. See chart on page 459 for the following variations:

1. Profit taking: A sudden decline that interrupts a strong climb in prices if fundamental conditions would suggest that a continued climb would be justified. It is attributed to traders who are nervous about how long the climb can be sustained and sell to preserve the profits gained by their stocks.

2. Rally: A period of healthy upward movement that extends the early up-reversal for a number of weeks. A rally may result from some good fundamental news, or it may result from bargain hunting that spreads enthusiasm among other investors to carry the technical move a little farther.

3. Turnaround: An abrupt change upward preceded by an extended decline or a consolation period. The same term is also applied to fundamental conditions within a company that could lead to improvement of a weak performance.

Technical rally: A rally or turnaround in the market that occurs during a period of generally declining prices. It does not reflect improving fundamental conditions, but more likely is the result of bargain hunting by some investors, which sparks additional buying by others. Some expectant moves can occur when the market has been depressed for some time, but no new bad news has been released to force things lower. Technical rallies seldom hold for more than a month and are usually terminated by profit taking by traders. Refer to chart on page 459.

Top: The highest point reached on a chart during any period of time. It is also called a peak. If a specific

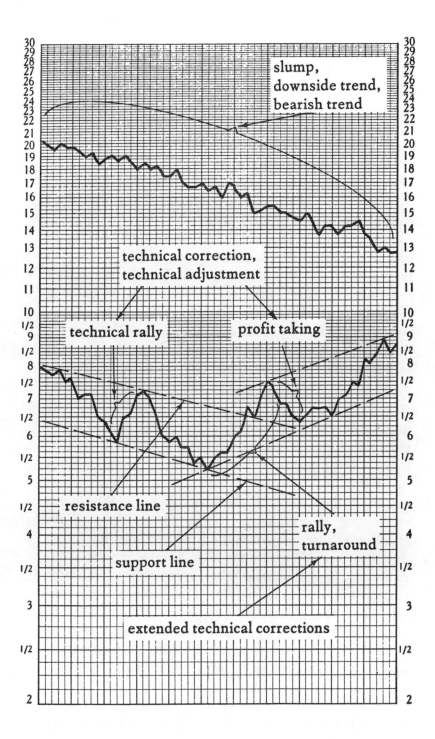

slump,
downside trend,
bearish trend

technical correction,
technical adjustment

technical rally

profit taking

resistance line

support line

rally,
turnaround

extended technical corrections

period is being discussed, such as a week, month, or a year, it may be called the high for that period. These terms can only be used in retrospect, and they must be followed by a decline. Also notice TOPPING OUT for a pattern that appears to be leading to a top. Refer to chart on page 461.

Topping out: A term that applies to the *apparent* condition of a chart that indicates a down reversal may soon be reached. This appears as a strong climb for an extended period that begins to moderate with smaller fluctuations and smaller net gains. It is an opinion of the chartist, but it cannot be verified until more time elapses, and the chart actually does turn down. Sometimes a flat area will appear on a chart following a rising period. This is a plateau and is the same as topping out. Such patterns are considered selling signals. Refer to chart on page 461.

Trend line: A device used by many chartists to determine expected areas of future price levels for stocks. There are two kinds of trend lines: support lines and resistance lines. They are developed in the same way and refer to the lowest or highest expected prices, respectively. A support line is a dotted line connecting two or three recent low points and extending for some time into the future on the chart. This defines the lowest limit for future prices. The resistance line is similarly constructed by connecting two or three recent high points and extending that line into the future. This will define the highest limit expected for a stock price. If prices penetrate these trend lines, it is interpreted as establishing a major trend and is considered a buy or sell signal depending on the direction of travel. This technique is based on the premise that once a pattern is begun, the tendency is for that trend to continue. It is a useful technique, but

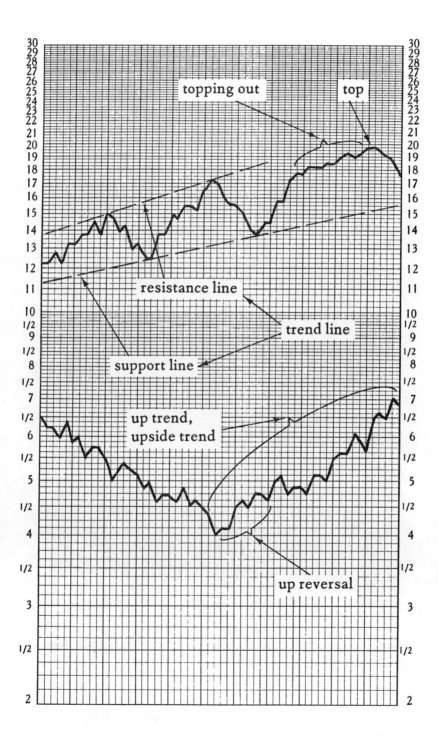

it is opposed to the Optimal Analysis tecnnique, which is based on the laws of averages that state that the longer a pattern continues in any given direction, the greater the odds become that a reversal will take place. Refer to chart on page 463.

Up reversal: A sudden change in the near term trend of market prices from a decline to rising prices. It is not said of day to day fluctuations, but the second or third day of upward movement is an up-reversal. If that upward direction continues for several weeks, it is called a rally, If it continues even longer following a long period of decline, it becomes a recovery. Refer to chart on page 463.

Up side trend: A period of time when prices are rising. The term usually carries with it an unspoken reference to a wave cycle which has both rising and declining sides. The upside, then, is the first half, which is rising. It may last a couple weeks in the case of a primary wave, or several years in the case of a fundamental wave, but always it infers that a decline has preceded the upside, and another decline will follow. Refer to chart on page 463.

Up trend: A period during which market prices are generally rising. If a long term trend shows rising prices, the overall trend would be upward, even though small down-reversals may interrupt from time to time. The upside of the short cycles would continue longer than the downside, so the net result is a rising market. Refer to chart on page 463.

Wave cycle: A pattern on a chart which contains both rising and falling prices with easily discernible tops and bottoms. These patterns look like ragged waves and will contain many small fluctuations. Waves, or cycles, will normally repeat in a very loose sense over a period of time. The cycles may extend for only a few

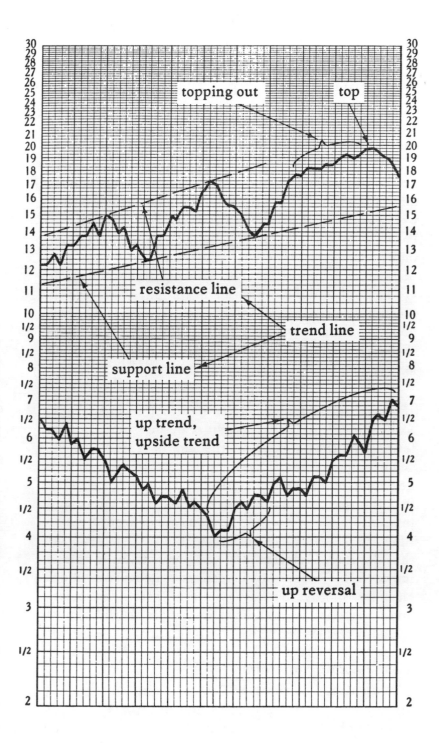

weeks, or they may extend for years. The high and low points may also be greatly different. Optimal analysis has identified three basic wave cycles that assist a chartist to interpret his charts. They are primary waves, secondary waves, and fundamental waves. Primary waves are the most important for traders since they are the most predictable and encompass easily workable time periods of two weeks to four months. Prices of volatile stocks may change 25% to 50% in this time. This cycle ignores daily fluctuations that are reactionary in nature and also the long term trends that are so hard to define in terms of timing. Wave cycles are quite important to traders, since profits depend upon buying at a low point and selling at a high point. Timing according to cycles will also improve profits for long term investors. Refer to chart on page 465.

Stock charts do much more than just record prices. Skilled investors and analysts can interpret various formations that appear on the charts to indicate investor emotion and even anticipate certain future developments. Using historical records, it is possible to determine typical reactions to certain conditions and influences. Since those conditions recur from time to time the chartist can recognize familiar patterns as they develop. Understanding the patterns, he is able to improve his odds on investment decisions. Stock charting is extremely valuable to all serious investors and indispensible to short term traders. It will almost certainly result in improved performance.

Stock clearing corporation

A subsidiary of the NYSE which acts as a central agency for security deliveries and payments between member firms of the exchange.

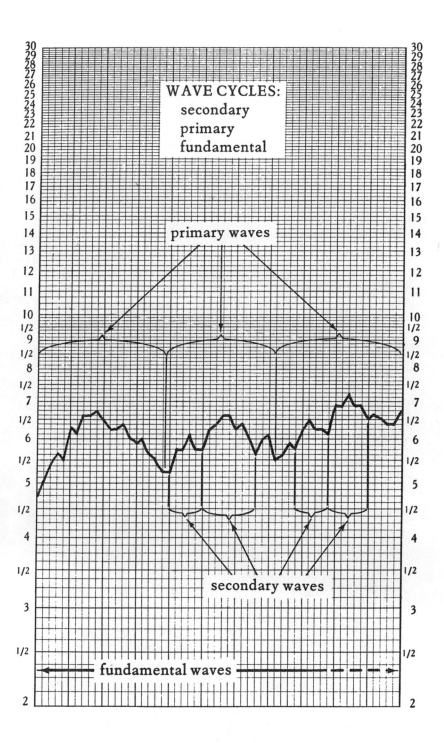

Stock dividends

Dividends which are paid in the form of stock. The dividend may offer as little as one share for each 100 currently owned, or as much as one share for each five shares owned. If the dividend is larger, for example, a ratio of 1 for 4, or 1 for 2, it is usually called a split. A stock dividend may be paid in the stock of another company. In that case it might be the stock of a subsidiary, and the distribution would be referred to as a spin-off.

Stock exchanges

A place where brokers and dealers transact securities trades for their customers. There are two national stock exchanges, the New York Stock Exchange and the American Stock Exchange, both located in New York. Also there are several regional exchanges located in major cities around the United States. Some are:
Boston Stock Exchange
Chicago Board of Trade
Cincinnati Stock Exchange
Detroit Stock Exchange
Midwest Stock Exchange (in Chicago)
National Stock Exchange (in New York)
Pacific Coast Exchange
(in Los Angeles and San Francisco)
Philadelphia-Baltimore-Washington Stock Exchange
Pittsburgh Stock Exchange
San Francisco Mining Exchange
Spokane Stock Exchange

In addition there are foreign stock exchanges located in major cities around the world. All exchanges admit only their members to use the facilities, who then conduct business on an auction basis, or with bid and asked prices for securities. 86% of all U. S. trading takes place in the New York Stock Exchange. See EXCHANGE SEAT for information about membership.

Stock market

The market or public demand for stock in publicly held corporations. This is not a physical location or an organization, as a few people think. Prices for securities are determined only by the public demand for them, so it is a true auction market. Most transactions in listed stocks take place in one of the stock exchanges, but the actual market is where the people are, because the market *is* the people. Over-the-counter stock transactions are handled in brokers' offices in all parts of the country. Since the market is the public *demand*, the market indexes measure attitudes, intentions, and emotional status of investors more than security values. Many of the stock transactions are long term investments, but, also, a large number of them represent short term trading. The trading activities contribute to liquidity and volatility of the market, which are desirable for both investors and the issuing companies.

Stock option

A contract between individuals or a corporation and an investor under which an investor obtains the right to purchase a given number of shares of stock within a given time.

1. This can be used as a method of speculating where the person buying the option is expecting the market price to move in his favor so he can realize a profit. If the market price, for example, on stock XYZ is at $20 a share when a speculator buys an

option with a striking price at $25 six months later, he is speculating that the price will rise above 25 during that time. If the price in fact rises to $30, he may exercise the option at the price of $25. Since options are written for round lots only, or 100 shares, he will have made $500 minus the cost of the option, which may have been about $1 per share. Thus, for a $100 investment he got $400 profit.

2. A corporation may offer options to its key personnel as perquisites, or added benefits in respect of their positions. These options may be priced quite low purposely to allow a generous profit to the person.

See RIGHTS and WARRANTS for other types of options. Also see PUTS, CALLS, STRIPS, STRAPS, STRADDLES, and SPREADS for various options used in speculating.

Stock power

A document that when signed by an investor gives authority to a second party, such as a broker or a banker, to transfer his stock certificates to another name. A banker may execute, or put into effect, that authorization if the stock was pledged against a loan which becomes in default. A broker will execute the authorization when transferring stock from your name to a street name account for you, or to another person when you sell the stock.

Stock pricing

Prices of stock vary widely at the time of issue and become more complex and bewildering after issue. The original issue price is called the subscription price. That price is determined by the issuer and the underwriter and is usually based on marketing considerations . . . any easy price to sell if it is a new company, or slightly below the market if the issuer has other shares out. Subscription prices include the underwriters' expenses, so no commission is charged to the buyer. When the issue is sold out or terminated, it can then be traded on the open market . . . over-the-counter if it is a new or small company, or on an exchange if it is a listed company. Supply and demand controls the prices on the open market, and, since the supply is limited, the price will rise if the demand increases. Higher earnings or favorable news that could lead to higher earnings are influences which tend to increase prices. Even a strong demand, by itself, tends to attract more buyers. This is the psychology of the winner. Almost anything can lead to falling market prices: reduced sales, shrinking profits, management problems, law suits, competition, political unrest, national economic decline, higher interest rates, even inactivity in the general market influences tend to push market prices downward.

If a company thinks its stock is too high for easy marketability, it may split the stock or issue new shares to all shareholders in proportion to their equity position. Splits may be in any proportion appropriate . . . If a 2:1 split is decided upon, for example, each shareholder will receive two new shares for each of the old shares he owns. Increasing the number of shares without a simultaneous increase in net worth or earnings cuts the market price by the same factor.

If the company thinks the price is too low, they may have a reverse split, or exchange the old shares with *fewer* new shares of *higher* value. This is sometimes done when market prices sag so low that investors shun it as being a sick stock.

All shares traded on the open market are sold at the

market price, plus a commission if the transaction is handled by a broker. If sold by a dealer out of his own account, it is at the market price plus a markup which approximates the broker's commission. When a new issue first goes on the open market, the price is somewhat related to its book value per share and includes all sales charges. Subsequently, the price is more related to earnings or *potential* earnings. If a company experiences difficulties which coincide with national economic problems, it may see its stock sink to a third of its book value. In times of prosperity and growth, public favor may push the market price to 10 or 20 times its book value.

Stock tables

Long columns of figures appearing on the financial pages of newspapers which report market data on thousands of stocks. They usually give high and low for the year, high and low for the day, closing price and change from the close of the previous day. Some newspapers include trading volume, price-earnings ratio, dividend payments, yield, and other information.

Stock ticker

An instrument which prints stock trading data on a continuous narrow paper tape within seconds after the actual transaction. It identifies the company by ticker symbol, then lists the number of shares traded, price, and, occasionally, some other important information for each transaction. Also see NEWS TICKER for difference and SYMBOLS for explanation of identification symbols used on the tape or other reporting media.

Stock valuation

A qualified opinion of the true value of a stock. Stock

values are judged on the basis of assets, earnings, and future prospects, independent of actual market price.

Stock ratings

A system for evaluating the financial strength behind a certain stock or the management performance of the issuing company. Ratings are made by numerous advisory services, but the most widely known are from *Standard and Poor's*. The actual ratings are listed under RATINGS OF SECURITIES. The words ratings, rankings, or grading are practically synonymous.

Stockholder

Also called shareholder. A person or organization who shares ownership of a corporation. Ownership is evidenced by stock certificates or shares which state the exact number of shares owned. Since the company may issue more shares of different classes of shares at a later time, the shares cannot state the percentage of ownership. Prices will vary with market demand, so the purchase price is not indicated on the certificate. A stockholder's rights are the same, regardless of the number of shares he owns. His voting power increases, however, with a larger number of shares. Shareholders elect a Board of Directors, who in turn elect the operating officers and set the major policy of the corporation. The stock purchased by the shareholder represents equity in the company and entitles each shareholder to his proportion of the assets in the event of liquidation. See SENIOR SECURITY and DEBT SECURITY for preferential ranking for some investors. Also see STOCK for a listing of different types of stock. See BONDS for non-equity securities.

Stockholder of record

A stockholder whose name is registered on the books

of the issuing corporation as of a certain date, called the record date. This date is important when dividends are paid, since payment is sent to the person recorded as the owner on that date. If the stock has been transferred to another party after the record date, but before the payment date for the dividend distribution, the check will go to the person on record on the record date. Often stock prices will be reported as ex-dividend during the period between the record and payment date, which will mean the trade is made without right to the dividend.

Stockholder proposal

A proposal by a shareholder, who may or may not be an officer or employee, which is brought before shareholders at an annual meeting.

Stockholders' equity

The net investment value of a corporation, or the net worth as it is carried on the books. Also called shareholders' equity. Notice that stockholders' equity applies to the worth of the entire company, while the term book value applies to the per share worth for a stockholder. See FINANCIAL STATEMENT for other related matters as they are recorded on the books of a company.

Stop limit order

A stop limit order to buy is an order issued by an investor to his broker to be executed at the stated price or less. A stop limit order to sell is an order to be executed at the stated price or higher if possible. A stop limit order is unlike the stop order in this respect; the stop limit order must be executed at the limit price or better when the stop price is reached. By contrast, the stop order becomes a market order once the stop price is reached, which permits the broker to accept any price obtainable. If the price recedes after reaching the stop price, the order, which is now a market order, may be filled at a less attractive price. See BUY or SELL ORDERS for a list of other kinds of orders used in securities trading.

Stop loss order

A sell order given by an investor to his broker to sell a security automatically if it falls to a pre-selected point. The stop becomes a market order when a specified price is reached so that the broker may then execute the order at the best price available. He may not be able to execute it at the stop price, but since it is now a market order, he may execute the order at a less attractive price. Also called a stop order. Note that the stop loss order differs from the stop limit order which does *not* become a market order when the stop is reached. It must be executed at the stop price or better. See BUY or SELL ORDERS for a list of other kinds of orders used in securities trading.

Stop order

An order to buy or sell a security when it reaches a specified price. The stop order to buy becomes a market order as soon as a transaction in the security occurs at or above the stop price. A stop order to sell becomes a market order as soon as a transaction in the security occurs at or below the stop price. A stop order may be used to protect a paper profit or to try to limit a possible loss to a certain amount. Since it becomes a market order when the stop price is reached, there is no certainty that it will be executed at that price, but it will be executed as soon as possible at any price available. See BUY or SELL ORDERS for a list of other kinds of orders used in securities trading.

Stopped stock

A stock which has been temporarily stopped or guaranteed in price to a broker by a specialist. It is a service which permits a broker a short time to seek out another seller at an advantageous price while being assured that the price will not rise in the meantime. If no better price is found, the broker can take his guaranteed price from the specialist. However, if he locates a seller willing to take less, he buys that stock and cancels the stop with the specialist.

Story

A recent happening which causes investors to turn to a particular industry seeking investment gain. In use you might hear a question, "What is the story about the computer industry?"

Straddle

Also called a spread. The practice of buying a put and a call (options to sell and to buy) for the same stock on the same day for the same price. It is done with the hope that a loss on one will be offset by a gain on the other. Sometimes the terms spread or combination are used to mean a straddle but they are not preferred meanings. See SPREAD for its common use in commodity trading.

Straight line depreciation

A very common method for calculating depreciation deductions for capital assets used in business. This amounts to reducing the value of the asset by a fixed amount each year throughout the expected life of the asset down to the salvage value. The amount of reduction each year is calculated by subtracting the estimated salvage value from the purchase price, then dividing the difference by the number of years of expected life. The result is the amount written off each year against gross profits before taxes. See DEPRECIATION for other methods of calculating depreciation with examples.

Straight line interest

A straight percentage of the unpaid balance on an annual basis. An example of this is as follows:

A $1,000 installment loan for two years at 8% would cost $79.85 in interest by the time it is paid off. The monthly payments would vary from $48.33 on the first payment to $41.86 on the last payment. A variation to this method would be to set a fixed amount for each monthly payment. To hold a fixed payment of $47, the interest for the first payment would be $6.67 and the principal would be $40.33. On the second month it would be $6.40 interest and $40.60 principal. The third month $6.13 interest and $40.87 principal. The final payment, the 24th, would total $48.01.

Interest is figured on the unpaid balance so that for each successive month there is a larger amount of the payment applied to the principal, and less is for interest. See INTEREST for other methods of interest and examples of each.

Strap

A form of straddle or combination purchase of puts and calls. The ordinary call is an option to buy a specified stock at a specified price within a specified time. If the investor is doubtful about the market he may hedge his position by purchasing a put at the same time. He now has a straddle. In this way, he offsets his loss if the stock price moves opposite to his expectation. If he feels strongly that the price will rise but he still wants to leave open a small road for retreat, he will buy *two* calls that will show him a profit if the price rises sufficiently, then he will also buy *one* put to offset the cost of the calls, just in case the price does decline instead. This combination of two calls and one put is referred to as a strap. Also see STRIP.

Street

A term which refers to the entire financial community which is concentrated in the Wall Street area of New York. Sometimes it is applied to mean the investing public.

Street name

The registration of stock in the broker's name, even though he is not the owner. This is a convenience to permit rapid transaction of business. Short term traders buy and sell frequently and find that hand delivery of certificates in their own name is extremely burdensome. Using a street name account, the investor need only use a telephone to complete his business.

Striking price

The predetermined price at which an option may be exercised. It is a fixed price established at the time the option is written. If the holder can exercise the option before the expiration date at a profit, the transaction takes place at the striking price. If the market, however, has moved contrary to the holder of the option, he merely lets it expire. His only loss is the cost of the option.

Strip

Another form of straddle or combination of puts and

calls. The ordinary put is an option to sell a certain stock at a given price within a given time. An investor expecting a price to decline may purchase a put with the hope of buying that stock at the lower price to make delivery at the higher price stated on the put. The difference between those prices is his profit. If he has some fears that the market may rise he may hedge by buying a simultaneous call that will offset the losses on his put. This combination is called a straddle. If his bearish feelings are strong enough, he may buy two puts to make a profit on the falling prices, and a single call which would offset his loss on the puts if the market does rise instead of fall. This combination of two puts and one call is called a strip. Also see STRAP.

Strong hands

A term sometimes applied to institutions and other sophisticated investors. It is thought that, at the bottom of a market decline stocks rest in strong hands, since the panic-stricken smaller investors have sold out. Perhaps the strong hands sold out earlier to avoid losses and are now back to buy in at bargain prices from small investors who were afraid to get out early in the decline.

Strong market

Another way of saying the market is rising or advancing. A bull market, up market, or rally.

Sub-chapter M

A section of the Internal Revenue Code which provides special tax treatment for regulated investment companies. Under this section, investment companies are exempt from income tax if 90% or more of their income is distributed to their shareholders. Prior to 1954, this section was called Supplement Q.

See INVESTMENT COMPANY ACT OF 1940 and
STATEMENT OF POLICY for other regulations and
limitations applying to investment companies.

Sub-chapter S
A section of the Internal Revenue Code under which
certain small corporations may be organized so that the
profits are not taxed to the company, but are passed on
to the owners to be taxed as personal income. Its
advantage comes from income averaging if the owners
had relatively low income in previous years. The
corporation's sudden high income may be averaged
over the past five years of low income.

Subject market
Estimated market for a security as stated by a broker
or dealer, not a firm quote or firm market. Also called
indicated market or subject to confirmation. A firm
order to buy or sell can be made only with further
checking by the broker. Sometimes called a workout
market.

Subordinate
Some stocks or bonds are issued with special conditions which permit one group of investors to hold
precedence over others in the event of liquidation.
Those in the lower order of rank are subordinated. The
arrangement is used at times to give added security to
a lending group. It may also sweeten a participation
offer for an especially risky venture.

Subordinated debenture
A debt security that ranks lower than some other
security issued by the same company. In case of
liquidation its claims on assets will wait until higher
ranking securities have been paid off. For example, a

company may float a first mortgage bond issue which will outrank the debenture bond. Subordinated debentures are also called overlaying bonds. See BONDS for other types of bonds and descriptions of each.

Subscription

A simple document which gives legal notice of intention to buy a specific number of shares of stock in a primary offering by the company indicated. The subscription form gives a few basic facts about the issue including prices and any restrictions or special conditions. It is given to prospective investors with a prospectus which gives very detailed information about the issue. The completed subscription form is turned in with the payment, but the investor may not get stock certificates for a number of weeks. In some cases, if there are not sufficient shares subscribed, the offering may be cancelled and the money returned.

Subscription price

The fixed price per share at which a new issue or even a secondary issue of stock is being offered to the public. This price includes the underwriter's expenses, so there is no commission charged, as is normally done in securities trading. This price is set and will not fluctuate with the market until the issue is sold out or terminated. When the offering is completed, it may then be traded on the open market at prices determined by supply and demand. At that time commissions will be charged by brokers.

Subscription rights

Usually shortened to rights. The privilege given to shareholders of a corporation to purchase their proper proportion of any new shares offered by the company, usually at a price below the market price of existing shares. The difference between the price stated on the right and going market price for the stock it represents is the market value of the right. If a shareholder is unable or unwilling to exercise the right by purchasing the new shares, he may sell the rights at the market value. Rights must usually be exercised within a few weeks or months. Warrants are similar pre-emptive privileges to purchase stock except that the warrant may be good for several years or even perpetually. Notice differences from OPTIONS.

Subsidiary

A company which is subject to the control of another. The control is established by ownership of a controlling interest of its stock. A statutory subsidiary, as defined by the Public Utility Holding Company Act, is any company in which there is 10 % or more ownership of the oustanding voting shares by another company.

Subsidy

Financial grant or aid. Generally applied to government payments made to individuals or organizations for services to the government or to comply with government planning. The term does not apply to all government compensation, but only to programs where the payment is only part of the total cost of the operation. For example, airlines receive subsidies for carrying mail, although most of their revenues come from other sources. Farmers have at various times received subsidies for complying with crop control plans which may call for not planting part of their land.

Sum-of-the-digits

1. Sometimes called the rule of 78. A method for calculating interest refunds if the original interest

was charged as add-on interest, that is, interest calculated as if the full amount of principal is held for the full time of a purchase contract. That total amount of interest is added to the principal before being divided by the number of payments to be made. If such a loan is paid off early, the interest refund must be calculated, but a different method is used which reduces the refund. Each monthly payment is numbered beginning with 12 for the current month, 11 for the next, 10 for the next, and so on until the last month is 1. Totaling these numbers gives 78 points for a 1 year loan contract, hence the Rule of 78. A two year contract totals 300 points and a three year contract equals 666 points. An example of a refund on a two year contract that is paid off early in the 20th month is as follows: $1,000 loan at 8% for 2 years. $1,000 x 8% x 2 = $160 interest + $1,000 principal = $1,160 total contract divided by 24 months = $48.41 for the first payment, then 23 payments of $48.33. Pay off is calculated in the 20th month as 4 + 3 + 2 + 1 = 10 (sum-of-the-digits for the last 4 months) out of a total of 300 points for a 24 month contract. $160 divided by 300 equals $.533 per point x 10 points for the last 4 months, equals a $5.33 refund. The interest refund for the final months is considerably less than the actual amount of interest charged for the same months. By using the add-on method of charging interest, the borrower paid $6.66 interest each month ($1,000 x 8% x 2 yrs. divided by 24 months) for a total of $26.66 for those final 4 months. See INTEREST for further discussions on the subject.

2. Also applied to a method for calculating accelerated depreciation. See DEPRECIATION for explanation.

Supervision

In mutual fund management it is continuous, professional management, using experience and knowledge to apply the products of research to the selection of securities for the fund portfolio.

Supplement Q

The section of the Internal Revenue Code which provided tax-exempt status to investment companies until 1954. Supplement Q was replaced in 1954 by Sub-Chapter M. See separate listing.

Support line

A technique used in technical analysis to forecast market trends. The chartist draws a dotted line across his stock chart connecting two recent low points and extending for some time into the future. He then declares that a declining trend will most likely not be able to penetrate that line. Many analysts will hedge that statement by finding two other low points that could generate a dotted line that would slope below the primary support line. Then his announcement would be that if the downward trend does in fact penetrate the first support line it would indicate sufficient downward pressure that it would push to the lower support line before halting. Penetration of the first support line is called a signal to sell. Buying is usually recommended whenever the price reaches a support line, and if it does reverse upward again it is interpreted as a strong buy signal. See RESISTANCE LINE and TREND LINE for related charting techniques. Also see PATTERNS and BUY SIGNALS for other charting signals, and STOCK CHARTS for illustrations of various patterns on sample charts.

Surplus

1. When this term is found on a financial statement of

a corporation it will be accompanied by any of several other words: *earned*, *earnings*, *capital* and *paid-in*. The meanings of each is precise but since they concern dissimilar subjects they are sometimes confusing.

A. Earned surplus:
Corporate earnings that are retained for growth *after* dividends are paid. This is the same thing as retained earnings.

B. Earnings surplus:
The same thing as earned surplus above.

C. Capital surplus:
The original cash received from the sale of securities to the extent of the difference between par or stated value and the actual cash received for the offering. The capital surplus can be calculated in later years by adding the net worth to the stated value of the stock, then subtracting earned surplus. Dividends cannot be paid from capital surplus except as a return of capital, or a tax free dividend. Capital surplus represents shareholder's equity.

D. Paid-in surplus:
The same as capital surplus above.

2. In personal finances surplus is less precise in meaning, but, in general, it refers to spendable income. Economists use different terms to define the variables such as:

A. Disposable income:
The total cash left after paying all *tax liabilities*.

B. Excess cash:
This usually means the cash available after paying normal living expenses such as food,

clothing, and housing. The excess is available for optional expenses like entertainment, luxuries, savings, investments, and other personal interests. This is often called discretionary income, and, by some people, mad money.

Suspension

A punitive action against a brokerage firm or one of its employees. The move is initiated by the National Association of Securities Dealers if it has discovered violations of regulations. Suspensions can be temporary . . . a few days or a few weeks, or they can be permanent if there is a serious violation. Suspension revokes the privileges of a securities license and trading privileges on the exchanges. Sometimes the action can prohibit the censured person from acting as a principal, but he will be permitted to serve as an employee of another member.

Suspension of trading

Stopping of all trading on an exchange of a certain listed stock because of abnormal conditions concerning that security. This type suspension, or even delisting, is not a punitive action as would be a suspension of a broker. Rather, it is a stabilizing action to prevent reactionary market runs that could follow some news announcement. The company may have legal problems that may trigger market runs, or an unfavorable news release may be the cause, but the suspension is enacted to allow time for rumors to subside and for facts to be digested. Even rumors may cause undue price changes leading to a suspension. Trading is resumed when the problem is eased. A permanent suspension, called delisting, could result if the issuing company falls below certain standards for financial strength, sales volume, and market breadth for its stock. See LISTED STOCK for details on listing requirements.

Sweetener
Some added benefit given to make a proposition more attractive. Sometimes a bond issue will have an added conversion privilege or have a warrant attached. The sweetener may be attractive enough on some bonds that investors will accept unusually low interest rates. Often key employees are given extra benefits beyond their salaries in an effort to attract a ready supply of new executive caliber people. These sweeteners are called PERQUISITES.

Switch order
An order issued by an investor to his broker for the purchase of one stock and the sale of another stock at a stipulated price difference. It is also called a contingent order. See BUY ORDERS and SELL ORDERS for a list of other kinds of orders used in securities trading.

Switching
In mutual funds switching is the practice of liquidating shares in one fund to purchase shares in another. Usually it is called *conversion* if the change is between two funds operated by the same management, and if the change is the choice of the shareholder. This type conversion is legal and desirable if the change is to better fit the investment circumstances of the investor. However, if the change is induced by a salesman to gain a new customer who was once with a different fund management, the term *switching* is then applied, and it is considered unethical and illegal. Notice another term, CROSS, which is sometimes called a switch order but pertains

to a special type negotiated trade for large orders on the exchange floor.

Symbol

A ticker symbol which is a set of identifying letters assigned to a security to speed reporting of market prices on the stock ticker. The ticker reports every trade within seconds after the transaction takes place. The report is printed on a narrow paper tape which includes the identifying symbol followed by the number of shares traded and finally the price. A few old companies have the envied position of possessing a single letter symbol, such as Ford with F and U. S. Steel with X. Most other listed stocks have two or three letter symbols which are the initials of the company or a phonetic abbreviation, as General Motors with GM, or Bowmar with BOM. Some are unrelated simply because of similarity of other company names, such as Leisure Technology with LUX or Yates Industries with YES. In print, the symbols for *listed* stocks are large, upper case letters, and they use one, two or three letters.

Early in the 1970's a move was begun to report prices of *over-the-counter* stocks along with the listed stocks on a unified tape. The first step was assigning symbols to the most widely traded OTC stocks. These symbols are called NASDAQ symbols for National Association of Securities Dealers Automatic Quotation. Several thousand of these stocks are now quoted electronically with the listed stocks. In print the NASDAQ symbols appear as upper case letters but in smaller type than the listed stocks. They will also use four or five letters for each symbol. Some examples are: Dairy Queen Stores with DQEN and Reynolds & Reynolds with REYNA.

Symbols

Newspapers and financial periodicals use numerous symbols to aid in keeping stock tables brief. Many publishers use some of their own symbols, but the following are fairly standard:

a	Adjusted
a	Extra dividend
c or cv	Convertible issue
cld	Called
ct	Certificate
d	Deficit
e or est	Estimated
f	Flat
fn	Foreign security which is subject to interest equalization tax
r	Registered bond
wd	When distributed
wi	When issued
wt or w	Warrants
ww	With warrants
xw	Without warrants
x or xd	Ex-dividend (without dividend)
nd	Next day delivery
nw	New issue
x or xi	Ex-interest (without interest)
x-dis	Ex-distribution (dividend paid to shareholder of record on that date)
xr	Ex-rights (without rights)

Syndicate

A group of investment bankers who join together to underwrite and distribute a new issue of securities or a large block of an outstanding issue that is too large for handling on the exchange floor. The syndicate will actually purchase the block, then attempt to resell it to the public. Notice the difference from selling group, selling concession, and participating brokers and dealers who only assist they syndicate but are not a part of it. The syndicate underwrites the issue and accepts the financial liability.

T

Taking a bath
Sustaining serious losses in investments. It is also expressed as being taken to the cleaners, wiped out and being murdered on Wall Street. When a stock suffers a sudden and serious decline in market price, perhaps 50%, 75% or even more in decline, it is said to fall out of bed, while the owners of the stock take a bath as a result.

Taking a cleaning
Sustaining serious losses in investments. Also expressed as taking a bath, as above.

Tape
A shortening of ticker tape. The tape is the actual narrow strip of paper on which the stock ticker prints information about every security transaction that takes place on the national exchanges. In recent years a

transition has been under way to report over-the-counter transactions as well on a new composite tape. Sometimes the term tape is used to mean only the outflow of information rather than the physical tape. A different term, broad tape, is a teletype printout in brokerage offices throughout the country. It is the output from the Dow Jones News Ticker and contains news information rather than market prices. See TICKER, TICKER SYMBOL, and TICKER TAPE for more information related to the tape.

Tape watcher

A person who spends a great deal of time in a brokerage house board room watching price changes on the electronic display board. Such a person is usually not a big investor, but he would like to give the impression that he is.

Tare weight

The weight of a container or packing materials used for packing bulk materials. It is used to calculate the weight of merchandise being packed for shipping. The full container and its contents are weighed to find the gross weight, then the tare weight of the container is subtracted to arrive at the net weight of the merchandise.

Tax avoidance

Managing your financial affairs to take advantage of the lowest possible tax liability for yourself. It is a perfectly legal activity and is even promoted by the Internal Revenue Service. Quite a different matter is TAX EVASION listed below.

Tax evasion

Failing to pay taxes that are due or falsifying records

to give the impression that less tax is due. This is a federal crime. Notice the difference from TAX AVOIDANCE above.

Tax-exempt

A term applied to certain types of bonds, also called municipals, which permit a special tax-free privilege on the dividends or interest income. The privilege was granted by the government in order to induce investment in local projects such as sewer systems, school construction, highway bridges and parks. Generally, interest rates on such bonds are substantially lower than on industrial bonds, so they do not have the appeal to people in the lower tax brackets. Also see BONDS for other types of bonds and comparisons between them.

Tax loss

Any loss which can be a deduction for income tax calculations. There are times when high income individuals have more advantage in reporting a loss for a deduction than if they would pay tax on the full income. Often at the year's end a decision is made to sell any stocks that are held at depressed prices if they are not expected to recover soon, and if the loss would assist in offsetting an abnormally high income from other sources. Businesses are allowed to carry losses from one year to another if the loss from any year exceeds the taxable income for that year. This is called a tax loss carry forward.

Tax loss carry forward

Business losses from prior years that are deducted from profits in current and subsequent years. In the filing of tax reports, businesses may deduct the losses of past years from the current year's income before calculating tax liabilities. If losses carried forward exceed the current year's profits, the balance is carried forward again the next year. Occasionally a company with a a heavy tax liability will acquire a tax loss situation, which means buying another company that has substantial losses from previous years. The purpose is to claim the tax loss credits and also to add new assets and product lines at bargain prices. These deductions are also known as tax credits, tax loss credits, loss carry forward, and carry forward.

Tax loss credits
The same as tax loss carry forward above.

Tax selling
Selling securities at the year's end if losses on the transactions would reduce income taxes. Also see TAX SWITCHING.

Tax shelter
Any investment plan that has government sanctioned provisions for special credits or allowances to reduce tax liability. Their purpose is to attract investors into some needed area that would normally not attract strong interest from large investors. Examples are development of natural resources and agriculture.

Tax switching
Selling a security at the year's end in order to realize a loss for tax deductions and then reinvesting in another security which shows a better potential for gain. This provides a savings on taxes and allows a profit from the other selection.

Technical adjustment
Any brief change in the direction of trend of market

prices that is contrary to the general trend, whether up or down. The term is similar to several other terms that describe various degrees of market reversals. Some of these terms are listed below:

1. Turnaround: An abrupt change of direction preceded by an extended declining trend. The brief period of a few days after the bottom is reached on the chart.

2. Rally: A longer period of healthy upward movement than the first reversal or the few days of turnaround. It will continue for a week or more, perhaps a month in duration.

3. Sell off or profit taking: Synonymous terms to describe a brief decline in market prices following a longer period of rising prices. It is so named because fundamental conditions do not justify a decline in price so it is assumed that speculators and traders are selling to take advantage of gains made in the preceding market rise. It is assumed that a profit taking dip in market prices will be very brief, and that prices will turn up shortly.

Notice the difference between the above terms which refer to brief changes in market trends and the terms BOTTOMING OUT, TOPPING OUT, BULL MARKET, BEAR MARKET, and RECOVERY. These latter terms describe longer term market moves, and they reflect basic or *fundamental* conditions in the market. The former, short term moves are called *technical* moves because they reflect short term efforts of the market to adjust itself for the emotional reactions and overreactions of investors. Technical moves do not concern true values for securities at all. See STOCK CHARTS for illustrations of some technical moves on sample stock charts.

Technical analysis

Studying charts of market prices and indexes, then interpreting them to forecast future price movements of individual stocks. Security analysts and investors who rely on charts for analysis are called technicians or chart readers, and they have devised complex charting systems with varying degrees of value and reliability. Technical analysts usually are interested in short term trading. Notice the difference from FUNDAMENTAL ANALYSIS and OPTIMAL ANALYSIS.

Techanical analyst

A security analyst who studies charts of stock prices and market indexes then makes market forecasts based on patterns and signals that appear on his charts. In the strictest sense he does not consider financial conditions in the company or economic conditions in general. Most analysts will combine the use of fundamental data with their technical data. Notice the contrast between a strict TECHNICAL ANALYST and a FUNDAMENTAL ANALYST. Also see OPTIMAL ANALYST for a different approach.

Technical correction

The term, which is sometimes shortened to correction, refers to a break in the trend of market prices as they appear on a chart. It would apply to a single stock or the entire market. Often it is an attempt by an observer to explain a market change when there is no other real reason discernible except the pressures of emotional trading. The term suggests that the trend has passed a level in keeping with fundamental strength and is adjusting itself to reality. Also notice the term CONSOLIDATION, a related term that suggests the self-stabilizing quality of market prices. See STOCK CHARTS for illustrated chart patterns.

Technical indicators

Indexes of statistics which reflect stock market trading, but are not measures of economic conditions. Some of these indexes which have a great deal of value in stock charting are market volume, new highs and new lows, advances and declines, odd-lot trades, short interest, and margin requirements. They provide data on market prices and various measurements of investor reactions to market prices. When used by a skilled analyst, such data can provide advanced indication of market trends. Also see INDEXES, AVERAGES, and COMPOSITES for comparisons of different types of indicators.

Technical move

A minor fluctuation within the general trend of stock market prices. Analysts apply the term to suggest that there is no real fundamental reason for the market pattern, so the market is adjusting itself toward normal. Often they talk of the charts adjusting themselves. This self-stabilizing characteristic is evidence that market prices actually measure emotional attitudes of investors as much or more than they measure true value in the securities that are being charted.

Technical position

In referring to market conditions, this term is applied to internal conditions on charts and in statistical indexes such as short-interest figures, margin statistics, uninterrupted rises or declines in the market, market volume, current prices related to previous chart patterns, etc. Opposed to fundamental conditions such as income, dividends, economic and political conditions, or other factors involving the ability of companies or whole industries to operate profitably. See TECHNICAL ANALYSIS and FUNDAMENTAL ANALYSIS.

Technical rally

A rally or turnaround in the stock market or commodities market that occurs in a generally declining market. If fundamental conditions cannot support a rise in prices, but the market recovers briefly anyway, it is said to be due to technical reasons. If the preceding prices have fallen sharply and steadily, there will often be a number of investors who begin buying with the thought that it cannot continue falling. The rally is evidence that there is an attempt by some investors to outguess the emotional reactions of the average investor. See STOCK CHARTS for illustrated chart patterns.

Technician

One who uses the technical approach to security analysis. That is, he is concerned only with price movements and indicators which appear on his charts to presage future price movements. He is usually a short term trader. Note the difference from FUNDAMENTALIST and OPTIMATICIAN.

Telequote

An automatic stock price quoting machine. It is a desk top device which can give up to the minute data on thousands of stocks traded on the national exchanges. It can give open, high, low, and close prices, latest trade, volume, earnings, and other pertinent information by pressing the appropriate stock ticker

symbol and information keys. Other machines used are
Quotron and Ultronic Stockmaster. There are also
others which give a continuous display of information
from the stock ticker. These include Lectrascan,
Teleregister, Video Master, and Translux. See each
listing separately.

Teleregister
An electronic display board built in various degrees of
complexity which displays continuously updated stock
market information of selected stocks. It is an
automatic display board, as are Lectrascan and
Translux. There are also electronic desk top machines
that will display specific information on thousands of
securities. Some of these are Video Master, Quotron,
Telequote, and Ultronic Stockmaster. See each listing
separately.

Tenant
1. The legal owner of any property with full rights to
   its use.
2. The person in whose name a stock certificate is
   registered.

Tender
To offer or submit something, as a resignation, or an
option. In securities it refers to a quantity of securities being offered to another person. See TENDER
OFFER.

Tender offer
A request submitted to stockholders of a certain
company by one party wishing to purchase a large
portion of that stock. Usually it is an attempt to gain
controlling interest of the company. The request is
announced publicly and usually offers to purchase the

stock at a price substantially higher than the existing market price. The shareholders are being asked to tender, or submit, their stock to be purchased by the principal making the request.

Term

The time of maturity or the life of a bond or some other form of debt. A bond may have a term of less than a year or over a hundred years, but most are from 10 to 30 years for maturity. Serial bonds will have different terms for different portions of the issue, so that there may be some bonds maturing each year for many years.

Testing the market

Referring to stock prices and chart patterns, this is a movement toward a given test point. An analyst may decide that a stock could normally proceed no more than a given amount without indicating that a major trend is being established. As the price approaches that point, he proclaims that it is testing the market. If it passes his appointed limit, he declares the trend to be in effect and proceeds to buy or sell on that basis.

Thin market

A market in which there are comparatively few bids to buy or offers to sell.

Third market

An off-the-board market for listed securities. While most listed stocks may be traded in the stock exchange, there are times when a trade of a large block may disrupt prices, so it may be negotiated privately. This is called a cross. There are also many small trades made off the exchange floor, simply because a customer may get a better price or a lower commission by negotiation. Lower prices may be available off the floor of an exchange, but the convenience and speed of trading on the exchange is more important to most traders. These off-the-board, or third market, transactions are conducted by brokers and dealers who are not members of the exchange which lists the securities being traded.

Third world

A broad and loose term that refers to the unaligned nations of the world. The aligned nations are in two camps; the capitalistic, industrial nations generally sympathetic to the United States are referred to as the West. The opposed nations, generally communistic, are aligned with Russia and are sometimes called the East, but more often the communist bloc. The many smaller nations which make up the third world, are usually not industrialized and prefer to avoid any dilution of national independence. Although intensely independent, those nations must rely on the larger nations in both the East and West for many types of goods and services, so they play a part in international trade policies and activities. They can affect economic conditions in the larger countries.

Ticker

An instrument which prints continually updated information on a continuous paper tape. There are two kinds in use in the securities industry, the stock ticker and the news ticker.

1. The *stock ticker* prints on a narrow strip of tape, a continuous record of all securities transactions that take place on the exchange floor, usually within seconds of the actual trade. Since early 1973, an

increasing number of over-the-counter stocks are also being reported by the ticker on a new composite tape. The tape shows the company name by its ticker symbol, trading volume, price, and, occasionally, some other pertinent information.

2. The *news ticker* is a teletype printer found in brokerages around the country which prints out a broad tape with news information about corporations and economic conditions which are published by Dow Jones. The news ticker has a bell which is used to signal the importance of some items being recorded on the tape. A signal of four bells may cause a broker to drop his pencil and rush to see what the tape is printing.

Ticker symbol

A letter symbol used to identify the various securities that are being traded on the stock exchanges and also a number of the over-the-counter stocks that are traded around the country. The symbols were developed to simplify the rapid reporting of trading by the stock ticker. The symbols are assigned to companies by choosing letters taken from their names, if at all possible, for easy identification. There are a few old line companies who still posses the envied single letter symbols such as Ford with F and U. S. Steel with X. Most are two and three letter symbols using initials or a phonetic abbreviation as in the case of General Motors with GM or Bowmar Instruments with BOM. Some are unrelated to the names, simply because other companies have used all possible choices that are closer. Note the case of Leisure Technology with LUX or Yates Industries with YES. In print, the symbols for *listed* stocks are large, upper case letters. Early in the 1970's when plans were laid out for the unified tape, the process of assigning symbols to *over-the-counter* stocks was begun. These NASDAQ symbols are now in use for several thousand stocks and they appear as upper case letters, but in a smaller size than the listed stocks. They are conspicuous in that they use four or five letters for each symbol. Some examples of these are Dairy Queen Stores with DQEN and Reynolds and Reynolds with REYNA.

Ticker tape
Often called simply the tape. It is the actual printout of a stock ticker which shows every transaction of all listed stocks immediately after they take place. The printout, on a narrow strip of paper, lists the company by its ticker symbol, the number of shares traded, and the price at which the trade was made. There is a move underway to replace the current ticker with a new unified tape, or composite tape. This new tape will show transactions in thousands of over-the-counter stocks as well as the listed stocks. Many of those OTC stocks have already been assigned NASDAQ symbols in preparation for the new system. Notice the difference from news ticker, which prints out news items on a much wider roll of paper. This news ticker is called the broad tape. Also see SYMBOLS for related information.

Tight money
The condition that exists when there is a short supply of lendable money. It can occur when reserve requirements decreed by the Federal Reserve Board force banks to increase the percentage of their deposits that they hold in reserve. The condition generally results in higher interest rates which then weaken the

demand for money. When the Federal Reserve Board decides to sell short term government securities, this will also take money out of circulation to tighten money markets.

Time certificate of deposit

A deposit which is evidenced by a certificate rather than a passbook. These cannot be withdrawn at will, but a written notice must be given to the bank sometime in advance of the date the withdrawal is planned. The certificate is not redeemable until maturity date, but it may be sold to another party. Also called certificates of deposit, or CD's. They earn higher interest than the ordinary passbook savings accounts.

Time deposit

A deposit in the bank which cannot be withdrawn before a specified date. See CERTIFICATE OF DEPOSIT.

Times earnings

The ratio between the market price of a stock and the issuer's earnings per share. Also called price-earnings ratio, P-E ratio, P-E, earnings multiple, or multiple. See PRICE-EARNINGS RATIO for additional information.

Time order

An order issued by an investor to his broker to buy or sell securities which becomes a market order, or limited price order, at a specified time. As a market order, the broker would execute the order at the best price available, and execution of the order is assured. As a limited price order, the broker would not be authorized to execute the order unless he could obtain a specific price or better. See BUY or SELL ORDERS for a list of other orders used in securities trading

Timing

The process of managing securities trading so as to take advantage of short term price changes. Usually investors keep charts to record daily prices and indicate trends. The aim is to buy at the lowest point of price cycles and to sell at the highest point of price cycles. The process requires study of market conditions so that intelligent interpretation may be made of various patterns and signals that appear on stock charts. Investors react to news reports and economic events in predictable ways, so a person studying the charts can anticipate some future moves as he sees the chart patterns take form. 100% accuracy in forecasts is not possible, because new influences constantly intervene to alter developing patterns, but the study definitely improves the odds for the studious chartist. See STOCK CHARTS for illustrations of various chart patterns that assist an investor who uses charts to improve his timing of investment decisions.

Tips

Supposedly inside information on corporation affairs. They are the most unreliable information an investor can use.

Tipster

A person who passes information, whether sound or only rumor, that is supposedly not known by the general public.

Today only order

A trading order issued by an investor to his broker,

which is to be executed before the close of trading on that day, or not at all. The same policy is applied to "this week only", which terminates at the close on Friday, or "this month only" which terminates on the last trading day of the month, regardless of what day of the week it might be. This type order can also be a limit order, a stop order, a contingent order, or one of several others at the same time, if other qualifications are added for the broker to follow. See BUY ORDERS or SELL ORDERS for a list of other kinds of orders used in securities trading.

Tombstone
A non-advertisment placed in some periodical to announce a stock or bond offering. The tombstone name is applied because they are completely devoid of the usual advertising techniques to attract attention. No claims are made; no selling is attempted. In fact, the statement is always inserted that it is not an offer to sell, but only an announcement of the fact it is being made available. Buyers are referred to a list of brokers which is included in the ad. Regulations prohibit advertising securities, so a tombstone is technically listed as an announcement only. Interested parties are referred to the underwriters and participating brokers for information about the security.

Top
Also called peak. In stock charting, the term is used to describe the highest point reached for a given period of time. It can only be said in retrospect and must be followed by a break. If the following break is brief, it is termed a correction. If the break continues a week or more, it is called a sell-off. If it continues several weeks, it becomes a downside trend which verfies that

the top was truly a top. If the top is followed by a short break and then the price recovers to another top in the same price range, it is called a double top, which is considered a resistance area that probably cannot be exceeded. It is considered a selling signal with the start of a long term downside trend assumed to be a certainty. See separate listings for these terms. See STOCK CHARTS for illustrated chart patterns.

Top management
The Board of Directors and the highest ranking officers of a corporation such as president, vice presidents, secretary, and treasurer. This level of management is responsible for setting company policy and all major plans. The next lower level of management would be the staff level, which is responsible for implementing and coordinating the major policy and plans. It would include some vice presidents if there are more than two, division managers, and their immediate subordinates. The third level of management is called line management and includes department heads and supervisors. They are responsible for production, sales, and other phases of actual operations. See LINE and STAFF under separate listings.

Topping out
A term that applies to an *apparent* condition which can be applied to the general market, to a group of stocks, or to an individual issue. The condition indicates that an uptrend appears to be coming to an end. It is an opinion by the person making the statement, but he cannot be certain until more time elapses. The indication is given when a stock chart shows a long period of rising prices ending with a

period when gains are small and possibly mixed with some short declines and flat periods of little or no change. A period of little change is called a plateau, and it illustrates a market mood that is called a sidewise market. If such conditions follow a strong upward period, it is assumed that the market is about to begin a general decline. See STOCK CHARTS for illustrations of various patterns on sample stock charts.

Trade date

The date on which a security transaction is made. The payment date or due date will usually come five trading days later. Also see DELIVERY DATE, RECORD DATE, and PAYABLE DATE for other dates of importance to an investor.

Trader

A person who buys and sells securities for his own account with the hope of making profit as market prices increase. He usually has little concern for income from his investments, but is seeking growth instead. Often his interests will be short term, that is, less than six months between a purchase and subsequent sale. Note the difference between the terms investing, trading, and speculating as listed under the heading INVESTING.

Trading

Buying and selling securities for a short term period (less than 6 months) in hopes of making profits. A trader is more aggressive and less concerned with income from the security than an investor, who seeks income and safety of the original capital. Trading does not suggest quite the extent of risk taking as speculating. Speculating is trading in securities without regard to the risk in order to obtain a much greater than usual amount of profit. Also contrast with PLAYING THE MARKET. Refer to separate headings for expanded definitions.

Trading crowd

Members of a stock exchange assembled at a trading post on an exchange floor to effect buy and sell orders. See TRADING FLOOR for description of the physical layout of the floor and trading posts.

Trading day

Days on which the exchanges are open. Generally, Monday through Friday, except holidays.

Trading floor

The trading area of any stock exchange. It is a large room, about half an acre in size, at the New York Stock Exchange, where stocks and bonds are sold. It provides space for 18 trading posts, which are horseshoe-shaped counters. Clerks occupy the posts to handle the records of transactions, and the specialists who conduct the actual trading stand outside the posts, where they can conduct the auction of securities by hand signals. The specialists are members of the exchange, just as the trading floor brokers and dealers are. In all, about 350 specialists are registered with the New York Exchange. Each specialist will carry an inventory of the securities in which he deals (about 75 different issues each) which he must buy with his own capital. Post 30 is different from the rest, consisting of a group of filing cabinets where a large number of infrequently traded securities are handled. It is called the inactive post. Brokers are admitted to the floor for trading by membership only. The memberships are called seats and are sold on an auction basis on the open market. Members must also meet certain requirements including NASD licensing, certain financial standards, and must comply with federal regulations for security dealers. Also see SEAT, EXCHANGE, and MEMBER for more information.

Trading post

One of eighteen horseshoe-shaped trading counters on the floor of the NYSE at which stocks assigned to that post are bought and sold. About 75 stocks are traded at each post. Each post is about 10 feet across and is occupied by clerks handling the necessary records. Actual trading is conducted by specialists on the floor area around the outside of the posts. The trading floor is connected to the member firms by telephones which surround the trading floor. Also, see POST 30 for a special post that is different from the others. This is where inactive stocks are traded.

Trading room

The over-the-counter department of a security brokerage which handles trades in unlisted securities.

Transaction slip

The same as confirmation slip. A brief form mailed to a securities trader listing financial information about his trade. It will show the name of the company issuing the shares, date of transaction, number of shares traded, the per share price, commission, federal taxes, transfer taxes, and the total amount due or payable with the due date. For traders on the commodities exchange, the document is called the purchase and sale memorandum.

Transfer
This term may refer to two different operations.

1. The delivery of a stock certificate from the seller's broker and legal change of ownership, normally accomplished within five days of the sale.
2. Recording the change of ownership on the books of the corporation by the transfer agent. This may require weeks or months.

Transfer agent
A person or agency which keeps the record of all shareholders of a security. When shares are sold, the transfer agent cancels old shares and issues the new shares to the proper investor.

Transfer tax
A tax imposed by the federal government and some states on every stock trading transaction, paid by the seller. The tax is small, ranging from one to four cents a share for New York's state tax, and from four to eight cents a share for the federal tax. Florida, South Carolina, and Texas also have transfer taxes. Tax liability is determined not by the state of residency or location of the transaction, but by the location of the transfer agent for the issuer of the security.

Translux
An electronic stock price quotation device which displays a magnified image of a moving ticker tape on a screen. Other display devices include Lectrascan, Teleregister, and Video Master. There are also desk top machines which provide up to the minute data on thousands of stocks. Some of these are Quotron, Telequote, and Ultronic Stockmaster. See separate listings for each.

Transportation index

Transportation index
Formerly called railroads or rails. A Dow Jones index
of 20 transportation stocks including railroads,
trucking firms, and shipping lines. The index itself is
considered of value in appraising the strength in the
economy. Some believe that comparing the transportation average with the industrial average can give
an indication of future trends. For example, in the
event of divergence or the condition when these two
indexes move opposite directions, it is interpreted as
meaning no change will occur in market trend.
However, when they move together, it means a major
trend is beginning, if that joint move is opposite to
previous trends.

Treasuries
Short for treasury bonds which mature in 5 to 28 years
with a maximum 4½% interest rate. To make the
bonds attractive to investors, they are sold at a
discount which makes the effective yield rise to as
much as 10%. See GOVERNMENT BONDS for other
types of government securities and BONDS for
comparisons with industrial bonds.

Treasury bill
A short term debt obligation sold by the U.S.
government with maturity in 13 to 26 weeks. Treasury
bills earn interest rates higher than the 7 to 10 year
government bonds. See GOVERNMENT BONDS for
comparisons to industrial bonds.

Treasury bond
A government bond that matures in 5 to 28 years with
a maximum 4½% interest rate. To make the bonds
attractive to investors they are sold at a discount,

which makes the effective yield rise to as much as 10 %. See GOVERNMENT BONDS for other types of government securities and BONDS for comparisons to industrial bonds.

Treasury certificate
A short term debt obligation sold by the U.S. government with maturity in 6 months to 1 year. They earn interest rates higher than the 7 to 10 year government bonds. Also see GOVERNMENT BONDS for other government securities and BONDS for comparisons to industrial bonds.

Treasury note
A short term debt obligation sold by the U.S. government with maturity in 1 to 5 years. Also see GOVERNMENT BONDS for other types of government securities and BONDS for comparisons to industrial bonds.

Treasury stock
Stock that has been issued and reacquired by the treasury of a corporation. It receives no dividend and has no voting rights. The purpose of the reacquisition may be to increase the book value of outstanding shares, or it may be to hold them in anticipation of use in acquisitions, bonuses, or other transactions. See STOCK for more information and a list of other types of stocks.

Trend
A long term pattern on a stock chart. Smaller patterns may appear, but the trend over months or years is what the long term investor is looking for.

Trend bucker

A company whose stock prices do not decline when the general economy declines. More often called a defensive issue.

Trend line

A device used in some charting techniques. It is a line drawn to connect any three of the lowest points in the irregular patterns of a charted stock price and extended into the future on the graph. It is also used to connect any three of the highest points and extend into the future. Any time in the future that the stock price crosses these lines it is interpreted as a sign that a new trend has been established and is expected to continue in that direction. The point at which the price crosses the trend line is called a breakout. These trend lines can be called support lines or resistance lines, depending upon the direction from which the price is approaching the line. If the price is rising and a line connecting high points lies above the current price, it is considered a resistance point. If the price can gather sufficient strength to penetrate the resistance line, it is a sign that a trend upward is confirmed. The same reasoning is used for falling prices. If the price penetrates the level of support, it is considered weak enough to establish a downward trend. See STOCK CHARTS for illustrations of various chart patterns and signals on sample stock charts.

Trend lines market barometer

A composite index composed of a number of other key indexes in weighted values. It indicates bullish and bearish conditions in general market attitudes.

Trust

1. An arrangement under law in which securities or

other property is held by one person, called the trustee, for the benefit of another person, called the beneficiary. The instrument itself is called a deed of trust, and the person establishing the trust is called the trustor or donor. The donor and trustee may be the same person, but the trustee cannot be the beneficiary. Trusts are frequently established by parents for their children for tax advantages and professional management of the financial affairs. Trusts can be created by agreement between the parties involved, by a will, or by an order of the court.

2. The term is also applied to a large monopolistic company which exercises effective control over some commodity or service. In this sense it becomes illegal and is fought by the government.

3. Many banks use the term to identify themselves as institutions which hold and administer funds for their clients.

Also see FIDUCIARY and LIVING TRUST.

Trustee

1. A person who undertakes administrative duties under a trust agreement.

2. A person holding title to property for the benefit of another person (beneficiary).

3. A person who holds the security for a bond issue and handles certain duties related to the issue.

4. A person who performs duties normally handled by an officer or director for an unincorporated mutual fund.

5. An administrator appointed by the court of a bankrupt or insolvent company.

Truth in Securities Act

Another name occasionally used for the Securities Act of 1933. Its primary purpose is to obtain full disclosure of all pertinent facts about the issuing company, its products, its financial status, its officers, the intended use of the proceeds of the offering, and any special conditions or limitations of ownership in a security which is being offered to the public. The term registration (of a security) refers to the process of complying with this Act of 1933.

Turnaround situation

The conditions existing when a company has solved whatever problem may have caused its stock to drop in price. For example, selling off unprofitable operations, thinning out excess personnel, modernizing facilities, a change in competition, or recapitalization.

Turnover

1. In the securities industry, turnover is the daily volume of business in either a single security or the entire market. The most common turnover, or trading volume figures, quoted are the total shares traded on the New York Stock Exchange, or on the American Exchange. Odd-lot volume is not included in that total.

2. In an investor's portfolio, the turnover figure refers to the number of trades made in a year's time divided by the average dollar amount involved per trade. It is roughly the number of times a given amount of money is invested in a series of different securities. Aggressive trading may move a given amount of money into and out of five or more stocks within a year. Long term investment may turn over the money only a few times in a lifetime, maybe not

at all. In commodities, turnover may be as frequent as several times a week.

3. In industry, an inventory turnover represents the number of times inventory must be replenished in a year's time. It is roughly measured by dividing gross sales by average inventory. It is generally considered bad to have a slow turnover, since it represents idle investment. Four times a year may be an average for industry but it can change dramatically for some industries. Makers of heavy equipment may have low turnover rates, while the food industry may be much higher.

Two dollar broker
A member of the New York Stock Exchange who executes orders for other brokers having more business at the time than they can handle themselves, or for firms who do not have their exchange member-partner on the floor. The term is derived from a time when these independent brokers received a fee of two dollars per 100 shares for such transactions. Today the fee will vary with the price of the stock, and the fee is paid by the broker who seeks out the independent.

Two-way commission
The *calculated* total commission on a round trip trade *if* the sale and purchase are at the same price. The condition rarely arises, but it is a convenient figure to keep in mind as a guide to the amount of gain that must be made in a stock in order to break even when it is sold. When the security is sold, the selling commission is calculated in the usual manner and added to the buying commission to arrive at a total in-and-out commission or cost for the round trip.

Two-way trade

Selling out of one security and buying into another at the same time so that the money is not idle. Occasionally the term is improperly used to mean a round trip, or an in-and-out trade in the same security.

U

Ultronic Stockmaster

A desk top stock quotation device which looks
somewhat like a calculator that gives information on
open, high, low, close, and latest price plus volume,
earnings, and dividends on 4,000 listed stocks by
pressing the proper buttons. Similar to Quotron and
Telequote. Also see Lectrascan, Videomaster,
Teleregister, and Translux for devices which give
continuous displays.

Undervalued situation

The conditions existing when a particular stock
justifies a higher market price and P-E ratio than it
has. Undervalued stocks are said to be depressed in
price and are called bargains. The condition often
occurs when a particular industry is down, and some of
its members are still strong in other fields, but their
stocks are depressed by association. Undervalued

stocks are sought out by sophisticated investors, since the prices are unrealistically low, and recovery is certain to produce profits.

Underwriter

A person or company who undertakes to guarantee a certain obligation.

1. Insurance firms are called underwriters because in the event of some casualty or loss they pay a stipulated amount of cash to offset the loss.

2. In securities, an underwriter is an individual or a company who guarantees the sale of a security issued by actually purchasing the entire issue and then offering it to the public. A securities underwriter is called an investment banker. Investment bankers frequently will form a syndicate to share the burden and risk of such a purchase and subsequent public offering. There are alternatives to underwriting in case the security appears doubtful in public interest. The offering may be made as a BEST EFFORTS offering or an ALL OR NONE offering. See separate listings for these terms.

Underwriting

The procedure used to bring a new issue to the market when investment bankers buy a new issue outright, then offer it for resale to the public. If the investment bankers believe the market is doubtful, they may accept the new issue on a best efforts basis or perhaps an all or none basis if the issuer feels that a complete sellout is critical to the success of the venture.

Unearned income

Income which has been received before it is actually earned, such as rent payments received in advance of the period of occupancy. For accounting purposes it is carried as a liability because it is really owed to the payer until the real earning period is complete. Also called deferred income.

Unified tape

A new stock ticker printout which reports transactions in all national and regional stock exchanges, as well as over-the-counter trades. A major advance from the traditional ticker tape which reports only transactions on the national exchanges. Also called the composite tape. See TICKER, TICKER TAPE, and SYMBOL for more information. Notice the difference between symbols for listed stocks and the NASDAQ stocks (over-the-counter).

Unissued common stock

Authorized stock which has not yet been issued to shareholders. It does not represent equity until it is sold. See STOCK for listing of other types of stock. Notice the difference from *treasury* stock and *retired* stock, both of which have been issued and repurchased by the issuing company.

Unit of trading

The number of shares that are normally handled as a basic package or unit. Most stocks are traded in round lots of 100 shares each. A few inactive shares may trade in 10, 25, or 50 share units. A trade involving 775 shares would be considered as 7 round lots and an odd-lot of 75 shares. Also see BLOCKS of stock for large transaction.

Unlisted stock

A security not listed on a stock exchange. The term does not necessarily refer to the value or quality of the security. While certain minimum standards must be met to become listed on an exchange, there are certain large corporations which do not choose to be listed. Many utilities, banks, and insurance companies are not listed. These securities will be traded in the over-the-counter market. See LISTED STOCK for requirements for listing and STOCK for other types of stock.

Unlisted trading privileges

Stocks which are properly listed on one exchange may, under certain circumstances, be admitted to another exchange. The request for such privilege is made by that exchange to the Securities Exchange Commission and does not require the approval of the company whose stock is to be listed. In some cases the company will request listing on the other exchange, in which case it is called dual listing.

Unrealized appreciation

Gains in the market prices for given securities held by an investor that will not be real, taxable profits until the security is sold. Also called paper profits.

Unrealized depreciation

Losses due to declining market prices of given securities being held by an investor that would become real losses if sold at that depressed price. Also called paper losses.

Unregistered stocks

Certain stocks issued on a limited basis, for special purposes or by small companies for sale to a limited number of people within one state. They are perfectly proper under the designated conditions but are often not permitted to be sold out of state or to larger numbers of people without registration with the Securities Exchange Commission. See STOCK for listing of other types of stock and REGISTRATION for requirements of preparing stock for sale to the public.

Up market

A period of generally rising stock prices. Also called a bull market, growing market, expanding market, strong market, advancing market. It is a reflection of growing investor optimism which by itself is related to growing business activities and profits.

Up reversal

A sudden change in the near term trend of market prices from a decline to rising prices. If the uptrend continues for several weeks it is then called a rally. If the rally occurs after a prolonged and serious decline and holds for several months, it is called a recovery. See STOCK CHARTS for illustrated chart patterns.

Up side

A period of time when stock prices are rising. The term is usually used with the unspoken reference to a wave cycle which has both rising and declining prices. The up side then refers to the rising half of the cycle. The up side trend may refer to a very short cycle of a week in duration, or it could refer to a very long fundamental wave of several years duration; but always it infers that a decline preceded the up movement, and another decline will follow.

Up tick

A term used to designate a transaction made at a price higher than the preceding transaction. Also

---

called plus tick. The term originates from the printout from a stock ticker. They come out in sequence as trades take place. Anyone wishing to make a short sale may do so only on an up tick, so the tape is watched closely for up or down moves. Also see ZERO PLUS TICK.

Up trend
A period during which market prices are generally rising. The charts may show cyclic wave patterns with some small declines, but the up side of the cycles usually extend farther than the down side.

Usury
An interest rate for loans that is either illegal or unconscionable. The point at which high interest becomes usury is arbitrary and may depend upon economic conditions, fluctuating legal standards, or interpretations and personal feelings.

Utilities
1. In speaking of market indicators, utilities refers to the Dow Jones utilities index, which is a composite of market prices of 15 large utility companies. There are other indexes of market conditions which use a composite of the entire utility industry.
2. When speaking of industry groups, utilities refer to the power companies.

Utility fund
An investment company or mutual fund which limits its investments to securities in the public utilities industry. Generally those funds are set up to serve individuals who seek maximum safety for their in-

vestments and good income. Retired investors are such individuals. See INVESTMENT COMPANIES for other types of funds and descriptions of each. Also see INVESTMENT COMPANY ACT OF 1940 for definitions, purposes and limitations.

Variable charges

The same as VARIABLE EXPENSES listed on next page.

Variable costs

The same as VARIABLE EXPENSES listed on next page.

Variable dollar investment

An investment like common stocks in which the value received at the time of sale depends upon market prices. In contrast, certain government securities and savings accounts will give a guaranteed return of the original principal, plus interest payments. Those are fixed dollar investments. In general, stocks are variable dollar investments, and bonds are fixed dollar investments. See FIXED DOLLAR INVESTMENT for more information.

Variable expenses

Also called variable costs and variable charges. The expenses of doing business that will vary with the volume of business, the economic climate, and the effectiveness of management. Items included are raw materials, labor, advertising, shipping, utilities, and legal expenses. These expenses are often listed separately from fixed expenses on a financial report. When variable expenses are added together with fixed expenses, they make up operating expenses. Also see EXTRAORDINARY EXPENSES.

Variable income security

Securities like common stock which yield earnings based upon the effectiveness of the issuer in making a profit. Dividends on common stock may vary from year to year and may not be paid at all if the Board of Directors decides to retain all earnings for operation of the business. Most growth type stocks pay little or no dividends. In contrast, bonds, savings accounts, and preferred stocks usually have a fixed income or dividend. See FIXED INCOME SECURITY.

Variable ratio plan

One method for formula investing, keeping a part of your investments in common stocks and the balance in bonds or preferred stock. The proportions are varied according to general market changes, usually holding a higher percentage of common stocks in rising markets and less in falling markets. Also see FORMULA INVESTING for other plans.

Venture capital

Money invested for equity in a new company or project. For some reason we apply the term risk capital to *all* stocks whether new or old companies; but when the company is new, and the risk is decidedly higher, we give it the more glamorous name of venture capital.

Vested interest

An established claim to some property or asset. Usually applied when referring to the rights or ownership privileges of an individual or a small group when discussing a large asset or pool of assets. For example, in many pension funds, employees have vested interests for all or some portion of the funds in their account. In the event they leave the company before retirement, they must be paid the full amount of their vested interest.

Videomaster

An electronic instrument used by brokers or other professionals to obtain stock quotations. By pressing the proper sequence of buttons the user can obtain a large amount of data on a screen much like a small television set. It is one of the most sophisticated such machines in use today and can give information on commodities and NASDAQ (over-the-counter) prices as well as listed stocks, and a vast amount of related data such as price-earnings ratios, volume, earnings, open and close prices, and many others.

Volatility

The characteristic of rapid and intense price changes, a mark of danger to some analysts and a fascination for others. Volatility in prices of securities is a measure of investor emotion and interest. Since securities markets are auction markets, the bids are matched with asked prices. If public interest increases following a favorable news announcement, investors will offer higher prices to secure their investments. Fears and uncertainty can also depress demand and prices. The resulting fluctuations produce interesting patterns when charted, and recognizable cycles may recur. Analysts and traders follow such patterns to help make investment decisions. See WAVE CYCLE for an interesting discussion of periodic price changes.

The short term trader wants volatility. The novice investor is attracted to the rapid climbs in price, so he often buys in a little belatedly, while the price is going up. When it falls, he is frightened and sells out, but not early enough to avoid taking a loss. This is why some professionals watch the odd-lot sales and move the opposite direction when the small investors move in large numbers. Odd-lot sales supposedly indicate transactions by the small investors.

Volume

The total number of shares traded during a specified period for either the entire market or a single issue being discussed. This figure is helpful in interpreting market trends. For example, a price decline on light volume is not as important to an analyst as a decline on heavy volume.

Voluntary plan

A program offered by some mutual funds under which an investor may purchase additional shares at any time. No limits are set on the number of shares purchased or on the time interval between purchases. Notice the difference from contractural plans, which require a person to purchase a fixed dollar amount of shares at fixed time intervals. Both of those plans are called periodic payment plans. See *special features* to select the Board of Directors and influence certain under the heading of INVESTMENT COMPANY for other variations.

Voting rights

Shareholders, being the real owners of a corporation, have the right to vote in the affairs of the corporation. Often when voting for directors, the vote is cumulative; that is, the shareholder is entitled to one vote for each seat on the board times the number of shares he owns. Thus if he owns 100 shares, and there are 10 seats on the board up for voting, he has 1,000 votes that he may cast in any way he wishes. In other corporate business, voting rights generally limit the vote to one vote for each share held by the shareholder.

If a shareholder is unable to attend or doesn't wish to attend the shareholders' meeting, he may delegate someone else to vote his shares by means of a proxy. Proxies are written authorizations for someone else to represent the stockholder in voting. Proxies may be given to management to vote in any manner suitable to management, or the stockholder may designate his desires, which obligates management to apply the vote in the manner stipulated. A third party may also be given the proxy as is often done in an attempt to unseat the present management and install new officers or directors.

For the most part shareholder voting is limited to electing directors and deciding any changes in capital structure or changes in the articles of incorporation. Directors of the company vote during their official meetings to decide major policy of the company and to elect officers. Directors usually have one vote per member.

Voting stock

Generally, common stock carries with it voting rights

major policies of a corporation. There are certain special classifications of common stock which do not have voting rights, but may instead have designated priorities concerning dividends, claims on assets in case of liquidation, etc. Preferred stocks are normally non-voting, but are called senior securities referring to liquidating priorities. See STOCK for listings of other types of stock.

Voting trust

An arrangement in which one or more stockholders of a corporation has placed his voting rights in the hands of a trustee for a limited time. This arrangement is sometimes used in cases where several large stockholders have differences of opinions which they cannot resolve. The parties in question agree to abide by the decisions of the trustee who votes their shares.

Warrant

A certificate issued to existing shareholders of a company that is offering a new issue of shares to the public. The warrant gives the shareholder the pre-emptive right to purchase additional shares at a price lower than the market price in order to maintain his original portion of equity. If the shareholder does not care to or is unable to purchase these shares, he may sell the warrant on the open market. Its value is the difference between the price of shares offered to the shareholder and the market price of previously issued shares. A warrant states a specific price at which it can be exercised and also gives a time limit for the warrant to be exercised. There are some warrants that are good perpetually. Warrants are similar to rights, except that rights may expire in a few weeks or months. Most warrants are good for many months or even years.

Both warrants and rights are forms of options. See OPTIONS for some differences.

Wash sale

1. Simultaneously buying and selling in a given stock. A purchase through one broker and a sale through another which artificially increases trading volume and may raise prices. It is considered as manipulating the market and is illegal.

2. For tax purposes a purchase within 31 days of a prior sale is considered no sale at all, so that losses on such trading cannot be claimed. The term wash sale is used in this case also, but it is not illegal to repurchase within 31 days. The investor merely loses the right to claim a short term loss if that is the original aim (as in the case of a year-end sale for tax loss with the intention of repurchase later.)

Watered stock

Stock that has been issued without adding corresponding value to the issuing company. A watered stock is said to be diluted. The condition occurs frequently when a company, particularly a new one, will issue shares to an individual in return for patents or production rights. Other investors supply the cash, while the inventor supplies the product and knowledge. The new product and knowledge are most important to the future of the company, so the dilution is not at all unfair. In fact, it is quite a bargain for investors. They do not have to pay out any cash to obtain the new product. The inventor gains only if the product is successful. In some cases organizers of new companies have issued themselves unfair portions of stock compared to the contribution made. This leaves a stock far overpriced in relation to the value of assets, and it may be a long time before the book value approaches the purchase price. See DILUTION for more information. Also see STOCK for other terms used for different types of stock.

Wave cycle

On stock charts the charted prices rise and fall continuously. Very often patterns become obvious that look like ragged waves. These waves may extend over a few days of the charted period, or they may cover months of time. They tend to repeat in a very loose sense; that is, they continue rising and falling although the time spans may be different, and the high and low points may be quite different. Since each wave does show a rising trend for a time, then a subsequent declining period, the waves are called cycles. The cause of the cyclical pattern is a certain amount of inertia in the attitude of investors and an intervening sequence of influencing factors such as political developments, international trade developments, interest rate changes, new product announcements, profit or loss announcements, law suits, and management changes. Statistics have shown that the cycles or waves tend to fall into three classifications as follows:

1. Secondary waves: very short periods up to a week in length. These are so called because they are secondary in importance. This type wave reflects the rapid reactionary traits in investors as they receive news, but they have little substance.

2. Primary waves: cycles that extend from a week to as much as four months. The great majority of these waves last three to six weeks and indicate the full release of investor inertia as they respond to current

conditions. These are the most important price patterns for traders to follow, as they may show price changes of 20 to 30% of the market price during any given cycle of volatile stocks.

3. Fundamental waves: major cycles that reflect the overall conditions in the economy or in a given corporation. They may continue from six months to a dozen years. The cycles are not particularly important as *cycles*, but the direction of trend for any portion of the cycle is quite valuable for setting investment objectives and policies. Long term investment plans must consider the fundamental conditions and fundamental cycles.

See CHARTS, CHARTING, OPTIMAL ANALYSIS, FUNDAMENTAL ANALYSIS, and TECHNICAL ANALYSIS for investment techniques that study cycles. Some samples of different charting techniques are shown under the heading STOCK CHARTS.

Wave theory

The theory that stock prices reflect investor emotion more than the true value of the stock. It cites the three basic wave patterns (secondary, primary, and fundamental) which recur regardless of the conditions in the company, the nation, or the world. See WAVE CYCLE above.

Investor's Systems, Inc. has scientifically analyzed the cyclical patterns on stock charts to devise a system to take advantage of those patterns in investment management. The system employs the optimal analysis method of selecting, monitoring, and forecasting price trends according to statistical probability graphs. See OPTIMAL ANALYSIS and STATISTICAL PROBABILITIES.

Weak hands
Supposedly the great numbers of unsophisticated small investors who panic easily and sell out after a stock market price slump.

Weekly list
A list of the less active over-the-counter stocks printed each Monday for distribution by the National Quotation Bureau. The more active issues are listed in a daily publication called the pink sheets.

Weighted average
1. A figure used for statistical reference which is determined by multiplying the base, or raw figures, by certain factors which allow for relative importance of each component of the average. For example, it could be said that, of a selected group of adult men, one fourth are unemployed. It is discovered that one half of those unemployed men are over 75 years of age and not looking for employment; therefore, the total unemployment figure would be inaccurate unless an allowance is made before comparison to other more average groups.

2. In accounting, the term is used to describe a method of calculating the costs in inventory. To obtain the average, the total cost of each commodity and product is divided by the number of each in stock. The average price of each is then added with others to give the total inventory value. For other methods of caluclating inventory values, see FIFO and LIFO.

When, as and if
A conditional transaction in a new issue of stock that

has been authorized for sale but not yet actually issued. The prices of such stocks are reported as "when issued", or will have the letters WI with the indicated price. This means that when the issue is finally made officially available, the transactions may be completed. As soon as it reaches the broker's hands, he may write orders for it (although he may have made reservations for certain clients in advance). If the security is not withdrawn for some reason before actual issue, a customer may finalize his order at the announced price. See BUY and SELL ORDERS for a list of other kinds of orders used in securities trading.

When issued
The same as WHEN, AS AND IF above.

Wholesale
In business it is the sale of large quantities of goods to a dealer, who in turn resells to the public. Wholesale prices are also called net, net cost, dealer cost, factory price, quantity price, or dealer invoice price. Discount retail stores often advertise that they are selling at or below wholesale which, of course, is impossible. They may discount, but they cannot sell below their cost unless it is truly a distress sale. Often there are a number of prices for a given product. Some supply houses may sell to consumers and to dealers, contractors, and job shops. They will then charge one price to consumers and another price to the quantity purchaser. It is possible also for dealers to receive overrides, rebates, or bonus payments if their sales attain a certain volume. This practice is what makes it possible for some businesses (auto dealers for example) to sell merchandise at a small but widely promoted mark up over their invoice price and still

make a substantial profit.

Wire house
A member firm of a stock exchange which maintains a communication network, linking either with its own branch offices, offices of correspondent firms, or a combination of both.

With interest
A term that is often used when quoting bond prices. It means that the buyer of a bond must also pay a pro-rated portion of the next interest payment to the seller of the bond. The interest may be paid quarterly, and, if the bond is sold a month before a payment date, the buyer is entitled to only that one month of interest. Thus, he pays the proper portion to the seller who held it for two months after his last interest payment. Sometimes a bond price is reported as ". . . and interest", as well as ". . . with interest".

Withdrawal plan
A plan offered by some mutual funds by which an investor can receive monthly or quarterly payments from the fund for his living expenses. It may be limited to dividend distributions or it may be fixed at a rate exceeding dividends and capital gains distributions. In this event, some shares are liquidated periodically to make the payments. This type plan is suitable for retired individuals who have sufficient investments to safely consume part of the principal. See sub-heading of *special features* under INVESTMENT COMPANIES for more information.

Working capital
Current assets less current liabilities, or the amount

of money available for use in the operation of a business. It is one measure of a company's financial strength and may be a critical factor if an economic downturn should strike.

Working control

Technically, control of a corporation is gained by owning 51% or more of the voting stock. In reality, it is sometimes possible to have effective control by much less than 50%. In some large corporations the stock is so widely held that only a small portion is owned by management. A person or a group of people working together can win sufficient support by proxies so that they can control the corporation. There may be many small stockholders who do not bother sending proxies, or, because of lack of information, simply give management free reign. In this way, less than a majority can formulate corporate policy.

Workout market

A price stated for a security which is not a firm quote but believed by the broker or dealer to be the going market price for a reasonable length of time. Very similar to subject market or indicated market. If the inquirer wishes to place an order, the dealer would check further for the firm prices. Note the difference from QUOTE, FIRM MARKET, and BID AND ASKED.

Write an option

The procedure of writing up a contract for a trader to buy or sell a security at some specified price on or before a specified date. The writer must own the shares that the option concerns, and he is, in effect, betting against the speculator who buys the option.

There has been a practice for a few option writers to write options without owning shares. This is called naked option writing. It is very risky for the writer and the speculator who buys the option. It is still legal, but, since the failure of some option writers and the loss of many millions of dollars to the buying public, there is a move to prohibit naked options. See OPTIONS, PUTS, and CALLS for definitions.

Write-down

An accounting term for reducing the value of an asset, similar to a write-off with some distinctions.

The *write-down* is usually a sudden reduction in value from the value carried on the books to whatever salvage price can be obtained. This is often used for obsolete equipment that has not been depreciated but is found to be less efficient or productive than newer equipment. A write-down is also used in retail trade where a selling price is reduced to clear out damaged merchandise or out-of-date merchandise.

The *write-off* is a deduction from earnings for a pro-rated wear and tear of the item, or the total remaining cost if its usefulness is ended. Losses from operations are said to be written-off from subsequent earnings. See OBSOLESCENCE and DEPRECIATION.

Write-off

Charging off an expense or loss to a specific time period of operations for tax purposes. For example, development costs for a new product may be amortized off over a period of years to offset profits for those years. However, if the product fails, all the expenses might be written off during the year the project is cancelled. That makes a large loss for the year. Also, some accounts receivable may have little prospect for collection, so they may be written off as a loss. Equipment which wears out is written off a little at a time by depreciation deductions. Notice some small distinctions from WRITE-DOWN. Also see DEPRECIATION for several methods of calculating the gradual reduction in value of equipment through wear and tear. See OBSOLESCENCE for replacement of equipment that is not worn out.

Write-up

An accounting term for increasing the value of some asset as it is carried on the books. The increase may result from rising market values or from an attempt to present a better picture to shareholders.

Writer

A person who writes or deals in options. He, in a sense, is betting against the person who buys the option from him. He sells his option contracts to speculators who are expecting market changes to move in their favor. See OPTIONS for definitions.

Y

Yield

Dividends or interest paid on securities. In discussing a security that you own, the yield is stated as a percentage of the price you paid. If you do not own it, the yield is stated as a percentage of the current market price. On stock dividends, the dividends over the past 12 months are divided into the market price to give the yield. On bonds the coupon rate is divided into either the market price or your acquisition price. This yield is also called return, or return on investment. Usually when observing from the viewpoint of the investor, the figures are stated as percentages. From the viewpoint of the issuing company, the amounts are called payouts and are stated in dollar amounts. A company will report earning $1.65 per share or paying $.35 per share in dividends. The investor will receive a yield of 4% on investment if his cost was 9 3/4 and he receives a $.35 dividend. Yield and payout are then the same thing, depending upon your vantage point.

Yield to maturity

Yield on bonds calculated by considering the securities' redemption price, time to maturity, current market price, and coupon yield. Any premium paid or discount received at purchase time is spread over the entire life of the bond.

Z

Zero basis

A condition that occurs when a convertible bond is attractive enough to investors that they pay a premium for it so high that any interest received is cancelled out by the premium paid to purchase the bond. The bond is said to be trading on a zero basis. The premium may even get so high that it is greater than the interest earned. In this case, the yield to maturity is negative, and the bond is said to be trading on a minus-yield basis. If the conditions change so that market prices decline enough to go below par value, the bond no longer sells at a premium, but at a discount.

Zero-minus tick

A transaction for a particular stock on a stock exchange which occurred at the same price as the last previous transaction, but lower than the most recent previous transaction with a different price. Regulations state that short sales are not permitted on a minus tick or a zero-minus tick.

Zero-plus tick

A transaction on a stock exchange which took place at the same price as the last previous trade but higher than the most recent previous trade which had a different price. Short sales are permitted only on a plus tick or zero-plus tick.